21 The Four Quarters of the Night
   The Life-Journey of an Emigrant Sikh
   Tara Singh Bains and Hugh Johnston

22 Cultural Power, Resistance, and Pluralism
   Colonial Guyana, 1838–1900
   Brian L. Moore

23 Search Out the Land
   *The Jews and the Growth of Equality in
   British Colonial America, 1740–1867*
   Sheldon J. Godfrey and Judith C. Godfrey

24 The Development of Elites in Acadian
   New Brunswick, 1861–1881
   Sheila M. Andrew

25 Journey to Vaja
   *Reconstructing the World of a Hungarian-
   Jewish Family*
   Elaine Kalman Naves

McGill-Queen's Studies
in Ethnic History
Series Two: John Zucchi, Editor

1 Inside Ethnic Families
   *Three Generations of
   Portuguese-Canadians*
   Edite Noivo

2 A House of Words
   Jewish Writing, Identity, and Memory
   Norman Ravvin

3 Oatmeal and the Catechism
   Scottish Gaelic Settlers in Quebec
   Margaret Bennett

4 With Scarcely a Ripple
   *Anglo-Canadian Migration into the United
   States and Western Canada, 1880–1920*
   Randy William Widdis

5 Creating Societies
   Immigrant Lives in Canada
   Dirk Hoerder

6 Social Discredit
   *Anti-Semitism, Social Credit, and the
   Jewish Response*
   Janine Stingel

7 Coalescence of Styles
   *The Ethnic Heritage of St John River Valley
   Regional Furniture, 1763–1851*
   Jane L. Cook

8 Brigh an Orain / A Story in Every Song
   The Songs and Tales of Lauchie MacLellan
   Translated and edited by John Shaw

9 Demography, State and Society
   Irish Migration to Britain, 1921–1971
   Enda Delaney

10 The West Indians of Costa Rica
   *Race, Class, and the Integration of an
   Ethnic Minority*
   Ronald N. Harpelle

11 Canada and the Ukrainian Question,
   1939–1945
   Bohdan S. Kordan

12 Tortillas and Tomatoes
   *Transmigrant Mexican Harvesters
   in Canada*
   Tanya Basok

13 Old and New World Highland Bagpiping
   John G. Gibson

14 Nationalism from the Margins
   *The Negotiation of Nationalism and Ethnic
   Identities among Italian Immigrants in
   Alberta and British Columbia*
   Patricia Wood

15 Colonization and Community
   *The Vancouver Island Coalfield and the
   Making of the British Columbia
   Working Class*
   John Douglas Belshaw

16 Enemy Aliens, Prisoners of War
   *Internment in Canada during the
   Great War*
   Bohdan S. Kordan

17 Like Our Mountains
   A History of Armenians in Canada
   Isabel Kaprielian-Churchill

18 Exiles and Islanders
   The Irish Settlers of Prince Edward Island
   Brendan O'Grady

19 Ethnic Relations in Canada
   Institutional Dynamics
   Raymond Breton
   Edited by Jeffrey G. Reitz

20 A Kingdom of the Mind
   *The Scots' Impact on the Development
   of Canada*
   Edited by Peter Rider and
   Heather McNabb

21 Vikings to U-Boats
   *The German Experience in Newfoundland
   and Labrador*
   Gerhard P. Bassler

22 Being Arab
   *Ethnic and Religious Identity Building
   among Second Generation Youth
   in Montreal*
   Paul Eid

23 From Peasants to Labourers
   *Ukrainian and Belarusan Immigration from
   the Russian Empire to Canada*
   Vadim Kukushkin

24 Emigrant Worlds and Transatlantic
   Communities
   *Migration to Upper Canada in the First
   Half of the Nineteenth Century*
   Elizabeth Jane Errington

25 Jerusalem on the Amur
   *Birobidzhan and the Canadian Jewish
   Communist Movement, 1924–1951*
   Henry Felix Srebrnik

26 Irish Nationalism in Canada
   Edited by David A. Wilson

27 Managing the Canadian Mosaic
   in Wartime
   Shaping Citizenship Policy, 1939–1945
   Ivana Caccia

28 Jewish Roots, Canadian Soil
   Yiddish Culture in Montreal, 1905–1945
   Rebecca Margolis

29 Imposing Their Will
   *An Organizational History of Jewish
   Toronto, 1933–1948*
   Jack Lipinsky

30 Ireland, Sweden, and the Great European
   Migration, 1815–1914
   Donald H. Akenson

31 The Punjabis in British Columbia
   *Location, Labour, First Nations,
   and Multiculturalism*
   Kamala Elizabeth Nayar

32 Growing Up Canadian
   Muslims, Hindus, Buddhists
   Edited by Peter Beyer and Rubina Ramji

33 Between Raid and Rebellion
   *The Irish in Buffalo and Toronto,
   1867–1916*
   William Jenkins

34 Unpacking the Kists
   The Scots in New Zealand
   Brad Patterson, Tom Brooking,
   and Jim McAloon

35 Building Nations from Diversity
   *Canadian and American Experience
   Compared*
   Garth Stevenson

36 Hurrah Revolutionaries
   *The Polish Canadian Communist
   Movement, 1918–1948*
   Patryk Polec

37 Alice in Shandehland
   *Scandal and Scorn in the Edelson/Horwitz
   Murder Case*
   Monda Halpern

ALICE

in

SHANDEHLAND

*Scandal and Scorn
in the Edelson/Horwitz Murder Case*

MONDA HALPERN

McGill-Queen's University Press

Montreal & Kingston | London | Ithaca

ISBN 9780773545595 (cloth)
ISBN 9780773583375 (ePDF)
ISBN 9780773583405 (ePUB)

Legal deposit second quarter 2015
Bibliothèque nationale du Québec

Printed in Canada on acid-free paper that is 100% ancient
forest free (100% post-consumer recycled), processed chlorine free

The author acknowledges the assistance of the J.B. Smallman Publication
Fund, and the Faculty of Social Science, The University of Western Ontario.

McGill-Queen's University Press acknowledges the support of the Canada
Council for the Arts for our publishing program. We also acknowledge the
financial support of the Government of Canada through the Canada Book
Fund for our publishing activities.

Library and Archives Canada Cataloguing in Publication

Halpern, Monda M., 1963–, author
Alice in Shandehland : scandal and scorn in the Edelson/Horwitz murder
case / Monda Halpern.

(McGill-Queen's studies in ethnic history. Series two ; 37)
Includes bibliographical references and index.
Issued in print and electronic formats.
ISBN 978-0-7735-4559-5 (bound).–ISBN 978-0-7735-8337-5
(PDF).–ISBN 978-0-7735-8340-5 (ePUB)

1. Edelson, Ben–Trials, litigation, etc. 2. Horwitz, Jack, –1931–
Death and burial. 3. Edelson, Alice. 4. Trials (Murder)–Ontario–
Ottawa–Case studies. 5. Adultery–Ontario–Ottawa–Case studies.
6. Sex scandals–Ontario–Ottawa–Case studies. 7. Triangles
(Interpersonal relations)–Ontario–Ottawa–Case studies. 8. Jews–
Ontario–Ottawa–Case studies. 9. Jewelers–Ontario–Ottawa–Case
studies. I. Title. II. Series: McGill-Queen's studies in ethnic history.
Series two ; 37

HV6535.C33088 2015   364.152'30971384   C2015-901543-X
                                               C2015-901907-9

To *my* miracle, Don Abelson

And in loving tribute to:

my mother, Clara Halpern Jeremias

my sister, Sonia Halpern

And in loving memory of:

my father, Dr George Halpern

my stepfather, Dr Martin Jeremias

Don's mother, Estelle Abelson

Contents

Illustrations follow pages xv and 67

Acknowledgments / xi

Introduction / 3

1

"This terrible drama of humanity":
An Affair, a Shooting, a Death, an Arrest / 13

2

"A prominent Ottawa jeweller" and "the jeweller's comely
young wife":
The Rise of the Edelsons / 37

3

"Startling evidence ... of a sensational character":
The Inquest, and Respectability Challenged / 53

4

"Her life was pure impulse without control":

Trial by Jewry, Community Anxiety, and the Spurning of Alice / 91

5

"In a court of British justice, sympathy has no place":

Trial by Jury, Respectability and Honour, and the Acquittal of Ben / 115

6

"A sudden silence fell":

The Legacy of the Case / 151

Conclusion / 172

A Note on Sources / 177

Notes / 183

Bibliography / 255

Index / 269

Acknowledgments

Books are written with the help of many people, and this one is no exception. First and foremost, I want to thank Philip Cercone of McGill-Queen's University Press, copy editor Susan Glickman, and the anonymous external readers.

I am especially indebted to Sharon Edelson, the wife of Joel Edelson, Ben and Alice's grandson. Sharon began investigating the case soon after she married into the family in the 1960s, and has accumulated heaps of family papers and photographs. After corresponding with me for several months through email, Sharon invited me to her home in Ottawa where she, Joel, and I spent the day sorting through her beloved basement archive, and talking candidly about the family and Jewish Ottawa. She and Joel also arranged my meeting the next day with Ben and Alice's eldest daughter, Dina, in her nineties at the time. Since this first visit in 2006, Sharon graciously hosted several more afternoons with me, and scanned and emailed me dozens of family documents and pictures. Our shared internet journey locating Jack Horwitz's widow and daughter was a highlight of my research. Determined and fearless, she supported this project in every way possible, even at the risk of alienating family members. I will never be able to thank her sufficiently for all that she contributed. In short, I had my very own research fairy-godmother.

The Edelson/Horwitz murder case was a traumatic event, and certainly a difficult and awkward one to discuss. For this reason, I am utterly indebted to those members of the Edelson and Horwitz families who graciously agreed to speak with me – in particular,

Ben and Alice's daughters the late Dina Edelson and the late Lillian Katznelson and Jack Horwitz's nephews Jack Horwitz and Jonathan Horwitz (all of Ottawa), all of whom professed understandable ambivalence about participating in this project, but who kindly did so nonetheless. As well, I am indebted to Yetta Horwitz's grandson Steven Chernove (Los Angeles) who in addition to relaying the fate of Yetta and Anita provided me with copies of family photographs. I am also grateful for the invaluable and spirited interviews, conversations, and correspondence with Alan Abelson (Ottawa), the late Estelle Abelson (Ottawa), the late Max Adler (Toronto), Murray Citron (Ottawa), Joel Edelson (Ottawa), Natalie Edelson (the Yukon), the late Adelene Sigler Hyman (Cambridge, Ontario), Suzie Gelman (Ottawa), the late Mary Goldberg (Ottawa), Tracey Kronick (Ottawa), Dr Sid Kronick (Ottawa), the late Abe Lieff (Victoria), Dr Lionel Metrick (Ottawa), Diane Payne (Victoria), Miriam Russ (Rego Park, New York), the late Francis Shaffer (Toronto), the late Michael Shaver (Ottawa), Eric Slone (Ameliasburgh, Ontario), Doreen Caplin Teichman (Toronto), and several others who preferred not to be mentioned by name.

Western University provided crucial research support and resources. I thank my colleagues in the Department of History, graduate student Nassisse Solomon, former undergraduate students Erica Gagnon, Madalena Kozachuk, Bayly Guslits, Michael Machlan, Michael Feiner, Heather Stevenson, Kiara Hart, Brahm Klar, and Adina Burden (University of Toronto), and Western's remarkable Work Study program. I am especially appreciative to Dr Sam Clark and the J.B. Smallman Research Fund, and of funding through The Agnes Cole Dark Award and the Alumni Research Award, all granted by the Faculty of Social Science.

Archive and library staff also proved tremendously helpful. Dawn Logan, Marcia Rak, and Laurie Dougherty, formerly of the Ottawa Jewish Archives, were indispensable to this project. The Ottawa Jewish Archives is a valuable resource, and Ottawa and the Jewish community are fortunate to have such a wonderful facility. This book could not have been written without it. Harriet Fried at the City of Ottawa Archives was also extremely knowledgeable and helpful, as was Barb Taylor at the Archives of Ontario, Rutgers University librarian Stephanie Bartz who volunteers with the South River Historical and Preservation Society (New Jersey), and retired master sleuth Walter Zimmerman (and the rest of the staff) at The D.B. Weldon Library at Western University.

At times, this project required some expertise beyond my own abilities and knowledge. For the translation of Yiddish, Hebrew, and Russian documents, thank you to my mother Clara Halpern Jeremias, my aunt Mary Blum Devor, Dr William Shaffir, the late Rivka Shaffir, Morry Koperwas, and Eiran Harris (Yiddish), to Dr Bill Klein and Rose Klein (Hebrew), and to Dr Chuck Ruud (Russian). For interpretation of the law and knowledge of legal history, thank you to my brother, lawyer Robert Halpern, lawyer William A.G. Simpson, law professor Hamish Stewart, legal scholars Jim Phillips, Constance Backhouse, and Caroline Dick, and criminologist Rosemary Gartner. For fascinating insights into the mechanics of guns and policing, thank you to Sergeant Stephen Dykeman of Western's Campus Community Police Service. For getting the photographs "camera-ready," thank you to Linda Zimmerman, and to Christine Wall at Western's Centre for American Studies. And special thanks to Danielle Demiantschuk.

On a more personal note, my fiancé Dr Don Abelson expressed tremendous support for this project, and assisted me in countless ways. He accompanied me to Ottawa on all of my research trips, facilitating my days of research in the archives by every means possible. And after arduous hours of examining documents there, there was no more welcome sight than Don and his father strolling cheerfully down the hall to pick me up. An academic himself, Don also graciously gave me the time and privacy needed for writing. In short, he has offered me constant encouragement and love, and, along with his children Rebecca and Seth, has infused my life with all things wonderful. As he launches his next project, I relish doing the same for him.

Don's parents were also indispensable to this project. His mother Estelle, who passed away in 2004, first told me of the Edelson/Horwitz story. Don's gregarious father Alan allowed me to stay at his home during almost all of my trips to Ottawa, and treated me to dinner more times than I can count. He also shed much light on Jewish Ottawa by happily answering my endless questions, and by taking me on a colourful driving tour of Ottawa's Lowertown neighborhood, indulging me as we retraced the route of Alice Edelson as she walked its streets the night of the shooting.

As always, my twin sister Sonia Halpern, also a professor at Western, expressed unconditional enthusiasm for my work. Throughout this project, she offered extremely keen insights and valuable (and rightly brutal) editorial suggestions, repeatedly reading over the manuscript despite her own heavy workload. She and her partner Lawrence Burden took much pleasure in the fact that when at home alone writing my book, "I was happy as a clam," and did everything they could to accommodate these times.

The rest of my family, my mother Clara Halpern Jeremias, and my siblings Shelley, Marnie, Lori, and Robert, and their families, all took an interest in the project. The persistent efforts of my mother to offer aid when she could during the loss of her husband, Dr Martin Jeremias, were especially meaningful. She knows better than anyone that as a bibliophile and storyteller, Martin would have enjoyed witnessing the publication of this book. My father, Dr George Halpern, who passed away in January 2011, had an abiding passion for all things historical, and he and his wife Barbara never failed to ask me about my progress on the "murder case."

And, finally, many thanks to my precious Havdalah, who routinely slept on my piles of paper, and then crawled into my lap, reminding me after hours of writing that I deserved a catnap too.

Ben and Alice during their courtship, 1910 or 1911.
Collection of Sharon Edelson

A love letter from Ben to Alice (front and back), 1911.
Collection of Sharon Edelson

TREMONT STATION

NEW YORK, N.Y.

Jul 24 11 19 PM

Miss. Alice Collent.
112 Rivington St,
New York. City.

I met a pretty Miss,
Whose lips compelled a kiss.
Her name you know I see
It starts with "A," but ends in "E."

Benjamin Edelson -

Alice and Ben during their courtship or early years of marriage,
about 1912. Collection of Sharon Edelson

Alice with her children, about 1927. Collection of Sharon Edelson

Alice with two of her children, early 1930s.
Collection of Sharon Edelson

Jack (superimposed, back row, middle) and Sam Berger (front row, middle) in the Boosters Club, Young Men's Hebrew Association (YMHA), 1921. Ottawa Jewish Archives, Individual Collections, File – Young Men's Hebrew Association, *The Booster*, January 1921.

Yetta, early to mid 1920s. Collection of Steven Chernove

Jack on his wedding day, 1924. Collection of Steven Chernove

Yetta on her wedding day, 1924. Collection of Steven Chernove

Jack and daughter Anita, 1931. This may be the
last photograph of him before his death.
Collection of Steven Chernove

The Horwitz home, 80 Stewart Street (today).
Collection of Sharon Edelson

ALICE

in

SHANDEHLAND

shandeh. Yiddish. n. shame or disgrace

Introduction

On the night of 24 November 1931, in Ottawa, Ontario, Ben, his wife Alice, and her lover Jack were determined to "settle the thing."[1] The Edelsons had been married for nearly two decades and had seven children, but, for years, Alice and Jack had been having an affair. Ben had long suspected his wife's adultery; that evening, it seemed that an exasperated Ben had finally had enough. The three of them met at Edelson Jewellers on Rideau Street, where words flew, a struggle ensued, and Jack Horwitz was shot. His death a few hours later would mark the start of a sensational legal case in which forty-one year-old Ben Edelson was accused of murder, and facing the gallows.[2]

For weeks, the case captured headlines in the city's two daily newspapers. *The Ottawa Evening Citizen* and *The Ottawa Evening Journal* covered the case extensively and in shocking detail. From the morning of Horwitz's death in late November to the coroner's inquest and preliminary hearing in December, to the trial in mid-January, the case was front-page news. The day after the shooting, page one of the *Journal* featured six separate stories about the incident. The articles often spanned several pages, filling dozens of lengthy columns. The *Journal* was especially dramatic in its coverage. It often referred to the shooting as a "mystery" and regularly employed the word "sensational" to describe both upcoming and previous court testimony.[3]

Of course, this was not the first infamous "love triangle" in recent history in which a man was accused of killing his wife's lover. In June of 1906, for example, millionaire Harry K. Thaw killed famed architect Stanford White for having an affair with Thaw's young wife, showgirl Evelyn Nesbit, an event described as "the crime of the century."[4] Unlike the Thaw/White case, however, which arose from the cosmopolitan, extravagant, and reckless world of the Manhattan Anglo-Protestant elite, the Edelson/Horwitz case took place in a small, industrious, Ontario Jewish community where such things simply didn't happen.

Both the Edelson and Horwitz families lived in or near Lowertown, the Ottawa neighbourhood inhabited largely by Eastern European immigrant Jews and their Canadian-born children. The lives of the Edelsons, as well as certain aspects of the case, were shaped by their participation in Lowertown's religious, philanthropic, and social institutions. And even if not all of Ottawa's Jews knew the families personally, they were linked to those who did. This intimate connection with the cast of characters made the case all that more captivating and heart-wrenching for Ottawa Jews.

Despite the rarity, sensationalism, and tragedy of the case, it has never been the focus of any scholarly or popular examination. This neglect is partly due to the fact that the story runs contrary to the conventional narrative regarding the dictates and practice of Judaism – one which has underscored the interconnected values of morality, sanctity of family, community standing and responsibility, philanthropy, and justice. Especially in the last fifty years, writers have emphasized the cultural expression of these religious tenets, and how they have facilitated both upward mobility and community-building.

A more recent trend in Jewish historical scholarship, however, is the examination of Jews accused of transgressing these values, including criminals such as mobsters, human traffickers, pimps, political and religious zealots, and even pirates.[5] This fascination with deviance may be attributable to several themes related to contemporary North American Jewish identity: Jews feel integrated, accepted, and comfortable enough to reveal their uglier side; liberal and increasingly secular Jews are uncomfortable with the notion of Jews as a "chosen people," so seek to demonstrate their fallibility and corruption; Jews want to rehabilitate their image as victims;[6] or, simply exasperated with persistent emphasis on the Holocaust and the Middle East, they want to learn about more "entertaining" aspects of their history.

Some of this new scholarship, including this book, explores Jew-on-Jew violence, a phenomenon, historical or otherwise, which many Jews find repulsive and painful.[7] They maintain that after suffering centuries of anti-Semitism and abuse, and exerting tremendous efforts to establish thriving, peaceful communities, Jews – whose numbers are diminishing – should be turning to, not against, each other. Although male murder of men is often endogenous, such inter-group violence has been so rare among Jews that it is all that more staggering when it strikes.[8] In 2007, for example, historian Michael Stanislawski expressed bewilderment reflecting on the 1995 assassination of Israeli prime minister Yitzhak Rabin: "How could this have happened? ... How could a Jew kill another Jew for political and religious reasons?"[9]

Like other social histories that focus on criminal cases, particularly murder, this book uses the Edelson/Horwitz case as a lens through which to investigate prevailing attitudes regarding the interconnected issues of gender, ethnicity, and class.[10] Two non-Canadian works that do so, and involve *imagined* Jewish killers, are worth noting. *The Leo Frank Case* (1987) and *The Butcher's Tale: Murder and Anti-Semitism in a German Town* (2002) profile early twentieth-century murders in Atlanta, Georgia and Konitz, Germany, respectively, in which Jews, in a climate of anti-Semitic fervor, were erroneously accused of brutally killing Christian children.[11]

With its Jewish landscape and cast of characters, the Edelson/Horwitz murder case might have been expected to serve as the ideal vehicle by which to examine the ways in which the dominant culture in 1930s Ontario expressed and espoused anti-Semitism. After all, in an era when non-Anglo immigrants were deemed prone to "brutish behaviour," the case could have been held up by the press and the Ottawa courtroom as an example of Jewish depravity – of Jewish rage, corruption, sexual debauchery, and

deceit by all three of its leading figures.[12] Particularly in crime reporting, "the racial or ethnic background of protagonists was
made prominent in a manner ranging from the patronizing ... to
the vicious."[13] For example, when an immigrant Jewish mother
in Wisconsin killed her husband in 1919, newspaper stories about
the case were "a mixture of scandal-mongering and sentimental-
ity, heightened by the fact that the people involved were Jews –
and therefore strange, almost by definition – which gives the
whole account a leering, condescending tone."[14] Certainly, the
Edelson/Horwitz case presented an opportunity for a racist press
and anti-Semites generally to celebrate the death of cunning, up-
start Jews like Horwitz, and to rally for the execution of amoral,
murdering Jews like Edelson.

There is no contesting that virulent expressions of anti-Semitism were pervasive at this time. As Richard Menkis notes, "The
1930s were the bleakest period for Canada's Jews."[15] Against the
backdrop of the Depression, and anxiety about the financial burden of ethnic immigrants, nationalist, fascist, and French-Catholic
rhetoric, immigration quotas, restrictive covenants, as well as professional, academic, and social barriers all served to reinforce the
inferior status of Jews in Canadian society.[16] In fact, the experience
of Canadian Jews in the 1930s has been studied almost exclusively
in the context of anti-Semitism, an historiographical trend which
should not be surprising with the 1933 start of the Holocaust in
Europe.[17] The 1933 riot at Christie Pits in Toronto was perhaps
the most dramatic incident, a violent brawl between Jewish boys
and teenage Nazi thugs.[18]

The most infamous Ottawa episode was spearheaded by Jean
Tissot, a detective on the Ottawa police force fixated on deposing
the prosperous Jewish owners of Freiman's Department Store,
prominent Zionists with powerful political connections.[19] He promoted the views of Quebec fascist Adrien Arcand, who regularly
spewed his anti-Semitic rhetoric in *Le Patriote*, a Montreal fascist
newspaper.[20] The Ottawa edition of the paper accused the Freimans of preferential hiring of Jews over non-Jews, and indicted
the other Jewish merchants on Rideau Street, among them Ben
Edelson, for usurping the formerly French Catholic business dis-

trict.[21] In 1935, *Le Patriote* solicited a boycott of all Jewish businesses in Ottawa, including Freiman's Department Store.[22] Tissot then called for a group of Gentile merchants in Ottawa to "help drive out the Jews."[23]

But remarkably, despite this climate of bigotry, the Edelson/Horwitz case elicited no anti-Semitic response in either the English- or French-language press. In fact, other than in the Ottawa press coverage surrounding the funerals of, and post-mortem tributes to, Jack Horwitz and, later, Edelson lawyer Moses Doctor, newspapers rarely mentioned the Jewish background of the case's leading figures, and the comments were never pejorative in nature.[24] Moreover, Ben's immigrant and religious background was never ridiculed in the courtroom, nor did it adversely affect the outcome of his case: in January 1932, six weeks following the shooting, Ben Edelson was acquitted.

It would be easy to suppose that this absence of anti-Semitic discourse was due solely to the fact that the homicide victim was himself Jewish, but this ignores crucial gender, ethnicity, and class considerations, especially as they relate to the respectability of Ben and Alice Edelson.[25] While anti-Semitism was an integral feature of Ottawa, for defendant Ben it only played a role to the extent that he was able to elude it by living his life according to Anglo-Protestant values. Ironically, this gave anti-Semites like Jean Tissot another reason to rail against ambitious Jews like him: they were helping, it seemed, to reinforce the hegemony of Anglo-Protestant mores. But the influence of Tissot and others would never eclipse that of an Anglo culture, which, however anti-Semitic, seemed ready to accept "quality" Jews like Edelson. Thus, the Edelson/Horwitz case can offer a significant glimpse of Jewish life in 1930s Ontario without placing aggressive anti-Semitism at the heart of the story. The case may speak to the possibility that despite the popular view that North American Jews "came of age" in the 1950s and 60s,[26] by 1931 men like Ben Edelson were generally viewed as valued citizens.

As a business- and home-owner, Ben Edelson was solidly middle-class (a Jew who was neither too prosperous nor poor) and represented the qualities associated with this status: he participated in the dominant culture, was a provider for his family, was a devoted husband and father, and personified manly respectability and honour, characteristics, this book contends, which helped inspire the all-male jury to acquit him. As Karen Dubinsky notes, "judges and juries drew from a vast pool of social assumptions regarding respectability and personal character when weighing the evidence in trials."[27] While it might not be unexpected that men of the middling classes received less frequent and less severe sentences than those of the lower classes,[28] what is surprising is that a Jewish man in 1930s Ontario was able to evade punishment altogether.[29]

Much scholarship has focused on the integration, success, and acceptance of North American immigrants, including Jews. Some scholars have referred to this achievement as becoming "white," a complex process in the early to mid-nineteenth century by which labourers who feared losing their distinct identity, independence, and influence under the capitalist system worked to become full and autonomous citizens. Although Noel Ignatiev notes that, for the Irish, this process did not necessarily mean "that they all became rich, or even 'middle class,'"[30] Karen Brodkin, in her book *How Jews Became White Folks* (1998), argues that by the mid-twentieth century, economic prosperity had "played a very powerful role in the whitening process" for Jews. Although this was also attributable to "a more inclusive version of whiteness," Brodkin asserts that the whitening of Jews was facilitated by their increasing middle-class status.[31] For Ben Edelson, middle-class status and respectability more than just "whitened" him – it saved his life.

But middle-class respectability alone did not vindicate Ben – an even greater factor was the "unwritten law." It really was no law at all, but a Victorian doctrine which claimed that a father, husband, or brother whose female kin was seduced by another man had the right to kill him in order to protect his property (that is, his women) and manly honour. To facilitate an acquittal, Ben's lawyer Moses Doctor argued that the gun had fired accidentally in the midst of a scuffle. But the accident theory that Doctor advanced might have been little more than a ruse for the jury's im-

plementation of the unwritten law. Influenced by his portrayal of
Ben as the loving husband to a selfish harlot, the jury's sympathy
for Ben and contempt for Alice overshadowed both his potential
guilt and any possible feelings of anti-Semitism. Their "not guilty"
verdict illustrates the powerful force of manly honour, especially
in combination with female sexual indecency.

This book argues that the unwritten law – according to which
betrayed men are entitled to avenge their wife's seducer – and not
modern notions of provocation informed the jury's decision, but
the two concepts are historically connected. "Provocation" relies
on the belief that the accused was only moved to kill due to sudden anger causing a momentary loss of self-control. This defence
is predicated on pre-modern ideas relating anger to moral indig-
nation, such as that experienced by an aggrieved man obliged to
kill to protect his honour. As legal doctrine evolved to set limits on
the provocation defence, which could decrease the charge of murder to one of manslaughter, objective standards regarding the tim-
ing and nature of the crime meant that what was "reasonable"
displaced what was honourable, and "loss of control" superseded
moral consciousness.[32] Ben's own testimony that he was in control
of his senses on the night of the shooting inspired the judge to instruct jurors to disregard "provocation," but that is not to say that
they didn't consider it. Their verdict of "not guilty" rather than
manslaughter suggests, however, that the jury was far more per-
suaded by the unwritten law, if only for the singular purpose of
rendering Ben's freedom.

Although the unwritten law, sometimes termed "southern justice," was utilized frequently in nineteenth-century America, it
was far less common in Canadian courtrooms, especially in the
twentieth century.[33] Indeed, jury nullification, which occurs when
a jury subverts the rule of law and elects to acquit, has been quietly but doggedly disparaged by the justice system, and thus has
seldom surfaced as a noteworthy issue.[34] Judges were under no
obligation to convey the possibility of this process to jurors, and
seldom did. But Canadian law, in the interest of protecting citizens
from unconstitutional laws and/or excessively harsh enforcement
of the law, did not prohibit it either.[35] Thus, the Edelson/Horwitz

case may be a rare instance in which jury nullification was imple-
mented in Canada.

There may, in fact, be more cases than we realize in which juries acquitted men guilty of killing their wives' lovers. Angus
McLaren, in "Males, Migrants, and Murder in British Columbia,
1900-1923," points to at least four cases in which the accused
was found not guilty. Although accident and self-defence theories
were asserted by the defence, juries seem really to have acquitted,
either covertly or overtly, because of their belief in a man's right
to protect his home and manly honour. As McLaren notes, "All
the evidence suggests that a husband who murdered to keep his
woman stood a very good chance of getting away with it."[36] As
with a "guilty" verdict, a "not guilty" verdict does not necessarily reflect the ways in which a jury chooses to understand "the
structural and/or ideological boundaries of *responsibility*."[37]

While Ben's middle-class status and the unwritten law worked
in his favour, Alice's middle-class standing did little to redeem her
in the eyes of the Jewish community and the courtroom. In fact,
it only raised the stakes for what was expected of her as a wife and
mother, and was trumped from the start by her sexual misconduct. It seems that for the jury, the potential for immigrant women
to become "white" was less about class, which was largely mediated through their husbands anyway, and more about conforming
to accepted standards of sexual decency. As adultery was deemed
among the most heinous acts that a wife could perpetrate, sexual
morality, while not the only gauge of a woman's character, was
certainly the chief one.[38] Indeed, "the double standard of sexual
behaviour was a social norm of such power it crossed race and
class lines. 'Bad girls' came in all classes and colours."[39] In fact, regarding Alice, neither the press nor the courtroom ever exploited
the once-popular image of the sexually loose "Jewess."[40] They
didn't have to – the ideology of respectable womanhood was powerful enough in the 1930s to deflect anti-Semitic rhetoric, a sign
perhaps that Jewish women, along with their husbands, and no
less than other women, had also "arrived."

This book argues that despite the shooting and death of Jack
Horwitz at the hands of Ben Edelson, Ben was the object of far

less contempt than was his wife Alice. While she endured the censure of both the Jewish community and the courtroom, Alice's
sexual immorality influenced both his better community standing
and his legal exoneration. Ben's middle-class status may be un-
derstood in the context of an ambitious immigrant community
that sought economic success and credibility, and in the context of
a dominant culture for which the badges of male respectability
during the emasculating Depression years were especially welcome. Alice's impropriety, for the Jewish community, may be un-
derstood in the context of shared, sacred, and increasingly tenuous
values concerning marriage and motherhood, and, for the jury,
Depression-era attitudes regarding women who were perceived as
undermining the value and self-respect of men.

Although Ben became somewhat alienated from the Jewish
community after the trial, it was Alice who was shunned. As a
wife and mother, and especially as a Jewish wife and mother, she
defied many of the era's gender expectations, and, as a result, bore
the brunt of the community's wrath. Although Ben's misdeeds
were more lethal, Alice's provoked more revulsion. The scorn leveled at Alice makes it easy to forget that Jack, too, was an adulterer. He also betrayed his marriage vows and subverted the
welfare of another man's family. But his otherwise glowing reputation was safeguarded by his untimely death.[41] Moreover, as was
typical in other extramarital affairs, women more than men
"could anticipate moral outrage."[42] As the treatment of both Ben
and Jack demonstrates, "standards of appropriate behaviour and
reputation were applied to men as well as women. But moral
scrutiny was applied more often and more harshly to women."[43]
As Dubinsky points out, "the label 'whore,' a social category that
could determine women's economic, family and community standing so completely, really had no male equivalent."[44]

Despite the significance the case still holds for some Ottawa residents, it has largely faded from collective consciousness. This is
partly attributable to the passage of time: the waning memories and
mounting deaths of an elderly population have taken their toll.
But the process began in 1932 with the Edelson and Horwitz families themselves, who saw no reason to dwell on the humiliating

event. After the trial was over, they rarely discussed it again. In fact, given public fascination surrounding the case, they and an embarrassed Jewish community were invested in silencing the scandal. Nobel Laureate Elie Wiesel once said, "I marvel at the resilience of the Jewish people. Their best characteristic is their desire to remember. No other people has such an obsession with memory."[45] In this case, resilience was expressed not through the imperative to remember but by the purposeful effort to forget. That Ottawa Jews were so complicit in publicly silencing the case in its aftermath speaks volumes about the power it had to expose cruel realities about the Jewish community, and about the anxiety that they provoked.

This book consists of six chapters and a conclusion. Chapter 1 uncovers the little-known circumstances surrounding the Edelson/ Horwitz scandal: Jack and Alice's affair, the shooting of Jack at Edelson Jewellers, his lingering death in the hospital, and Ben's arrest; Chapter 2 traces the upward mobility of the immigrant Edelson family in the ambitious Jewish enclave of Lowertown; Chapter 3 chronicles Ben Edelson's inquest, and shows how this process served to challenge his respectability; Chapter 4 describes an intimate and interconnected network of relatives and friends in Lowertown for whom the case proved especially shocking, and who rejected the Edelsons, especially Alice; Chapter 5 explores the trial, highlighting issues related to class and gender that contributed to the acquittal of Ben and the condemnation of Alice; Chapter 6 confirms the conspiracy of silence in the days, years, and decades which followed the verdict, and relies largely on interviews and memoirs to demonstrate that the case was both selectively remembered and deliberately "forgotten." Either way, Alice bore the contempt of Jewish Ottawa not only during the scandal, but in the community's collective memory.

1

"This terrible drama of humanity": An Affair, a Shooting, a Death, an Arrest

In an era before self-help groups, TV "reality" and talk shows, and regular confessions by politicians and celebrities, public disclosure involving immorality and misconduct was not usual, expected, or even desirable. Of course, newspapers were increasingly in the business of reporting such indignities, but both perpetrators and victims would have resisted exposure at every cost. But a scandal is not just about them – it necessarily requires community standards, and a receptive public who will react to the news with gossip, judgments, and consequences. Any one of adultery, assault, untimely death, or arrest would merit a scandal in a small community, but the Edelson/Horwitz incident was especially notable and tragic for featuring all four.

An Affair

On the evening of 24 November 1931, Jack Horwitz dropped off his brother Charles, Charles's wife Ann, and his sister-in-law at the Regent Theatre at the corner of Bank and Sparks Streets, and then drove to his next appointment. Smartly dressed in a blue-striped shirt, vest, jacket, and a grey overcoat,[1] he had a rendezvous planned with Alice Edelson, the thirty-five-year-old married mother of seven with whom he had been having an eight-year affair. As she waited to be picked up, Alice was walking through Lowertown. The November evening was unusually mild as she meandered through the familiar streets.[2] It seemed that even under the cover of night, she endeavoured to keep moving. If she sensed that someone was following her, she was right.

Almost three years before, in early 1929, Jack's wife, Yetta, and Alice's husband, Ben, had learned of the affair. Yetta and Ben each maintained that they had first heard the news from the other.[3] Once in the know, they had a meeting at Union Station near the Edelson store to discuss the matter and decided to keep an eye on their respective spouses to find out more. Soon after the meeting Jack contacted Ben, angry at the sordid story that he felt Ben was concocting and relaying to his wife.[4]

Perhaps the Edelson children had suspected something too. Daughter Lillian remembered Jack visiting Alice at the house in the mid-1920s. "Looking back at it," reflected Lillian, "I wondered why of all of their friends, I just remembered him being there ... If I noticed him ... that one time, he must have been there during the day when my father wasn't home." But Lillian did not see him just that one time. When a fire broke out in the broom closet under the stairs, Jack suddenly appeared, and rushed in to extinguish the flames.[5] The eldest Edelson daughter, Dina, deduced more. She remembered Jack regularly phoning the house and offering a fake name. One time, Dina raised her mother's ire when she hung up and dubbed the call a wrong number. Dina didn't remember him around the house often, but recalled a very kind Jack taking Alice and the children to Strathcona Park for ice cream.[6] The park was outside the purview of Lowertown's Jewish gossip-mongers, and safely away from Edelson Jewellers.

In February 1929, several weeks after Jack's nasty communication with Ben, and at the urging of Jack himself, the two families convened for a Sunday afternoon meeting at the house of Jack's father Max to thrash out the issue.[7] Present were Max, Jack's brother Philip, Yetta, and Ben and Alice. Ben later testified that "no sooner were we there than Mrs. Edelson and Mrs. Horwitz started to argue. Mrs. Horwitz leveled accusations at Mrs. Edelson and Mrs. Edelson told her she was crazy."[8] According to Ben, even in the face of his direct questioning for thirty minutes, Jack steadfastly refused to acknowledge the affair, insisting that he "had not been going out" with Alice.[9] Edelson later recounted that at the conclusion of the meeting, "nothing definite was arrived at."[10] Yetta testified, however, that the outcome was more certain: Alice "had declared she would never give up Jack Horwitz," and then, pressured by family members to end the relationship, she and Jack reluctantly conceded that "all the intimacies would be discontinued."[11]

The antagonism between Yetta and Alice at the family conference did not only surround the affair, but the youngest of the Edelson children. Yetta later testified that "Mrs. Edelson said, I think it was the last three, or two, or one, I don't remember, of the children belonged to my husband."[12] Rather than Alice confessing to this damaging secret, and in keeping with Ben's testimony above, it was more likely Yetta who hurled the allegation at Alice. After all, Yetta surely would have recalled a specific claim by Alice regarding how many and which children were fathered by Jack. Whether any other family members questioned the children's paternity is impossible to know. But Jack himself denied that he fathered any of the Edelson children, though he had no way of knowing for sure.[13]

Although they initially kept their promise to part ways, Jack and Alice rekindled the affair and, by November 1931, had likely been together again for over a year.[14] Alice's girlfriends knew that the affair had resumed – they were "in cahoots with her" and "covering for her" when she was off with Jack.[15] Nonetheless, in October 1930, Yetta informed Ben of her shocking discovery – Alice hiding in the cellar of Jack Horwitz's Bank Street store.[16] Yetta had walked toward the coal bin and, although blocked by Jack, attempted to open the door. Finally she "heard Mrs. Edelson's voice say 'Let me out.' Mr. Horwitz opened the door and she ran up the stairs and out of the store. I immediately went down to Mr. Edelson's store and told him about it."[17] There, Yetta found Alice behind the counter, but when she reported the incident to Ben, Alice denied it had ever happened. An obviously skeptical Ben departed with Yetta for the Horwitz store. Alice, worried for Jack's safety, picked up the phone to warn him. Suspecting as much, an enraged Ben returned momentarily to the store, grabbed the receiver out of her hand, and severed the phone wires.[18] At the murder trial, Yetta would claim that Ben actually ripped the phone off the wall.[19] At the Horwitz store Yetta showed Ben the coal bin, but when the pair confronted Jack, he, like Alice, denied that she had been there. Ben returned to his store without incident.[20]

Yetta also testified that for several months after the coal bin episode, an increasingly suspicious Ben repeatedly called her. He asked where her husband had been the previous night, or for the last several nights. Or he told her that while he was away on business, she should keep her "eyes open." Over a two-month period, he called her a dozen times, making similar inquiries and requests.[21]

In the fall of 1931, Yetta enlisted the help of her brother-in-law, Jack's eldest brother Charles. Charles' motivation to intercede was likely to assist Jack, whom he knew "was being nagged with regards to this affair." But when Charles spoke to Ben, Ben declared that he did not believe his wife was seeing Jack. Furthermore, he blamed Yetta for fanning the rumour, telling Charles that all of her accusations were "tommy rot" and that "if Mrs. Horwitz would mind her husband he would mind his wife." When Charles approached Jack about the veracity of the rumour, he too said "there was nothing to it at all."[22]

Clearly, poor Yetta tried to substantiate her suspicions about the reprised affair, but in her search for the truth, she faced disagreement and deceit from all sides. She admitted to interrogating Jack about his adultery, but "he denied it to the last minute."[23] She was blamed for both fabricating stories and mishandling her husband. In the end, as she later testified regarding the affair, "it was impossible to stop it."[24]

Conflicting stories arose as to both who initiated and renewed the affair. Yetta would later testify that Jack asserted "Mrs. Edelson would not leave him alone," and that she "was always after him." Yetta also claimed that "Mrs. Edelson said she would not give up my husband."[25] According to another version, however, Jack proved infatuated with Alice, and seduced her even before his 1924 wedding.[26] His family "tried to marry him off" because "there was a scandal brewing. He was hanging around all the time." Indeed, it was Alice, along with her sister, who had tried to convince Jack to leave her alone, proceed with the marriage, and settle down. Seemingly, Jack's marriage to Yetta was one "of convenience" to placate his worried family, but it certainly didn't stop his pursuit of Alice. While he might not have "followed" or "stalked" her, "obviously he couldn't let go."[27] It was likely this situation that prompted Yetta in 1926 to leave Ottawa with her baby and stay with her parents in Montreal for nearly three months.[28]

According to Ben's testimony, Alice believed that Jack was dangerously obsessed. When she told him that the rekindled affair had to end, he threatened to expose it to Ben and all of her friends, and cautioned that if she left him, "she would be sorry." Alice couldn't bear the thought of everyone knowing, and so continued the relationship under duress.[29] Regardless of whether Alice or Jack was the aggressor, "obviously," daughter Lillian later reflected, there was a deep "emotional attraction."[30]

A Shooting

Once and for all, Ben needed to know where he stood. On 23 November, his resolve was especially strong. He testified that on that afternoon he had received a humiliating anonymous phone call at the store from a woman who said "she was surprised that a respectable business man like myself should allow my wife to go out with another man. She said the man was Jack Horwitz."[31] Witness testimony would indicate later, however, that the caller was none other than Yetta.[32] When Edelson was later asked on the stand if he knew who was calling and why, he responded vaguely that before he could inquire, "she either hung up or was disconnected."[33]

That night, he enlisted the help of Lorenzo Lemieux, a trusted employee.[34] After closing at 6:30, Ben, planning to walk home and retrieve his car to pick up Alice at the store (presumably to relieve her of the cold five-block walk), hitched a ride with Lemieux. Once in the car, Ben asked him if he would have access to a vehicle the next evening, and if he could serve as Ben's driver, and the two men arranged to meet. Lemieux then dropped off his boss at home so he could return to the store to pick up Alice.[35]

Ben's ominous plan conflicted with his more cheerful Tuesday night ritual. Ben usually played bridge in a club whose members met at each other's homes. As Ben typically looked forward to the weekly gathering, and had not missed a single one in the last two years, his absence would arouse concern.[36] But on 24 November, he drove Alice home from the store, and ate dinner with her and the children.[37] He then drove to Lemieux's father's house at 634 St Patrick Street in Lowertown. At about 8:30 pm, he parked his car in the garage, got into Lemieux's car, and put on a pair of thick-rimmed glasses to obscure his identity. When Lemieux questioned the purpose of their excursion, Ben replied that he had been told "someone was stepping out with my wife."[38]

Ben knew just where to find her. The Edelsons lived on Friel Street in Lowertown, and the Horwitzes lived on Stewart Street in neighbouring Sandy Hill, only about six blocks away. Lemieux traversed Lowertown, driving north along Friel Street, crossing Rideau, and then parking for ten minutes between Rideau and York. He then drove south to Besserer Street, to Nelson, and back to Rideau within sight of its intersection with Friel. Ben thought it was at this location where Alice might wait for a street car, and, as he suspected, she appeared there at about 9:00 pm. But she didn't linger. Instead, she walked one block east on Rideau Street to the corner of Chapel, and then north toward St Patrick. Suddenly, Jack Horwitz's car appeared, stopped quickly for Alice, and then sped off. On Ben's instruction, Lemieux tracked it to nearby Myrand Street, a small deserted block.[39]

He and Lemieux got out of the car, and approached Jack and Alice. The oblivious couple had just emerged from their car, but when they spotted the two men coming toward them they quickly retreated inside, and Jack revved the motor. A frenzied Ben jumped on the running board but Jack shoved him off. Ben jumped on again, reached inside the open window, and pulled up on the hand brake. When the engine stalled, he ordered Alice out and implored her to come home, threatening to lock her out of their house if she refused. Jack declared that Alice would stay. He retorted that there were plenty of available hotels if Ben would not let her return home, whereupon Ben replied, "Yes, and I don't doubt that you have been using some of them." Alice begged Ben to come into Jack's car so that the three of them could talk at the Edelson house. Ben rejected the proposal, pointing out, "You can't come home and bring him. The children are old enough to understand." So Alice and Jack suggested they talk instead at the Edelson store. Ben agreed, and at about 9:15, they made their way to 24 Rideau Street. Lemieux followed, and after the unlikely trio went inside, he dropped by the Chateau Pharmacy next door.[40]

Montreal jewellry salesman Nate Alexander, who was staying across the street at the Château Laurier, was looking to do business with Ben that night, but finding the store locked and vacant, walked away. As it turned out, he travelled to the Horwitz store downtown on Bank Street. When he arrived, he "was told by the girl there that there had been an accident at the Edelson store."[41] Had Alexander stopped by Edelson Jewellers just a few moments later, he might have unwittingly averted – or at the very least witnessed – the tragedy.

As Ben was the only eyewitness to testify in court, the following account of what happened next is largely based on his testimony. Once in the store he locked the glass door from inside, and the two men squared off as Alice stood quietly by. Ben immediately had the upper hand. He walked to the phone, informing Jack that he was calling Yetta to invite her to the meeting. Jack told Ben that he would leave the store if he continued the call, so Ben hung up the phone. Alice confessed to Ben that although she initially kept her promise three years ago to end the affair, it had resumed. In an effort to exonerate herself, she explained that Jack had shown up at her door one night and, though she did not allow him in, he "'managed to get me out of the house and asked me to go for a drive." She revived the affair, but it was his threats to disclose it to Ben and their friends that forced her to stay with him. As Jack stood by in silence, an emotional Alice cried, "Why did I have to come to all this? Why did I not die when I was so sick last year?" She begged her husband to take pity on their children, but Ben's attention turned to Jack. He asked, "Jack, why did you have to do that? Why do you not leave Alice alone? Do you realize that for 20 years we have been married?" Ben first reminded Jack that the couple had seven children who needed their mother, then stated that he was willing to divorce his wife if Jack also divorced his wife and married Alice. Jack did not call Ben's bluff, however; instead, he claimed that he and Alice were through. But Ben had heard this all before, and doubted his every word. Ben testified that he then walked to his workbench, opened a drawer, and brandished a gun. Standing behind a glass counter, he pulled back on the gun's chamber to demonstrate it was loaded, prompting a live round to fall to the floor. Resting his elbow on the showcase, and pointing the gun upward, Ben warned, "Jack, if I ever see you with my wife again, if I ever see you speaking to her or hear of you telephoning her, I will walk into your store in broad daylight and shoot you." Instinctively, a terrified Alice shrieked "Jack, he is going to shoot you!"[42]

Edelson later described a struggle which Horwitz both initiated and intensified. Jack, with the showcase between him and Ben, was the first to make contact by grabbing Ben's wrist with his left hand, and attempting to seize the gun with his right. Jack kept twisting Ben's wrist, and despite Ben's plea to release it, wouldn't let go. As they continued to brawl, a shot rang out, the bullet piercing the wall behind a display case. Edelson testified:

> I said, "Jack, leave go and I will put the gun away." He said "Like hell I will. We'll see who's going to shoot who." His eyes went red and bulged out of his head. He pushed Mrs. Edelson to one side and swung his right hand and punched me under the right eye. I think his ring slashed me. He then continued to twist my wrist and I removed my finger from the trigger because I was afraid the gun might go off again. While we were struggling I heard another shot and he grabbed his side, slumping against the counter and walked towards the rear of the store.[43]

As Jack fell to the floor, Lemieux peered into the locked glass door, responding to the two gun shots he had heard from next door. According to Edelson, he opened the door, and ordered Lemieux to call for a doctor. Lemieux ran back to the Chateau Pharmacy and asked the owner to get medical help. When Laframboise was unsuccessful in securing his brother, a doctor, Lemieux ran back to the store, and, at the suggestion of Edelson, returned to the pharmacy to contact Dr S.L. Everett Danby, a surgeon who lived nearby. Lemieux then re-entered Edelson Jewellers to wait for the doctor, wondering perhaps why neither he nor Edelson used the telephone inside the store.[44]

Alice immediately went to Jack's aid. She bathed his face with a wet towel. She then tried to open his shirt to place the cloth on his wound, but her gloved hands fumbled so she ripped the shirt open, causing the severed buttons to fly onto the floor. She reassured Jack that all would be fine, and offered him some water that Ben had fetched.[45] According to Lemieux, Alice said "'Jack, I'll do anything for you.' And she was kissing him."[46] Lemieux also recollected that Alice warned, "You'll pay for that," but he could not say to whom she was directing this promise of revenge.[47] Ben later testified that it was Lemieux himself, for serving as Ben's chauffeur that night.[48]

Lemieux and Ben would recollect several facts differently. Lemieux testified that when he appeared at the store after hearing the shots, and Ben unlocked the front door, it was Alice, not Ben, who initially insisted that Lemieux call for a doctor. In fact, according to Lemieux, except for his subsequent request for Dr Danby, Edelson "was standing there without a word."[49] Although Edelson claimed that he fetched the glass of water for Jack, Lemieux later testified that it was he who had retrieved it.[50] And, according to Lemieux, when a wounded Jack requested that his brother be informed of his injury, it was Alice, not Ben (as the accused later claimed) who would instruct him to locate Charles at the Regent Theatre.[51]

By the time Dr Danby arrived, only five minutes after he was called, Jack's clothes were "half saturated" with blood.[52] After viewing the bullet wound, he immediately telephoned for help, but had problems reaching the ambulance dispatch office, which caused a considerable delay. In the meantime, he contacted the

hospital, also with "some difficulty," and requested that an operating room be readied.[53] Aware of the precious passing moments,
Alice was "running up and down the store" between Dr Danby
and Jack, pleading with Danby "to hurry and do something for
him."[54] Jack himself urged someone to retrieve his car and drive
him to the hospital, but Danby insisted he stay put until the ambulance arrived.[55]

Dr Danby would later offer detailed recollections of his time at
the crime scene. He detected no smell of gunpowder, no evidence
of a scuffle, and no gun. Danby also noted that throughout the
crisis, neither Edelson nor Horwitz referred to the shooting: "I
asked no questions and they said nothing."[56] Indeed, when the
prosecutor later asked Danby if he inquired of Edelson what had
happened, Danby replied "I took particular care not to."[57] It was
Danby who, by way of a hospital nurse, would finally contact
police after 12:15 am to report the incident, deciding to call only
when Horwitz's condition "was becoming serious."[58]

At about 9:45, fifteen minutes after the shooting, the ambulance
finally arrived. With neither the attendants nor Danby adminis-
tering drugs, the ambulance transported Jack, with Alice by his side,
to the Ottawa General Hospital on Water Street. As Danby readied to leave, Ben retrieved the doctor's watch, which was at the
store for repair, and returned it to its owner. Ben explained "you
better take it when you can; there may be some trouble," alluding
to the possibility that he could be detained or the store could be
closed with a police investigation. With the departure of Dr Danby,
and with Lemieux at the Regent Theatre, Ben was left at the store
on his own.[59]

Ben then simply locked up his shop and stood outside. As he
waited for Lemieux to return to pick him up, he spoke casually
with Laframboise of the Chateau Pharmacy. Laframboise later
testified that "he said there had been an accident and then we
began to talk about the weather." Strangely, Laframboise did not
probe Edelson for further details, including those related to the
identity of the victim and his physical condition. When Lemieux
returned at around 10:30 pm, Edelson showed him his battle

scar: a cut, bruised right eye received in his tussle with Jack. "See," said Edelson, "he hit me."[60]

A silent Ben spent the next part of the night driving with Lemieux, looking to contact lawyer Moses Doctor, an acquaintance in the Jewish community.[61] They drove first to Doctor's Lady Grey Drive house, but no one was home, so he left a message for the lawyer to call him at the Chateau Pharmacy. When Lemieux and Edelson returned to the pharmacy at about 11:30 pm, the lawyer was on the line, and Lemieux and Edelson drove back to his house, picked him up, and went to the hospital, where the two jewellers waited outside as Doctor inquired about Horwitz's condition. After they drove the lawyer home, they returned to Lemieux's father's house where Ben picked up his car and reminded Lemieux to show up for work at 8:30 the next morning.[62]

On that anxious drive home, perhaps Ben's greatest preoccupation was not Jack's potentially fatal injury, or even his own dire circumstances, but trying to protect his wife from criminal charges. Ben's court testimony describing the shooting would hint at this objective: to remove Alice from the proximity of the scuffle. In Ben's account, Horwitz "pushed" Alice "to one side," protecting her from the brawl;[63] in another more dramatic version Ben later relayed to the prosecutor, Horwitz even "punched Mrs. Edelson, knocking her to the floor."[64] Either way, Ben would make it clear that Alice was well away from the action once the first shot was fired.

Clearly, Ben knew something that no one outside the crime scene did – that Alice might have played a part in the shooting. On rare but separate occasions decades later, daughters Lillian and Dina both learned that in the fateful scuffle between the men, and in a failed attempt to prevent their harm, Alice might have pushed Ben's hand, inadvertently causing the weapon to fire, or grabbed the gun from Ben's hand, also unwittingly causing the gun to go off.[65] In either case, the fact that Alice sought to intercept Ben's actions suggests that she believed Ben was readying to shoot Jack Horwitz. In Dina's view, "my father didn't kill him – my mother did."[66]

Whether Ben disclosed Alice's possible role in the shooting in his discussion with Moses Doctor that night can't be known. But his story might have given Doctor the confidence he needed to argue the case as an accident – even if it wasn't Ben's accident, but Alice's. There certainly was no hard evidence to preclude Alice's involvement. In fact, there was a "suggestion made in legal circles that Mrs. Edelson might be arraigned on a criminal charge." Crown attorney J.A. Ritchie responded, however, that "the Crown has not yet considered bringing in Mrs. Edelson as an accessory or anything else as yet into the case," only vaguely promising to "look into every aspect that will bring the case to completion."[67]

But in the days that followed, there was barely an implication by the police, the press, or the public that Alice either wittingly or not caused Ben to pull the trigger or pulled it herself. This was partly due to the fact that investigation of the shooting had been compromised in significant ways. First, the police were not called to the scene that night, and didn't even learn of the shooting until hours after it happened.[68] Secondly, when they finally examined the gun for fingerprints none were retrieved, due both to the "corrugated" butt of the gun and "the checkered grip making such impressions valueless."[69] Only at the trial did police acknowledge that they could have lifted fingerprints from other parts of the pistol, although this, too, might have proved fruitless given that Detective-Sergeant MacDonald had transported the gun in his coat pocket.[70] Charges against Alice would never be laid, and her possible role in the shooting was never introduced by the defence during the trial as a strategy to help Ben.

So Alice's culpability in the homicide, whether as a prime suspect or an accessory, proved irrelevant. In the popular view, a woman could incite crime, but rarely committed it.[71] Indeed, it was less than a day after the incident when police surmised that the shooting "was due to domestic relations. It is alleged that Horwitz was thought to have been too attentive to Mrs. Edelson, who is an exceptionally attractive young woman."[72] Inherent in this statement was that Alice (and her beauty) was complicit in the homicide, but not the perpetrator of it. What's more, the foremost suspect in the case never contested that it was he who fired the gun, another reason that police felt no compulsion to investigate Alice. No matter what her true part in the shooting, Ben covered for her, and, likely in an effort to protect the woman he still loved, as well as their seven children, "took the entire blame."[73] It was Ben, the proprietor of both the crime site and the weapon, who went home after the tragedy and waited to be arrested.

A Death

At the Regent Theatre, Jack's brother Charles, his wife Ann, and his sister-in-law had settled into their seats. Ironically, the feature film was *The Guardsman*, a mediocre farce about a husband who suspects his wife of adultery.[74] At about 10:00 pm, only fifteen minutes into the movie, an emergency message flashed on the screen summoning Charles to the Regent's box office where he was met by Lorenzo Lemieux, who drove the anxious Horwitzes to the Water Street branch of the Ottawa General Hospital. There, Charles discovered that his brother Jack had been gravely injured, not in a motor car accident as he had first feared, but by a gunshot to the stomach.[75]

   Treatment for Jack was swift. Dr Danby had ensured that Jack was treated for shock, and that he was administered morphine, an abdominal X-ray, and a blood transfusion.[76] When Charles arrived at the hospital, he found his brother-in-law Harry Hertz donating blood for the transfusion in a last desperate attempt to save Jack's life.[77] The X-ray results, showing that the bullet had traversed the abdomen from the left and lodged itself on the right, confirmed the severity of the wound, and the need for surgery. By about 11:40 pm, however, a newly arrived Dr Shapiro observed that Horwitz, pallid with a faint pulse and blue fingertips, "was dying." In an attempt to placate his patient, Shapiro told him that his condition was manageable, and that surgery could wait, but the doctor knew that it was "impossible to operate." Horwitz would never receive the surgery, whose outcome, in any case, would have been fatal, and by 12:15 am, his condition had drastically worsened.[78]

A surprisingly alert Jack had focused on getting his affairs in order. He told Harry to pick up his car, parked at 24 Rideau Street in front of Edelson Jewellers, and instructed him on how to dispose of some assets. He also discussed his estate with his lawyer and childhood friend Sam Berger, whom he had summoned to his bedside at around 11:00 pm in order to hurriedly draw up his will.[79] At thirty-one years of age, Berger had only been a lawyer for four years, but he was tough and shrewd, and protective of Jack's interests.[80] Horwitz prevailed upon Berger: "Sam, please make my will. Hurry. I think I'm done."[81] Berger tended to the will, although Jack's eleventh-hour effort to bequest part of his estate to Charles would prove futile. Berger remained with Jack for about fifteen minutes, trying to reassure him that he would be fine. But Jack knew otherwise: he stated to his older brother, "I'm getting paralyzed. I can hear you but I can't see you,"[82] and tried to comfort him by concluding "it is an easy death Charlie."[83]

Jack also offered a variety of reasons for the cause of his injury. To Charles, he simply labeled it "an accident." To Berger, he stated that the gunshot had been accidentally self-inflicted – that he "had been toying with his revolver when it was discharged." And to Harry, he affirmed plainly "he shot me," making no specific reference to the shooter.[84] Given that Jack was preoccupied with issues related to assets and wills, he might have branded his injury an accident to protect his family's entitlement to the life and business insurance, which, as his brothers would later discover, would not pay out if Jack were culpable in the shooting. Another possibility is that his reference to his own misuse of his gun (which he was not toting that night) and then to a male shooter was a strategy to shield Alice from blame.

But the police would never get a chance to question Jack. By the time they arrived at the hospital at 12:50 am, he was slipping out of consciousness, and they were unable to obtain an official statement. Why the police were not called to the crime scene, and why they arrived too late to secure an ante-mortem statement from Jack would raise some serious questions.[85] Dr Danby later stated that he did not call the police while at the Edelson store because he "was too busy attempting to save Horwitz' [sic] life."[86]

Yetta also made it to her husband's bedside, but, unlike the police, arrived in time to converse with Jack. On Tuesday night, she had gone out to play bridge and returned home sometime between 11:00 and 11:45. Her maid informed her that there had been several telephone calls – hang-ups. Jack's brother Phil called at around midnight, and reported that Jack had been in "an accident." Arriving at the hospital sometime before 12:25 am, Yetta found Jack struggling to breathe. She did not ask him about how his injury was inflicted; instead she urged him "to fight for his life," and for their five-year-old daughter, Anita, and pleaded for him to kiss her. Jack obliged Yetta, asked her to kiss Anita goodbye, and then passed away in Yetta's arms.[87]

On 25 November 1931, at 1:05 am, Jack died of internal bleeding.[88] The gunshot had severed the iliac artery, a large blood vessel in the pelvis.[89] The death certificate was less clinical, citing the cause of death as "gun shot wound in abdomen – 'Murder.'"[90] Predating both the coroner's inquest and the trial, the certificate's allegation of "murder," even if placed in quotation marks, seemed highly inappropriate, but contrary to Jack's declaration to Berger, it did confirm that the wound had not been self-inflicted. Indeed, police investigators had located no powder burns on the victim, and concluded the fatal shot had been fired from several feet away.

Jack's body was taken to Gauthier's Undertaking Parlors on St Patrick Street. Here, relatives and friends, including brothers Charles, Phil, and Jacie, came to pay their respects, but also to attend the coroner's inquest set to begin prior to Jack's burial the next day.[91] In an interview before the inquest, Charles maintained that "I did not know of any trouble between my brother and Mr. Edelson," concealing his meeting with a distraught Yetta just a month or so earlier.[92] The inquest jury viewed the body, although the hearing would be adjourned until the following Tuesday.[93]

Jack's stores at 74 Bank Street and 168 Sparks Street were shut for several days. Notices on the doors announced that they were "closed through the death of the owner."[94] At the urging of the

Horwitz family lawyer, city police posted officers outside the two locked stores as a "precautionary measure" until after the funeral.[95] It was unclear whether this step was taken to protect the stores against opportunistic thieves or, as proved prescient, against Jack's shrewd widow Yetta.

Yetta was heartbroken, but still kept herself busy. In the early morning of 25 November, only hours after Jack's death, she was granting interviews to the press. Unlike Ben and Alice, who weren't talking, Yetta chronicled her actions the previous night, described her final moments with Jack, and lamented her unfortunate fate, sobbing to the newspapers that her life was "ruined."[96]

Astonishingly, Yetta also referred to her husband's indiscretion, which she blamed entirely on Alice. She described her Ottawa home with Jack and daughter Anita as her "own little nest here which has been broken up," attributing this devastation to her husband's long-term affair, Alice's sexual maturity and allure, and, ultimately, Jack's exploitation.[97] Yetta cryptically commented to reporters that she "was fighting this all along but I fought a losing battle. He was only a kid and they were more experienced hands."[98] Indeed, that night following Jack's death, an overwrought Yetta ran into Charles' house frantically screaming "They killed my Jackie! They killed my Jackie!" her use of the word "they" alluding to both Ben and Alice's involvement.[99]

Clearly, Yetta, who saw herself as the primary victim of the tragedy, was seeking to garner public sympathy. Her lawyer, Sam Berger, showed up at her home during the interview, either to encourage her or to rein her in. In any case, Yetta got what she wanted: the *Journal* described her as "looking haggard" following "a night of mental agony."[100] But the *Citizen* did one better, describing a heart-wrenching scene in which "youthful Anita called for her dad." The newspaper reflected sadly that "little did the youngster realize that her father was no more."[101]

Given her elevated status as the grieving widow, as well as her absence from Edelson Jewellers the night of the shooting, Yetta was regarded in the press and in court as nothing more than an unwitting victim. But her multiple meetings and phone calls with Ben, her snitching to him about Alice in the coal bin, and her possible identity as the "anonymous caller" reveal her complicity in the escalation of events even though it was motivated by a desperate desire for her accusations to be validated, and for her own degradation to end. While there is no evidence that Yetta collaborated with Ben to hatch a murder plot, or that she wanted her husband dead, the generous amount of money she believed was left to her in Jack's will could at least cushion her mistreatment and disgrace.

In keeping with Jewish law, Jack Horwitz's funeral was held the next day, on Thursday, 26 November at 1:30 pm. Perched on neighbouring verandas and stoops, about one thousand people gathered outside the Horwitzes' Stewart Street home.[102] Hundreds more of the "morbidly curious" lined the route of the cortège where police officers controlled the crowd and the traffic.[103] The funeral procession travelled past the King Edward Synagogue, whose doors were opened in tribute, to the Jewish cemetery on Bank Street, where over three hundred people attended the graveside service.[104] It included no eulogy, which was not surprising given the disreputable circumstances of his death.[105]

The tombstone, erected almost a year after Jack's burial as prescribed by Jewish custom, would disclose the brevity of his life. The stone did not record his date of birth, only that of his death, but the Hebrew epitaph lamented a precious life that ended too soon – a man "who was plucked in the youth of his life / a tender fragrant young flower / whose thread [or wick] of life was suddenly disconnected." Indeed, just thirty-three years old, he was prospering both professionally and personally. As well, the handsome, light-haired Horwitz exuded boyish innocence and charm; the elder, dark-haired Edelson, in contrast, had sharper, more chiseled features that could make him appear serious and stern, and older than his years.

The Ottawa papers eulogized Jack primarily as a flourishing and honourable entrepreneur.[106] While first working for his father, he possessed "keen business initiative," and went into business

for himself, operating the two thriving jewellery stores on Bank
and Sparks Streets, and for several years running a store in Hull,
Quebec.[107] As a businessman, he was most admired for his un-
derstated charm, graciousness, and likeability. The *Citizen* noted
that "his quiet, unassuming personality" early on "gained for him
a large clientele," and that his "rise to success was attributable to
an ever-courteous manner."[108] The *Journal* reported that he was
"possessed of a striking personality," and "was always known to
be courteous and obliging."[109] His fine reputation in the business
community explains, stated the *Citizen*, why on the day of his funeral "business firms throughout the city ... were closed out of
respect."[110] The newspapers reprinted only one photograph of
Jack, but it was a flattering picture in which he donned a suit and
tie, and which conveyed his pleasant and boyish good looks.[111]

But it was Jack's tragic widow Yetta, dressed entirely in black
at the funeral, who was the object of great interest by the press. It
could not help but notice that her eyes were "red and swollen with
weeping," and that she was completely inconsolable and "pros-
trated with grief." [112] Another report indicated, however, that she
seemed relatively composed in light of her deep bereavement, a
mark of her prudent approach to life.[113]

In fact, Yetta was "a tough cookie" who was nothing if not
pragmatic. In later years, she would become obsessively frugal,
saving plastic enclosures from bread bags, reading only newspapers that were discarded by others, and keeping a record of gift-
giving so she wouldn't spend more on friends than they did on
her.[114] Even in the days that followed the shooting, her anguish
did not distract her – or her brothers-in-law – from the practical
implications of Jack's death. Only three days after the shooting,
they were embroiled in a bitter legal dispute over the ownership
of Jack's two stores, a life insurance policy worth almost $22,000,
and other assets.[115] The *Citizen* first reported that Jack left his
entire estate to Yetta;[116] however, a reading of his deathbed will
described as "pathetic and terse," hinting at Jack's desperate condition, stated that Jack's estate was to be divided equally three
ways – among widow Yetta, daughter Anita, and brother Charles,
with Charles and brother Phil as executors.[117]

Yetta, significantly disadvantaged by the revised will, was infuriated that Charles had been named an equal beneficiary. Her position as Jack's wife had been undermined first by Jack's affair and now by his seemingly vindictive will, and there was talk that she would contest it. It was almost certainly Yetta who insisted to the press that given that "the dead man was suffering intense pain when it was drawn up, and was under the influence of powerful narcotics to relieve his agony while on the operating table, his mental faculties were impaired to a great degree."[118]

Although clearly a conflict of interest, Yetta was represented in the dispute by her husband's lawyer and friend Sam Berger. Berger asserted the widow's full claim to Jack's two stores. He even had locksmiths change the original locks, for which she had not possessed keys. Earlier that day, he had requested the keys from Benjamin Goldfield, lawyer for the Horwitz brothers. When Goldfield refused, Berger, with a police constable and locksmiths in tow, seized the Sparks Street store, and demanded that the store's staff, including Jack's two brothers-in-law, vacate the premises. Berger instructed the police officer to remove the men "by force if necessary" if they refused to comply. Berger and his entourage only left after Charles, the manager of the store, arrived on the scene. Later that day the Horwitz brothers reinstated the old locks, and sat vigil that evening at the stores after documents, money, and other items were discovered missing from the Bank Street store safe. Charles accused Berger of stealing the stores' insurance policies, as well as some cash.[119] As Yetta was the secretary-treasurer of the business,[120] a position which offered her ready access to the safe, Charles unequivocally implicated her in the scheme.[121]

The next day, on 28 November, a "sensation was sprung" when Berger suddenly resigned as Yetta's attorney.[122] He maintained that, as both Yetta's lawyer and a longtime friend of the Horwitz family, he felt too conflicted, and encouraged Yetta to engage an "independent lawyer."[123] He might also have quit the case because of his close acquaintance with Horwitz family lawyer Goldfield.[124] Even more significantly, Berger was running for alderman of St George's Ward (Sandy Hill) in the upcoming December municipal elections,[125] and must have realized that the publicity related to his role in the family feud was bad for his political campaign, especially as the reported dispute more than hinted at his influence with police, and at his character as a bully. What's worse, Berger had no legal authority to change the Horwitz store locks, and Charles and Harry Hertz were threatening a warrant for his arrest for illegally procuring and possessing the documents which disappeared from the Bank Street shop.[126] In renouncing his role as Yetta's lawyer, Berger wisely distanced himself both from possible criminal charges (and discipline or disbarment by the Law Society) and from inflammatory family conflicts.[127]

Berger was also at the centre of his own controversy. According to the The Canadian Jewish Chronicle, "legal circles of the Capital were agog ... with speculation over the position of Sam Berger." As he had witnessed the only ante-mortem statement given by Jack, Ottawa lawyers debated whether Berger, as Jack's counsel, would be legally obligated to disclose their conversation in a courtroom or whether he would be spared due to lawyer-client privilege.[128]

Following the nasty feud with Jack's brothers, and deserted by Sam Berger, Yetta and her daughter Anita would abandon Ottawa almost immediately after the January trial.[129] As a grief-stricken young widow humiliated by her husband's adulterous affair, his carved-up will, and her lawyer's resignation, she no doubt felt demoralized. But Yetta would be redeemed. The Journal disclosed on 8 January that she and Jack, having been married in Montreal, had a marriage contract, as was customary in Quebec to protect wives under provincial community of property laws. According to its terms, Yetta was entitled to Jack's life insurance left to her, plus an extra $10,000. Ultimately she would inherit Jack's entire estate, her position as a "creditor" (as the Journal called her) overriding the standing of the other beneficiaries, including her daughter Anita.[130] The existence of this contract helps explain why Jack consistently rejected the idea of divorcing Yetta. With Yetta appropriating Charles' share of the inheritance and suspected of looting the store safe, it is no wonder that, in the end, she was alienated from her husband's family and friends, and moved back with her daughter to Montreal.[131]

The Horwitz family was now in ruins. Young Jack was dead, and for the seven remaining Horwitz siblings, it was the third family death in as many years: in January of 1929, their mother Rebecca had died from liver and stomach cancer at the age of fifty-four, and in May of 1930, their father Max had died of amyotrophic lateral sclerosis (ALS) at the age of fifty-six.[132] Moreover, Jack's brothers and widow had waged war, forcing the alienation and desertion of the humiliated Yetta, and the permanent estrangement of Anita from her Ottawa family. Unlike the actions of Ben Edelson, however, and especially those of the adulterous Alice, the conduct of Jack Horwitz, which helped set off these heartbreaking events, would never be the object of severe scrutiny and contempt among those who knew something of his unseemly demise.

An Arrest

On the advice of his lawyer, Ben Edelson returned home after the shooting, and waited anxiously for the knock by police.[133] At 1:30 am, Detective-Sergeant Aubrey MacDonald and Sergeant-Major Joseph Hardon, along with Moses Doctor, arrived at the Edelson home. About an hour earlier, they had conferred with Jack Horwitz's doctors, and learned that the shooting victim was dying. Now they were here to escort Ben to the Queen Street police station.[134]

Once at the station, the police informed him that Jack was dead, and Ben Edelson was charged with murder. Perhaps due to his co-operative disposition and his middle-class respectability, the police offered him some latitude: they never placed him in handcuffs, and he was permitted to confer with Doctor for fifteen minutes in a private office. Hardon then booked Ben, emptying his pockets of some cash and small possessions, and placed him in a police cell overnight. The *Citizen*, already at the station, reported that "Mr. Edelson naturally showed signs of nervousness, twitching his hands, but he answered the questions ... in a clear and steady voice."[135]

It wasn't until after 2:00 am, four and a half hours after the shooting, that the police themselves knew enough to show up at Edelson Jewellers. Patrolling his Rideau Street beat, Constable Reginald Raby joined Detective-Sergeant Macdonald and Sergeant-Major Hardon in the Edelson store.[136] In addition to locating the live round that had dropped to the floor, Raby and Hardon located two spent .32 caliber casings and two shirt buttons. In a drawer in the workbench, Macdonald discovered a gun, a .32 caliber automatic with the safety catch off and a live round inside, and observed broken glass that had been part of an upright display case. They also spotted the glass and dish of water used to administer help to Horwitz, as well as his grey felt hat on a counter. What struck them most during their forty-five minute investigation was "the absence of disorder or signs of a struggle," and the dearth of blood stains except for those that appeared on a rubber mat.[137]

Leaving the store without securing the crime scene, the police would not visit Edelson Jewellers again until the following day, after Ben and Alice's teenage son Samuel had already reported for work. It was Samuel who showed them the bullet lodged in the wall, a glaring police oversight the preceding night given the extra spent casing found on the floor, the nearby shattered glass, and possible information by the newly arrested Edelson that there had indeed been two shots. Samuel then unceremoniously plucked the bullet out of the woodwork.[138]

Alice Edelson arrived home over an hour after Ben had been arrested, at 2:40 am.[139] For a short time at least, she had remained with Jack at the hospital, likely encountering his brother Charles and brother-in-law Harry Hertz.[140] As Yetta hadn't seen her when she arrived after midnight, however, it seems likely that Alice had left the hospital by this time, or that she remained as unobtrusive as possible.[141] Except for Dr Danby, who later testified that he spotted Alice there, witnesses claimed that they hadn't recalled seeing her, or they simply didn't mention her presence at all.[142] Looking to commiserate with the Horwitz family, and perhaps to offer penance, Alice then stopped in at Charles' home where Charles' wife Ann and probably other family members were waiting for reports about Jack. Although Charles and Harry never saw Alice there, they later arrived at the house to "considerable excitement,"[143] caused not only by news of Jack's death, but also, no doubt, by the unwelcome visit of an anguished Alice. There is no record of how long Alice stayed there, or how she was treated, but in the immediate aftermath of such a tragedy, she surely couldn't have expected a kindly reception.

Once home, Alice was obviously in shock: she had witnessed a shooting, her lover was dead, and her husband, whom she hadn't seen since the incident, had been hauled off by police. What's more, the press was already at the house, and had even spoken with Alice's sixteen-year-old daughter Dina.[144] Daughter Lillian remembered that her mother was so frenzied as she got out of a taxi in front of the house, family members had to help her up the walk. From inside the house, Lillian heard her mother's unforgettable screams: "I killed him! I killed him!"[145] Bombarded with questions by her frightened children, who had been awoken by their father's unusually late arrival home, and by the intrusion of police and the press, a "hysterical" and sobbing Alice proved incoherent, and was "on the verge of collapse" as she was finally helped upstairs.[146] In the days that followed, even the police didn't interview her due to her delicate health.[147] For the next two weeks, Alice would be in self-imposed seclusion, suffering from some sort of breakdown.[148]

In addition to signifying trauma and loss, Alice's frantic declaration could have held a variety of meanings. It could have indicated that she felt complicit in Jack's death because of the illicit affair, her decision to step out with him the night before, or because of her gun-wielding husband. Or it could have been a confession related to the shooting itself, suggestive of a direct, albeit accidental, hand in her lover's death, and in fear that she herself could face criminal charges.[149]

With Jack's death, Ben's arrest, and Alice's infirmity, the scandal that began with Jack and Alice's affair became far more public and salacious. As the jailed Ben awaited a coroner's inquest and then a murder trial, and as Alice's wifely and maternal presence grew elusive, it took no time at all for the newspapers to make matters worse. They reviewed the shocking events in lurid detail, offering up overtly sexualized descriptions of Alice, which, while ostensibly flattering, highlighted her adulterous image. The *Citizen* referred to her as "an exceptionally attractive young woman," while the *Journal* described her as "the jeweller's comely young wife," and as "petite and distinctively attractive."[150] The papers also reported on her relationship with Jack in the last hours of his life. A headline in *The Toronto Daily Star* announced that "Mrs. Edelson Kissed Dying Man."[151] When one paper described the injured Jack sprawled on the floor, it noted that she "was bathing his face."[152] Another made special mention of the fact that she escorted her paramour in the ambulance while her husband drove himself home.[153] From this point on, innuendo and judgments about Alice's behaviour before, during, and after the shooting would be a feature not only of press coverage about the case, but of her nasty treatment both by the Jewish community and inside the courtroom.

2

"A prominent Ottawa jeweller" and "the jeweller's comely young wife": The Rise of the Edelsons

Like most Canadian Jews, those living in Ottawa were part of a large wave who fled Eastern Europe between 1881 and 1920. Their numbers rose dramatically in these years: between 1911 and 1921, while the general population of Canada rose by 22 per cent, its Jewish population rose by 67 per cent; in Ontario, while the general population rose by 16 per cent, its Jewish population increased by 77 per cent.[1] In the 1920s and 30s, the Jews of Ottawa sought integration into the larger community, eager to establish themselves professionally, and to be deemed full and contributing members of the dominant culture. At the same time, however, they were never shy about wearing their Judaism on their sleeve. They were acutely aware of anti-Semitism, and how it could impede their upward mobility, and devoted countless volunteer hours to elevating the quality of their lives in the thriving Jewish enclave of Lowertown.

Once a struggling immigrant, Benjamin Simon Edelson could be counted among Ottawa's many Jewish success stories. He was born in Friedrichstadt, Russia (today Jaunjelgava, Latvia) on 27 March 1890. By 1897, Friedrichstadt, a small town fifty miles southeast of Riga, had about five thousand residents, over three thousand of whom were Jews.[2] Ben's father Joseph Pinchus owned an inn and served as *shammes* (sexton) of his synagogue; he and his wife Zelda Lehrman Edelson had five children.[3] Youngest son Ben was studious and intellectual, and his parents wanted him to become a rabbi. But the entrepreneurial Ben had different ideas. His older brothers had gone to Moscow to train as jewellers and had prospered, impressing Ben on their visits back home with expensive gold chains and watches. At fifteen years of age, Ben declared that he too wanted to be a jeweller, and in 1905 he apprenticed in Warsaw, becoming a skilled watchmaker and engraver.[4]

With his two eldest brothers in New York, and boasting a trade, Ben also sought to immigrate to America. In the summer of 1907, the seventeen-year-old left Riga on the steamship *Ivan Asbelef*, and disembarked in Philadelphia on 29 July, arriving in New York the next day.[5] Seven years later, the rest of the Edelson family would follow him there.[6]

Once again, Ben worked as an apprentice watchmaker. Like other such artisans, he aspired to be a retail merchant who employed junior craftsmen.[7] But for now, Ben laboured for others, working in 1908 for eight months at the Emanuel Gershuny jewellery store in South River, New Jersey, a town of about four thousand people.[8] Located at Main and Ferry Streets in the heart of South River's business district, the store seems to have eluded the July 1908 fire that devastated much of downtown.[9] Still, it's possible that in November of 1908, when Ben requested a letter of reference from his boss, the destruction of the downtown core induced him to seek employment elsewhere. Gershuny wrote that Ben was "capable of taking full charge" of his "business and work bench," and thought him "honest and truthfull [*sic*] in every respect."[10] Ben was then employed at the jewellery shop of Alfred Sorenson in Jersey City, New Jersey, one of about sixty-five jewellery stores in this relatively large city.[11]

At around the same time, in 1909, Ben fell in love with Alice Coblentz. They had met through their mothers who were distantly related, possibly cousins.[12] Their mothers had planned for Ben to court Alice's older sister Lillian, but when he laid eyes on the prettier Alice, he was "smitten by her." But Lillian would not to be left in the cold: in 1917, she would marry Ben's older brother Isidore.[13]

Alice was born 15 October 1896 in Ponevezh, Russia (today Panevežys, Lithuania), in Kovno guberniia.[14] At this time, 13,044 people resided in Ponevezh, just over half of them Jewish.[15] Successive fires that ravaged the town, combined with an 1883

Russian dictate that prohibited Ponevezh Jews from residing in outlying areas and forced them into the overcrowded city, motivated Ponevezh's many poor Jews to emigrate. With the additional incentive to flee political unrest and pogroms, most of them, perhaps as many as eighty percent in the years after 1905, moved to South Africa or America.[16] Chaya Coblentz and her four children arrived in America around 1905. Alice's father Samuel was already dead by this time, possibly as the result of a riding accident.[17]

Alice Coblentz, thirteen years old at the close of 1909, was a youthful love interest for the nineteen-year-old Ben, a fact which may account for variations in her date of birth. In the little book where he recorded family milestones, Ben wrote that Alice was born in 1894. The 1964 reissue of the Edelson marriage certificate also indicates that Alice's birth year was 1894. This date meant Alice would have been four years instead of six years younger than Ben, which made her a more respectable fifteen years old when they met.[18]

In other papers, however, Alice appears younger. A Canadian passport and corresponding citizenship papers issued in 1961 records her birth year as 1900.[19] (This date would have made her a shocking nine years old at the start of the courtship, and just under twelve years old when she married.) Confusion about Alice's age might stem from imperfect Russian birth or immigration records, from her birth month positioned at year's end, or from her vanity in later life.[20] In any event, it seems Alice didn't concern herself too much with the math, or with the discrepancy in official documents. All of this ambiguity might help to explain why her tombstone omits her date of birth altogether.

No matter her age, Ben was a man in love. He wrote love poems whenever he had the chance, scribbling them on the back of his Sorenson business card and on a customer repair ticket.[21] He also regularly sent her postcards covered with romantic illustrations and filled with expressions of his longing. On one 1911 postcard, a blissful young farm couple gazes at their new homestead as large, windswept clouds take the shape of their faces about to kiss. The printed caption reads "There's Love in the Air," which Ben personalized with "There's Love FOR YOU in the Air."[22] Another, typical of nineteenth-century French erotic postcards, depicts an oversized "A" for Alice decorated with portraits of ethereal women and girls baring their shoulders, their loose, thick wavy hair like hers. On the back, Ben wrote a poem that referenced the monogram:

I met a pretty Miss,
Whose lips compelled a kiss.
Her name you know I see
It starts with "A," but ends in "e".[23]

Ben's postcards and newsy notes to Alice several times a week belie the fact that the couple lived in relative proximity. Like hundreds of thousands of Eastern European Jewish immigrants, Alice lived in Manhattan's unsavory Bowery district (East 3rd Street), and, later, on the equally squalid Lower East Side (Rivington Street). Jersey City, New Jersey, where Ben resided, was located on the left bank of the Hudson River parallel to Lower Manhattan, and had direct access to the island by ferry, and after 1911, by rail via a new tunnel under the river. According to the 1910 census, twenty-year-old Ben also lived even closer to Alice on the Lower East Side where he stayed with his twenty-five-year-old brother Samuel, Samuel's wife, and a male boarder – possibly a relative.[24] Despite being identified as a watchmaker in the Jersey City 1910 City Directory, Ben, along with his brother and the boarder, was listed in the census that year as a presser in a clothing factory, an occupation deemed less skilled than watchmaker.[25] It is difficult to know whether Ben moved from place to place and job to job, or held down two residences and two posts concurrently. Whatever the circumstance, one can be certain that it was motivated by economic necessity, and perhaps by his desire to be nearer to Alice.

A year or two after meeting, Ben and Alice made their commitment official. In February 1911 they established a "mutual understanding," becoming formally engaged eight months later, on Alice's fifteenth birthday. On 17 August 1912, in The Bronx, New

York, twenty-two-year-old Ben Edelson and an almost sixteen-year-old Alice Coblentz married.[26]

Less than a year later, in April 1913, at the invitation of Ben's uncle, the couple settled in Montreal. Luckily for the Edelsons, this was before Canada enacted stricter immigration policies for Jews; between 1921 and 1931, while the general population growth for both Canada and Ontario remained somewhat consistent, the Jewish percentages dropped by more than half.[27]

In Montreal, Ben continued as a watchmaker and Alice worked as a milliner. Soon they owned their own store, where Ben repaired, cleaned, and built watches, and Alice, still a teenager, designed and created hats, and established a beauty salon.[28] Alice also worked as a saleswoman for Ben, educating herself about both costume and precious jewellery, and modeling it for customers. Through her revenue at her hat and beauty shop, and her labour (likely unpaid) in the jewellery store, Alice helped facilitate the couple's upward mobility. But it wasn't long before she assumed additional responsibilities, giving birth to the first of four children in Montreal.[29]

In September of 1920, thirty-year-old Ben, an almost twenty-four-year-old Alice, and their four children moved from Montreal to Ottawa. By 1931, Ottawa, a city of 146,509 people, had the fourth largest Jewish community in Canada, but it lagged far behind the third-ranking city. Both Montreal and Toronto had more than 45,000 Jews, Winnipeg had just over 17,000, and Ottawa had only 3,319. Interestingly, however, the Jewish population of Ottawa comprised 2.6 per cent of the city's total, a percentage higher than most other Canadian cities.[30]

Most Ottawa Jews resided in Lowertown. Lowertown (otherwise known as "below Rideau") was an enclave with Rideau Street to the south, Sussex Drive and the Ottawa River to the north, Rideau Canal to the west, and the Rideau River to the east. Elm-lined King Edward Avenue cut through the centre of the area as a major north-south boulevard. A working-class neighbourhood since the nineteenth century, largely comprised of French Canadians and Irish immigrants, Lowertown had earned a notorious reputation at that time as an unruly, hard-drinking, crime-infested area.[31] By

the early twentieth-century, however, most of Ottawa's Jews resided in a relatively tamer Lowertown.

After renting places first on Friel Street and then on Nelson
Street, the Edelsons bought a home in 1924 at 203 Friel, on the
northeast corner at Rideau.[32] Thanks to affordable properties in
Ottawa requiring only a small down payment, they were able to
purchase a house from Caspar Caplan, a wealthy Jewish entrepreneur who owned a small department store.[33] The house was a
side-by-side triplex, which fronted a huge yard with a small orchard. The Edelsons occupied one unit, which was large and comfortable, and rented out the other two spaces. With an expanding
family – three more children were born that decade – and during
the Depression's tough times, these housing units provided Ben
with much needed rental income. During the Depression it was
commonplace for even middle-class families to rent instead of purchase a house, which meant they were never short of tenants.[34]

The Jews in Lowertown lived alongside French Canadians.[35]
On Friel Street, Jews dominated the west side and the French the
east side.[36] They were also neighbours in the duplex and triplex
houses that pervaded the area. In 1931, for example, the Edelsons'
tenants were both Jewish and French Canadian.[37]

Despite the extensive French Canadian presence, Lowertown in
the early twentieth century, especially along Murray and Clarence
Streets, became something of a *shtetl* (an eastern European village
significantly populated by Jews) where Jews constituted 70 per
cent of the population.[38] The area incorporated the Byward Market, which boasted numerous Jewish-owned, family-run produce,
clothing, and dry goods stores, as well as dairies, bakeries, and
at least one kosher butcher with a *shochet* (ritual slaughterer).[39]
Jewish women shopped at the market on Thursdays when they
bought their kosher chickens in preparation for Sabbath dinner.[40]

Other pockets of Lowertown, as well as the downtown district,
were also abundant with Jewish-owned businesses and services.
They included hardware stores, delicatessens, pawn shops, and
the local *shvitz* (steam bath). Many Jews unable to afford their
own shops earned their living as peddlers. The mostly male peddlers hocked fresh produce, household wares, clothes, or rags from

their horse-drawn wagons, and, especially during the Depression, sold pre-bundled dry goods door-to-door.[41] Because Ottawa's Jewish population was smaller than that of many urban centres, peddlers went outside the community to sell their wares, relying heavily on Francophone customers.[42] Many peddlers' wives also kept a boarder in their homes, mostly recent Jewish immigrants, to make ends meet.[43] Due to the city having few factories and sweatshops, peddling as an occupation for Jews lasted longer in Ottawa than in other cities: as late as 1939, 43 per cent of all peddlers in Ottawa were Jewish.[44]

The jewellery trade was also heavily populated by Jews. Indeed, the first Jewish resident of Ottawa, Moses Bilsky, had been a jeweller. In 1931 Ottawa, Jews constituted about 20 per cent of the jewellery retailers, an extraordinary number given that Jews made up less than 3 per cent of the city's population.[45] Ben established a jewellery business in various locations. He first set up shop at 588 Sussex Street and 158 Nelson Street. The Sussex Street location was really more of a booth, in Union Station next to a fruit stand, but it was frequented by train workers whose jobs demanded that their watches be precise.[46] In 1925, he purchased a much larger, established jewellery and pawnbroker's store at 24 Rideau Street, about eight blocks west of his home.[47] He hired Alice's brother Samuel to help manage the business.[48] By 1932, Ben sold the tiny Sussex Street store, and long-since abandoned Nelson Street, and focused all his attention on 24 Rideau.

The store on Rideau occupied a choice location. It was on the street level of the Corry Block, an expansive seven-floor building of retail and office space. Directly across the street were the Rotary Club, the Château Laurier Beauty Salon, the Department of Pensions and National Health, and the famed and opulent Château Laurier Hotel, all of which were filled with hundreds of potential customers.[49] Proximity to the Château Laurier was especially profitable. Established in 1912, it underwent extensive renovations in the mid-1920s to double the number of rooms to five hundred and fifty. By 1929, the hotel was a celebrated, elegant, modern, full-service facility. This expansion and renewal meant the prestigious hotel did brisk business among a prosperous clientele, many of whom arrived in Ottawa via rail at Union Station, steps away from Edelson Jewellers.⁵⁰ Directly next to the store were the Chateau Pharmacy to the west, and the Banque Canadienne Nationale to the east, as well as more businesses and offices at the nearby central intersection of Rideau and Sussex.⁵¹ The proximity of Edelson Jewellers to these sights contributed to the store thriving, which is just what Ben had anticipated.⁵²

The store offered a variety of merchandise and services. It sold the usual giftware, including china place-settings, sterling silver, and fancy pen sets; jewellery, either from reputable jewellery companies or designed in-store; and fine diamonds. It also restored and engraved jewelry. First and foremost, however, the store provided expert watch repairs.⁵³

Even when the Depression hit, Ben did relatively well. Indeed, jewellers like Edelson and the Horwitz brothers, although struggling, fared better than most merchants, as people always were in need of a watch or a gift.⁵⁴ The Edelsons routinely had female vagrants knocking at their door begging for work, and over the years were able to employ some of them as live-in maids.⁵⁵ By 1931, there were seven Edelson children – Samuel, aged eighteen; Dina, sixteen; Lillian, fourteen; Vivian, twelve; Isaac Jacob (Jack), seven; Shirley (Joyce), five; and Elihu (Eli), four – but unlike many Jewish parents during the Depression, Ben and Alice were able to keep their teenage children in high school instead of compelling them to obtain full-time jobs.⁵⁶ Their part-time work in the store certainly helped Ben keep the money in the family, although he was always able to afford other employees. Except for her occasional work in the store, Alice was also able to avoid labour outside the home, a badge of honour for Ben as "middle class status was defined in the Jewish community by the absence of wage-earning wives."⁵⁷ Although Ben did experience some financial troubles, and required assistance from the bank when his tenants were unable to pay their rent, he never went bankrupt, and always earned a decent living.⁵⁸

Ben's entrepreneurship, work ethic, and professional integrity earned him a solid reputation in Ottawa's business community.⁵⁹ The Rabbi would note in Ben's eulogy over a half-century later that "certainly the success of his business emanated from a clear idea of what he wanted to attain ... He was careful as he developed his enterprise, with a sense of self discipline."[60] Even after the shooting, the Ottawa press often addressed Ben's status as a professional. He was repeatedly described as a "prominent Ottawa jeweler," and both he and Jack were characterized as "among the best known merchants in the Ottawa Valley."[61]

Some of Ottawa's Jews, including Jack and Yetta Horwitz, resided in Sandy Hill, the more upscale and largely Anglo-Protestant district that bordered Lowertown, and a neighbourhood where many Jews aspired to settle. Canadian acculturation partly determined residency there. Many Sandy Hill Jews, like Jack and Yetta, had been severed from Eastern Europe for at least a generation or two, and bore no trace of an immigrant accent or the struggle to fit in.[62] Still, in some cases, it was finances alone that dictated a family's prospects in Sandy Hill.[63] Certainly the perception by many was that genteel Sandy Hill was a considerable step up. When Abe Lieff knocked door to door down its charming avenues, and failed to hock his fly paper, his father remarked, "You are stupid, don't you know that there are no flies on those streets? You go where there are some flies."[64]

In the case of Ben and Jack, the neighbourhoods reflected some tangible distinctions. Lowertown's Ben Edelson was an immigrant, a self-made man, and reduced his business to one store. Sandy Hill's Jack Horwitz, in contrast, was Canadian-born, able to avail himself of a family business (as well as his father's legacy after 1930), owned two stores, and was contemplating expansion. No doubt, having to support seven children also kept Ben in Lowertown, just as Jack's status-seeking wife likely kept him in Sandy Hill.

In some ways, however, the divide between the two neighbourhoods was tenuous. On Friel Street at Rideau, for example, Ben Edelson actually lived just a stone's-throw from Sandy Hill, while Jack Horwitz's Stewart Street home was just a few blocks from Lowertown. Ben oversaw a tract of land and a large dwelling but was forced to rent out apartments, while Jack lived in the upper unit of a small, unassuming house. Indeed, despite the Edelsons' residence in Lowertown, Lillian remembered her parents being "socialites" and "a prominent family," an elevated status which, for Lillian, made their rejection by friends after the shooting and their general fall from grace all the more devastating. She remembered their Friel Street home as an "elegant" showpiece with striking, original paintings. In contrast, her sister Dina remembered their house as "mediocre," and "not especially elegant," and friend Adelene Hyman recalled it as "nothing special."[65] In recollecting the press' aggressive pursuit of her family in the days after the shooting, Lillian even referred to reporters as "paparazzi," as if her parents had been Hollywood celebrities.[66] Lillian's perception that her parents were part of Ottawa's Jewish elite was rooted not only in her own affinity for social status, but in the integrated social scene of the small Jewish community, the greater struggles of others during the Depression, and the fluid class and spatial boundaries of Ottawa neighbourhoods.

Whether from Lowertown or Sandy Hill, the Jewish population was industrious, organized, and activist in the name of Jewish causes. They seemed to have internalized the message asserted by New York guest lecturer Chaim Greenberg in his November 1931 talk at the Château Laurier that "those Jews who cared not to admit their identification or affiliation with the race of their birth were the deadliest enemies of the Jewish nation."[67]

Virulent anti-Semitism in Ottawa helped strengthen the Jewish community. Although it was forced to endure informal brands of anti-Semitism,[68] it did not submit to its systemic expression, instead creating its own institutions and asserting its social-standing in the city.[69] In the 1930s, for example, Jewish applicants were routinely spurned by non-Jewish law firms, so they established their own successful partnerships.[70] Benjamin Goldfield, only the second Jewish barrister in Ottawa, "built up for himself a large legal practice in his city," and was recognized by 1926 "as one of the leaders among the younger lawyers."[71] He regularly engaged Jewish law-school graduates as articling students or, as in the case of Moses Doctor, as partners in his firm.[72] But as most big businesses would not retain Jewish firms, their practices were generally limited to criminal law, litigation, and finalizing property transactions.[73]

Jews were also denied membership at the Ottawa golf and tennis establishments. Charismatic men's clothing proprietor Jess Abelson raised money from local businessmen to rent four courts for one year at the Victoria Tennis Club so that Jews could play. He then parlayed the membership and funds into the creation of a new institution. Its executive wanted to give their association a generic, innocuous name, but Abelson, its first president, wouldn't have it: he insisted that it be called the Tel Aviv Tennis Club "to let the Gentiles know that it was a Jewish club," and to convey the community's strong Zionist affinity. Eventually, the club took over the old Riverdale Tennis Club and boasted eight clay courts, as well as changing rooms, a games room, musical nights, and weekly dances. The Tel Aviv Tennis Club proved an important social outlet for the Jewish community, especially for singles. Abelson proudly claimed that in its twenty-five years, the club spawned at least two hundred marriages.[74]

In the infamous Detective Tissot case (as described in the Introduction), the Jewish community responded with equal force. In April of 1935, Lillian Freiman lodged an official complaint with Emile Joliat, chief constable of the Ottawa Police Department and member of the Board of Commissioners of Police. Mrs Freiman alleged that two officers "acted in such a manner as to ... provoke racial hate," charging that a Constable H. Boehmer, while on duty, had made anti-Semitic remarks, and that Detective Tissot had distributed anti-Semitic literature.[75] Unlike Boehmer, Tissot owned up to the accusations leveled against him, but both men were reprimanded by Joliat. He informed them that "any recurrence of their conduct along these lines would mean instant dismissal." In an April 1935 letter to Mrs Freiman, the Board of Commissioners of Police regretted the incident, and pledged that it would never happen again.[76] Tissot, however, preoccupied over the next several weeks with organizing a boycott of Jewish stores, and promoting the expulsion of Jews from Ottawa, was soon suspended from duty.[77]

Incensed by Tissot's defamatory writings and illustrations, and no doubt seeking to make an example of him, A.J. Freiman filed libel charges against him.[78] The Jewish community followed the case closely: as an editorial in the *Canadian Jewish Chronicle* noted, "this is not Freiman's battle, but rather the battle of all Jews in Canada." The paper urged them "to consolidate our forces" as "today it is Mr. Freiman, tomorrow it may be someone else."[79] That the Freimans fought back clearly demonstrated that the Ottawa Jewish community would simply not tolerate organized persecution from anti-Semitic agitators. Tissot was found guilty on two counts of publishing libelous material, and fined fifty dollars.[80]

Challenging the contention by some historians that Canada's Jewish communities were unorganized and discordant in the years before the war, Ottawa Jews claimed a remarkably established and ordered network of Jewish philanthropic, cultural, and religious organizations.[81] Beginning in 1934, the Jewish Community Council, known as the *Vaad Ha'Ir*, served to coordinate these many groups, which worked tirelessly and collectively on behalf of Jews in Europe and Palestine, and in aid of their own community.[82]

Ottawa Jews were particularly dedicated to the cause of Palestine. Journalist Max Bookman wrote in 1933 that "the Jewish community of Ottawa is one of the strongest and most ardent Zionist centres on the American continent."[83] Hadassah was the leading Zionist organization in Ottawa. Beginning in 1901 as the Young Ladies Progressive Zionist Society and re-forming in 1910 as The Herzl Ladies Society, Hadassah's first of more than a dozen chapters in Ottawa was founded in 1920. With Lillian Freiman as president (she would be national president for twenty-one years), Ottawa Hadassah in the early years contributed funds, clothing, foodstuffs, and medical provisions to Palestine, particularly to its Jewish women and children. Along with Hadassah chapters throughout Canada, it would also raise funds for the establishment of countless social welfare and educational institutions, programs, and buildings in the fledgling state of Israel. By 1948, Ottawa Hadassah, including the popular Junior Hadassah for young, single girls, claimed an impressive membership of five hundred women.[84]

As exemplified by the resounding popularity of Hadassah, women were central to Jewish charity work. As they had been virtually excluded from meaningful participation in the many male-centred benevolent organizations, they became "professional volunteers," and created their own fundraising associations.[85] Men happily allowed their wives to engage in philanthropic work: it conformed to the religious dictate of *tzedakah* (giving to charity), helped fortify the community with new institutions (and free female labour), was a socially acceptable extension of female domesticity and nurturing, left men the time they needed to build up their businesses, and helped affirm a couple's social status.[86] Certainly, Hadassah women by the 1920s "had risen into the ranks of the middle class."[87]

Like most respectable, married Jewish women, Alice belonged to Hadassah. A member of the Lillian Freiman Chapter, Alice devotedly participated in every facet of the group's activities in the 1920s. In November of 1927, for example, she helped with the Hadassah Bazaar in the old cafeteria of the Russell Hotel which was decorated in blue and white "Zionist colors."[88]

There was resentment by some that so many fundraising efforts were aimed at Eastern Europe and Palestine, but philanthropy was also directed home.[89] Indeed, Lillian Freiman noted at one charitable event that "we must look after the poor of Ottawa first."[90] Certainly, during the Depression, the Jewish community in Ottawa was struggling.[91] With banks averse to offering loans to those with no assets, the community's many peddlers, whose broken English hindered their success, especially required financial help.[92] The Ottawa Hebrew Benefit Society, founded in 1912, offered aid to new immigrants to care for the sick, and for burial. In the 1930s, about fifty aspiring entrepreneurs formed a self-help organization, the Actzia, that offered loans to members. They recruited the assistance of affluent Jews who secured loans from banks, and then passed on the funds to Actzia who distributed money to members in need.[93]

By 1906, the small area of Lowertown also offered spiritual support, boasting three synagogues. Rabbi Saul Aranov, in his history on the Ottawa Jewish community, characterizes the years between 1902 and 1911 as "the decade of the synagogues."[94] They were commonly known by the streets on which they were located:

Adath Jeshurun ("the King Edward" or "King Street *shul*"), founded
in 1892; Agudath Achim ("the Rideau Street *shul*"), founded in
1902; and Machziki Hadath ("the Murray Street *shul*"), founded
in 1906. All of these synagogues were located near one another, but
their shared popularity meant they "were able to thrive compet-
itively for many decades."⁹⁵

Various issues determined which *shul* a family attended. Because,
in accordance with Jewish law, adherents walked to synagogue
on the Sabbath, they often attended the congregation closest to
where they lived. A family might also attend a certain synagogue
because their parents were members there, and they went there as
children.⁹⁶ The reputation of a synagogue was also a factor. The
long-established King Edward *shul* claimed Ottawa's few wealthy
Jews as members, most notably the Freimans, as well as a crop of
younger Canadian-born professionals, so it possessed more pres-
tige than the other two *shuls* in Lowertown.⁹⁷

Partly as a testament to their success, the Edelsons were active
members of the King Edward *shul*. In 1930, Ben sat on the executive of the men's club, Alice volunteered for Sisterhood, their
eldest son Sam sang in the choir, and their small children attended
Sunday school.⁹⁸ A year later, in December 1931, the King Edward's
spiritual leader, Rabbi Nathan Kollin, would seek to comfort a
languishing Ben at the Nicholas Street Jail by bringing him a book
of Hebrew Scriptures.⁹⁹

Ben was also involved in other Jewish groups. He was a member of the B'nai Brith, a Jewish men's social and philanthropic
organization,¹⁰⁰ and was a founder of Ottawa's Young Men's
Hebrew Association (YMHA). In both groups, Ben distinguished
himself as an athlete and coach.¹⁰¹ In the early 1920s, the YMHA
was an especially popular social and athletic club that boasted its
own basketball league. Ben had coached youngsters in both YMHA
basketball and gymnastics at a rented gym at the local fire station.
The club also had its own bowling league of six to eight teams in
which Ben had participated.¹⁰² After the YMHA disbanded, Young
Judaea became the chief organization in the 1920s and 30s for
Jewish youth in Ottawa, and Ben continued coaching.¹⁰³ Indeed,
Ben made quite a name for himself in the sporting life of Jewish

Ottawa, conforming to the dominant culture's appreciation for
male athleticism while affiliating with Jewish clubs as an expression of community belonging.[104]

Ben was also a learned man. In New York he had attended
night-school, but he was mostly self-taught. He knew a variety of
languages, including Yiddish, Hebrew, Russian, English, and German, and voraciously read works in all of them. He loved the
German classics, as well as Shakespeare and the Bible.[105] He "was
also well acquainted with the giants of North American literature
and greatly encouraged his children to become [as] addicted to
them as he was."[106]

He also appreciated the outdoors and expressed this passion
through rugged and manly pursuits. His large Friel Street back-
yard, with its exotic plants and thriving apple orchard, allowed
him to indulge his passion for agriculture. Although he would
never achieve his dream of owning a farm, he trained homing
pigeons and raised police dogs.[107]

And Ben took great pleasure in his stunning wife. With her
black hair, fair skin, and green eyes, the diminutive but shapely
Alice was a stylish dresser and took pride in her appearance. Adelene Hyman remembered that when she visited the Edelson home,
Alice "was always wearing a hat," and was neatly and smartly
dressed.[108] This was partly thanks to Ben who, on his trips to New
York twice a year to visit family, regularly brought back a trunk
of designer clothes from discount wholesale stores for Alice and
the children. Daughter Lillian remembered that Ben "loved to see
my mother dressed up in very fashionable clothes."[109] Not only
did this high style delight Alice and enhance her good looks, it
also announced Ben's professional success during the Depression
(even if the clothes weren't bought retail), and helped affirm his
worth as the husband of a beautiful woman.

In addition to being pretty, Alice was bright and talented. Like
Ben, she knew Russian, Yiddish, English, and German fluently, as
well as Polish and French.[110] Even after she retired from shop-
keeping full-time to raise her growing family, Alice remained
creative, lending her artistic flair to virtually everything she
touched. She constructed and redesigned hats, sewed clothes for

her family, and made all of the dance costumes for her young daughter Lillian. And she worked on decorative projects for the home, such as embellishing lamp shades and the baby bassinette.[111] Alice was also known for her superb cooking and baking, which her Hadassah chapter, friends, and family all routinely enjoyed thanks to her warm and gracious hospitality.[112] Moreover, by 1931, Alice could regularly be found at Edelson Jewellers where she worked behind the counter part-time.[113] Clearly, Alice proved herself a capable household manager, a wonderful hostess, a dedicated volunteer, a devoted mother, and an able assistant in the family business, all attributes which contributed to her and her husband's community standing.

Throughout the 1920s and into the following decade, as Ben and Alice enjoyed a successful business and a thriving family of seven children, they integrated into the social scene of the Ottawa Jewish community, and life seemed good. When Ben whirled Alice around the dance floor at the many parties they attended, she in one of her stylish New York gowns, the handsome couple captured the notice of everyone in the room.[114]

Whether Ottawa Jews were peddlers, merchants, or manufacturers, whether they lived in Lowertown or Sandy Hill, virtually all of them hailed from modest beginnings and shared a formula for success: sensitivity to, and flexibility within, a shifting economy, and dedication to the Jewish community.[115] These traits, as well as commitment to family life, garnered respectability for men like Ben Edelson, who went from apprentice to business owner, tenant to landlord, bachelor to family man, community outsider to insider, and greenhorn to citizen. In all the ways that mattered, Ben and Alice Edelson were living the immigrant dream, one which a November night in 1931 would abruptly and dramatically shatter.

3

"Startling evidence ... of a sensational character": The Inquest, and Respectability Challenged

Ben Edelson's arrest was only the beginning of an intense legal journey that he would have to navigate over the next three weeks. Before he faced a murder trial, he had to endure incarceration and a coroner's inquest, as well as a preliminary hearing. During the inquest he suffered public humiliation as details of Alice's affair and Jack's shooting were revealed, and as the scrutiny of rapt spectators and a relentless press mounted. And all the while he had to live with the fact that he was inflicting harm upon his family, and that his wife was virtually nowhere in sight, appearing unwilling to help him. The reputation that he had worked so hard to achieve was fading fast.

The morning after the shooting, he stood in the prisoners' box at the Police Court with his lawyer at the ready. Moses Doctor, only thirty years of age, already enjoyed a reputation as one of the most brilliant criminal lawyers in Ottawa. He was consistently praised for his sharp mind, his extensive legal knowledge, his experience in a variety of courts, and for his honour and integrity. He was also known as a civic leader, involved in city politics as a prominent Conservative, and in a variety of citizenship, charitable, educational, and athletic organizations.[1] It didn't hurt that he was thought to be irresistibly handsome and charming.[2] Clearly, if anyone could offer Ben Edelson credibility and successfully defend him, it was Moses Doctor – never mind that the Edelson case was his first crack at defending a murder charge.[3]

By 1931, Doctor had participated in several high-profile cases, perhaps most notably the 1929 case against Canada's youngest

Member of Parliament, Louis Auger. The twenty-seven-year-old Auger was accused of raping seventeen-year-old Laurence Martel when she was interviewed for a secretarial job by the Hawkesbury, Ontario, MP at his parliamentary office. Auger turned to Doctor for the third of his five trials, and was acquitted of the rape charge.[4]

As Ben Edelson stood in the prisoners' box that first day, Detective-Sergeant MacDonald, representing the Crown, requested an adjournment.[5] Presumably MacDonald, a highly respected twenty-year veteran of the force, needed more time to probe the shooting further, although the next day he reported that the investigation was "in good shape," and nearly complete.[6] Magistrate Glenn E. Strike remanded Ben for one week without plea. Within minutes, Ben, along with eight defendants from other cases, was escorted back to the nearby Nicholas Street Jail.[7]

The Nicholas Street Jail, otherwise known as the Carleton County Jail, located a few blocks south of Rideau Street, had an infamous reputation. Built in 1862 as a maximum-security detention center, it boasted impressive architecture according to a reformist philosophy which made it seem a modern, progressive, and humane facility. In reality, conditions were appalling. The jail had been constructed to house one hundred prisoners, but regularly exceeded this number. Cells were small, dark, and dreary – frigid in the winter and stifling in the summer. A single cell typically measured nine feet long by three feet wide, just enough room for a small cot; cells designed to hold three inmates were only slightly larger. There were also several solitary confinement cells with shackles built into the floor. The ceilings of all the cells were vaulted so that noise could readily travel along corridors, allowing for subversive conversations among prisoners to be overheard by guards. There were no work or rehabilitation programs for otherwise bored and restless prisoners. Instead, they spent their days either performing hard labour or aimlessly roaming the hall. They were then confined to their cells from evening to early morning.[8] Not surprisingly, the jail was repeatedly likened to a "medieval dungeon" and eventually labeled a "monstrous relic."[9]

The jail had its own death row of four cells and a permanent on-site gallows. The shuttered window of the upper-floor gallows was viewable from one of two exercise yards, and served as a morbid reminder of the fate that could befall the hardcore criminal. Indeed, in January 1933, Edelson's prison-mate William Seabrooke, also charged with murder, would become the second of three men hanged there.[10] For many Canadians, capital punishment was perceived as an especially effective antidote to unlawful "foreign elements," a fact potentially relevant to Ben.[11]

For Edelson, a proud businessman, homeowner, and family man with no criminal record, the prison experience must have been horrific. Perhaps only his voyage in steerage to America came remotely close to the demoralizing conditions he faced in jail. Neither fellow inmates nor guards would have been used to having a Jew in their midst, let alone one who was middle-class. Possible mistreatment by them would have added to the physical and mental toll of incarceration.[12]

But Ben was accorded some privileges. Possibly in an attempt to keep kosher while in jail, he asked that friends be allowed to bring him one meal per day, a request that was granted by prison officials. The *Citizen* reassured readers, however, that "his other meals will be the prison fare as served out to the rest of the inmates."[13] That Ben's request for homemade meals was not directed at his wife, an excellent cook, is suggestive of several possible explanations: her extreme despondence, her wrath toward him, his desire to protect her from the ugliness of jail, or his lack of interest in seeing her. In any case, his morale was no doubt suffering from their ongoing estrangement.

During the first nine days of December, however, Ben had to stay focused on the coroner's inquest. An inquest was required to investigate unnatural, unexpected, unattended, or preventable deaths – not to determine legal liability.[14] It sought to establish the identity of the deceased, and the time, location, cause, and means of death.[15] Presided over by a coroner and attended by Crown counsel and a jury, the inquest was an open, public forum.[16] Unlike today, when criminal proceedings surrounding a death must be resolved before an inquest can be initiated or resumed, the coroner's inquest in 1931 was a parallel process that could be held at any time, including prior to legal proceedings as in the Edelson case.[17]

The coroner's inquest lined up at least fifteen witnesses. They included Edelson employee and driver Lorenzo Lemieux, Chateau Pharmacy owner J.B. Laframboise, attending physician at the store, hospital, and autopsy, Dr Danby, Jack's brother Charles and brother-in-law Harry Hertz, Montreal jewellery salesman Nate Alexander, lawyers Sam Berger and Moses Doctor, various police officers and hospital workers, and others who had yet to be identified. Yetta and Alice were also scheduled to be witnesses, despite Yetta "suffering from grief prostration."[18]

By Monday 30 November, however, it was clear that Alice, in fragile condition, would not be prepared to testify the next evening.[19] Her physician, Dr Danby, had reported that he urged her not to appear due to her state of "absolute collapse."[20] Knowing of her weakened condition, even Crown attorney Ritchie had stated that he would not force her to attend "if she is indisposed."[21] Lillian later recalled that during this time, "my mother wasn't doing very much of anything. She was in bed, doing a lot of crying, reading the papers … She was pretty much out of it."[22] Alice had been absent from her Hadassah chapter's regular Tuesday tea social on 1 December, which was to be expected; more glaring was her continued absence from the jail to visit the husband she hadn't seen since the shooting.[23]

Alice's condition, attributed to shock and grief, included symptoms of exhaustion, depression, and anger. By all accounts her illness was real, but there is no doubt that she benefitted from its severity and duration. In a culture that generally perceived women as unfit, frail, and prone to disease, Alice's ill health gave her permission for the next several months not only to dodge public appearances and testifying at the inquest, but to sidestep her onerous responsibilities as a mother, and, she hoped in vain, from the obligation to visit her husband in jail. This is not to say that Alice feigned illness but simply to suggest that she might have exploited her illness to achieve privacy, rest, and quiet.

In addition to Alice's frail health, her standing as the wife of the accused would help release her from testifying at the inquest. As will be discussed in Chapter 5, and as the *Citizen* pointed out, under the Criminal Code of Canada, one spouse, with few exceptions, could not give evidence against the other in a criminal case. It was mainly for this reason that police would never question her in anticipation of Ben's murder trial.[24] Because the coroner's inquest was a separate medical investigation, Alice could be legally compelled to take the stand there (and had been summoned to do so), but Ritchie was well aware that even if Alice did testify at the inquest, her testimony would not be admissible in the preliminary hearing and trial.[25]

With Alice no longer a witness, the testimony of Lemieux was especially anticipated.[26] Not only was he in the store immediately after the shooting, but the newspapers discovered that he had lied in an earlier interview with them. On 25 November, Lemieux had told reporters that he was nowhere near Edelson Jewellers the night before, and then claimed he was there "in order to arrange some Christmas displays."[27] When the press asked him the next day about these and other conflicting statements, he retorted, "I was not forced to tell you the truth. I was protecting my job." He directed members of the press to Moses Doctor if they wanted to know more, and pledged that he would say nothing else until the inquest.[28]

Commencing on the evening of Tuesday 1 December at the police station courtroom, and presided over by coroner J.E. Craig, the inquest heard "startling evidence … of a sensational character" – the beginning of Ben's courtroom humiliation. As anticipated, Lemieux, considered the evening's "star witness," offered explosive testimony.[29] He claimed that as an ailing Jack Horwitz waited for help on the floor of Ben's shop, he said "Lemieux, you never thought your boss was a murderer."[30] This shocking testimony diverged sharply from early reports that Jack mistakenly fired the gun, and established Jack's own belief in Ben's sinister intentions. Lemieux also stated that, after the shooting, Edelson said of the victim, "he deserved it. He had been going with my wife for eight years."[31] Not only did this statement sound vengeful, suggestive of a motivation for murder, but, according to Lemiex's testimony, confirmed Ben's knowledge of his wife's illicit affair. Failing to recall certain facts, Lemieux often provoked the ire of Crown prosecutor J.A. Ritchie, who had tried dozens of criminal cases over the last two decades. With Lemieux's repeated excuse of being "excited" [frantic] following the shooting, an irritated Ritchie retorted, "Why should you be excited? ... You weren't shot."[32] Lemieux was on the stand for just over an hour, during which time Edelson offered both "a quizzical smile" and "signs of strain."[33]

Although the testimony of Laframboise, the proprietor of the Chateau Pharmacy, inspired less fanfare, it revealed one point of significance. Laframboise testified that in speaking to Edelson outside after the shooting, Ben had referred to the incident as an "accident." Although the credibility of Laframboise's testimony was shaky due to his apparent indifference that night, there was no mistaking his recollection that Edelson employed the term "accident."[34] This suggests that the accident defence was not necessarily a strategy contrived by lawyer Moses Doctor for the murder trial, but was a version of the incident initially put forth by Edelson. Of course, there is always the possibility that Laframboise's use of the word could instead have been the product of witness-coaching by Doctor, and that Edelson never utilized the term when he spoke to Laframboise after the shooting.

Yetta also had the opportunity to testify at the inquest about "relations between her husband and Mrs. Edelson."[35] Yetta was described in the press as "pretty," but also as "a pathetic figure in black and extremely pale."[36] Authorities offered her a chair and a glass of water, "afraid the strain of giving evidence might be too much for her."[37] Although her testimony would not directly implicate Ben in the shooting, it cast him as a man unable to manage his wife. It also inspired the sympathy of the press and the courtroom for a young widow who, due partly to his actions, needlessly lost her husband. The Journal reported that she "so pathetically told of offering her husband a divorce and having the offer refused," and that "as she related the story of her husband's death tears were brought to many eyes who visualized her pleading with her husband to fight for his life, if not for her sake at least for the sake of their daughter."[38] Yetta spoke "in a clear, firm voice, without hesitation," but, as feared, ultimately became so distraught during her eight-minute testimony that she had to be escorted temporarily from the courtroom.[39] Later, upon hearing that Alice had kissed Jack as he lay wounded, she fainted.[40] It was reported the next day that "Mrs. Horwitz has not yet recovered from the strain she underwent after giving evidence at the inquest last night."[41]

At almost midnight, with several witnesses yet to be heard, coroner Craig called an adjournment. The proceedings were to resume 9 December, the following Wednesday.[42] Because of the late hour, Ben was escorted not to the Nicholas Street Jail, but to a cell in the police station basement where he spent the night.[43] The next morning, at the request of Sergeant MacDonald who was acting for the Crown, Magistrate Strike officially remanded Ben Edelson for another week.[44] A hearing pertaining to the murder charge would not proceed until the conclusion and verdict of the inquest.[45]

The delay in the coroner's inquest meant additional miserable jail-time for Ben, but it served two functions in pursuit of the truth. The first was to allow further investigation into the shooting, particularly into evidence related to the bullet and the gun. Firearms expert Charles H. Howe had yet to determine if the bullet retrieved at the Horwitz autopsy matched those in the gun. The second was to buy time for the recovery of Alice, who was "still confined to her bed." The *Citizen* reported that "the crown is still hopeful of being able to call Mrs. Edelson as a vital witness at the resumption of the inquest on Wednesday night next." The Crown was very much aware that "her medical advisers are of the opinion that she is not fit physically to undergo what must necessarily be for her a great ordeal."[46]

When the inquest reconvened the following week, the courtroom heard some riveting testimony. The most compelling witness was Jack's brother-in-law, Harry Hertz, who testified that as he stood at Jack's bedside at the hospital, Jack uttered "He shot me," although he never named the perpetrator. Other witnesses included several police officers who arrived later at the crime scene, and those who could identify the clothing that Jack wore the evening he was shot. Firearms expert Howe, with thirty-five years of experience behind him, described numerous experiments he conducted with Edelson's pistol and bullets: for example, he fired into "rolled blankets, waste cotton and pieces of linen" intended to replicate Jack's clothing, and concluded that "the markings on the fatal bullet were similar to the marks on the bullets he fired into the rolled blanket."[47]

Conspicuous by their absence were Jack Horwitz's lawyer Sam Berger and Alice, both of whom had been rumoured to testify, but never did.[48] On this second and final night of the inquest, Ritchie was particularly irritated by Alice's absence, as "the jury would have had much more first-hand evidence if the other eye-witness to the shooting, Mrs. Edelson, had told her story."[49] Like an apparition, Alice inexplicably showed up at the police station that evening, her first public appearance since the incident, but she sought refuge in a private downstairs office.[50] The *Citizen* noted that "the curious were not given any opportunity of viewing this almost tragic central figure in the drama" as Alice "shrank visibly and hung her head as she hurried through to the stairs."[51]

On 9 December, at 9:45 pm, the coroner's jury finally delivered its verdict.[52] It declared that Ben Edelson fatally shot Jack Horwitz at the Edelson store. After a five-hour proceeding over two nights, it took only twenty-nine minutes for the eight-man jury to deliberate based on the nineteen witnesses who testified on both 1 December and earlier that evening.[53] Although throngs of spectators and reporters had earlier flooded the courtroom, because of the late hour it was near empty when the verdict was read. Even Ben was absent. He had been escorted to a cell in the police station basement to be readied for transport to the Nicholas Street Jail.[54]

After the courtroom was cleared, Alice, accompanied by her brother Sam and a sister, had "emerged from her seclusion in the locked office of the court clerk." Both the *Journal* and *The Renfrew Mercury* identically reported that after she was told of the judgment that implicated Ben, she "was obviously very weak, and despite warnings of 'wet paint' on some of the walls of the police station, she persisted in leaning against one of them." She ultimately collapsed and, having had no contact with Ben that night, was hurried home in a taxi.[55] Her feelings of guilt must have been unbearable. Not only was she at least partly responsible for the killing of Jack but now her husband was officially declared the shooter, bearing the full weight of a murder charge, and nearing the gallows.

In his closing arguments, Ritchie had emphasized Ben Edelson's culpability as the shooter, and advised the jury to do the same. He declared that "there is no doubt that Jacob Horwitz was shot in that store," noting "it is a reasonable inference, I think, that he was shot by a pistol in the hands of Edelson." Ritchie instructed the jury that given that no one yet knew the full story, it should not "characterize the shooting" of Horwitz "by describing it as a particular offence or crime." The jury needed only to conclude that "the wound was inflicted by Edelson"; it would be up to another court to determine his motivation and intent. Contravening his own advice, however, in an attempt to more fully implicate Edelson, Ritchie had noted that "bad feeling" existed between the men, and that after Jack was shot, "there is no evidence that Edelson did anything to succor Horwitz or did anything more than have a doctor sent for."[56]

Ritchie had also expressed his frustration over the scanty evidence garnered by witnesses at the crime scene. First, he regretted that neither Lemieux nor attending physician Danby asked simply "What has happened?" – an obvious question that would have yielded crucial information about the case generally, and Edelson's culpability specifically.

Although conflict-of-interest issues would never be addressed by inquest or trial lawyers, Dr Danby assumed a peculiar position in the case. Danby held multiple roles and functions: he was Jack's attending physician as he lay injured, performed Jack's autopsy, and – although he was a surgeon – served as Alice's doctor in the weeks after the shooting. As well, the reluctance by Danby to inquire about the scene, to call the police, and to expedite Alice's recovery so that she could testify suggests that Danby sought to shield the Edelsons. That it took him some time to contact an ambulance could be deemed suspect. At the inquest, moreover, he testified, against all common sense, that he had no knowledge of Alice's whereabouts once the ambulance left or of how she turned up at the hospital, not wanting to reveal, it seems, that she had accompanied Jack there.[57] Ritchie, too, found Danby's behaviour and responses odd. In his summation to the coroner's jury, after referring to Danby's actions at the crime scene, Ritchie had admitted "just what his idea was I do not know. It was quite obvious the man [Horwitz] had been dangerously wounded. But he [Danby] did not choose to make any inquiries. That is his concern, not yours."[58] Clearly, Danby had compromised medical standards of care, as well as his credibility as a legal witness. And it seemed that Ben knew from the start that he could expect this kind of protection: Lorenzo Lemieux had testified at the inquest that when he returned to the Edelson store from the Chateau Pharmacy without having contacted Dr Laframboise, "he [Edelson] said he didn't want Dr. Laframboise, but Dr. Danby."[59] Ben would later testify that his request for Danby only rested in the fact that he lived closer to the store.[60]

At 2:40 pm on Tuesday 15 December, almost a week after the inquest, Ben had to endure yet another humiliating proceeding: the preliminary hearing. Its purpose was to determine through the prosecution's examination of crown witnesses if there was enough evidence for the case to stand trial. Presided over by Magistrate Glenn E. Strike, and with J.A. Ritchie again representing the Crown, the hearing opened with the court clerk announcing the charge that Edelson "did unlawfully murder one Jack Horwitz."[61] As it was anticipated that the testimony would generally reiterate what was relayed at the inquest, courtroom attendance, although large, was not overwhelming. Partly because of the proceeding's workday hours, the crowd was largely absent of men.[62]

The roster of fifteen witnesses was predictable and familiar. It began with Lemieux who recounted to Ritchie with relative consistency the evening of 24 November, and who repeated Horwitz's inflammatory words at the scene: "Lemieux, you never thought your boss was a murderer."[63] In an effort to temper the impact of this statement, Doctor, who was not obligated as defence counsel to participate in the hearing, asked Lemieux, "Isn't it possible

Horwitz said to you: 'Your boss isn't a murderer?'" Lemieux insisted that this was not possible. Doctor also asked if Mrs Edelson said "any endearing words to Horwitz," to which a presumably discomfited Lemieux replied in hushed tones, "I remember she was kissing him." Lemieux's response was so quiet that Ritchie objected that he could barely hear it.[64] Yetta Horwitz also testified, and when she relayed the story of finding Alice in the coal bin at Horwitz Jewellers, Doctor asked if Edelson at the time had believed her account. Yetta replied that she did not know.[65] At the conclusion of this incriminating hearing, Ben's murder trial was set for January of 1932.

As with most early twentieth-century murder cases which were public spectacles, interest in the inquest and later hearing had been "aroused to a high pitch," attracting large courtroom audiences and a captivated press.[66] In response to this fervor, "authorities" had warned that "only persons having business within the courtroom" would be admitted.[67] Even with this restriction, "the room was crowded to its utmost," and "many of the spectators [some of whom were lawyers[68]] had to stand throughout the whole proceedings." The police "had one of the busiest evenings they have ever had in their work of seating the crowd."[69]

The Jewish community, as well as the rest of Ottawa, were fascinated by every aspect of the testimony, and from the very beginning "rumours" were "rife."[70] The papers noted that "the majority present were women, who chattered excitedly as each different witness was called to the stand."[71] The coroner cautioned the jury "against taking into consideration the great amount of comment and gossip that had most certainly taken place on the street and everywhere about the city regarding the case." In fact, "outside in the corridors a great hubbub arose as various groups of men and women gathered discussing the evidence."[72] The *Journal* reported the next day that "the startling testimony brought out at the inquest last night when domestic troubles between the Edelson and Horwitz families over a long period were revealed was the subject of conversation everywhere in the city this morning."[73]

Like the soap operas on the radio and the grand romances on the silver screen, the Edelson/Horwitz coverage highlighted those themes of love, disloyalty, and vengeance that were all the rage in popular culture. These melodramatic and titillating themes were at the heart of the gripping "love-triangle" and "husband kills lover"/"crime of passion" plot lines and provided high entertainment value for the courtroom crowd.[74] With little extra money to spend for public amusements in the Depression years, spectators treated the inquest and later trial as theatre, fighting for and reserving the best seats, and eating, giggling, crying, and even applauding.[75] The legal spectacle became life imitating art, featuring a *femme fatale* who would rival the leading lady in any play or picture show.

Alice's presence on 9 December aroused great excitement. The *Citizen* had observed that "a whisper flashed round the packed room that Mrs. Edelson had arrived and there were many curious looks directed at the door guarded by a burly policeman."[76] The women were especially energized. The *Citizen* noted that "a crowd of about 60 people, mostly women, were clamouring for admission to the police building as she arrived," all "craning their necks to get a glimpse of her."[77] The *Journal* had also observed that "more women and girls were in the audience, apparently drawn by the possible chance of seeing Mrs. Edelson and of hearing more sensational disclosures than those given in the earlier evidence."[78] Not prepared to miss a sighting of the infamous woman as she ran to the downstairs office, "many, learning where Mrs. Edelson was, clustered outside the door, while many other men and women attempted to get into the room but were immediately refused admission."[79] The paper had the opportunity to only quickly observe that she was "attired in black which enhanced the extreme pallor of her face."[80]

In the otherwise hyper-masculine arena of the courtroom's legal proceedings, a turn by Alice on the stand would have served several functions for the women spectators who excitedly anticipated her appearance. First, she would have offered them a glamorous figure to watch and study, and from whom they could garner, first-hand, the formula for inspiring such intense adoration by two men. Second, she would have brought a feminine sensibility – heretofore absent except for the brief appearance of Yetta – to the feminine topics of love, romance, and marriage. Third, she would have affirmed for them the significant role that women could play in men's lives – a role, in this instance, that was central not only to the feud between Ben and Jack, but to the official and important work of doctors, police, lawyers, and judges. Alice reminded women of their essential place in a patriarchal culture that generally relegated them to the sidelines. Although Alice would never appear on the stand, women continued to flood the courtroom, hopeful for her presence and intrigued by her absence, and watchful of a husband deprived of her support.

Ben's vulnerable appearance and disposition were tangible evidence of the high courtroom drama, and were early on a focus of the press. With his Police Court hearing, the forty-one-year-old Edelson, described as a "middle-aged man of slight build [he was 5' 7"] with a small moustache ... and hair thinning slightly over the left temple,"[81] was portrayed as being in an anxious and weakened state. The *Journal* observed that he was wearing a navy blue suit and a blue tie, "which accentuated the pallor of his face," while the *Citizen* noted that he looked "unkempt and worried," and that friends reported the "haggard and unshaven" Edelson looked "ten years older since the time of his arrest."[82]

On 9 December, Ben seemed relieved that the inquest was concluding that night. Both the *Journal* and *Citizen* concurred that Ben "was nattily dressed and appeared quite unconcerned and in the best of humor," and that he was "well groomed and neatly attired," with "little sign of nervousness, and "looking better than he had any time since his arrest."[83] That evening, "he smiled frequently to many friends who crowded the court room and corridors."[84] Closely monitoring his relaxed disposition were press tables of local and out-of-town reporters, as well as more than a few interested lawyers.[85]

Despite Ben's periodic bright moods, however, he no doubt lamented the harm that he was causing his family over the long winter months. One member bearing the burden was his elderly and pious father, Joseph Pinchus. He had recently written a brief but encouraging letter to Ben and Alice, indicating that Ben's mother Zelda knew nothing of the incident. According to Joseph

Pinchus, this was "good news" because if she knew, "she would definitely collapse."[86] A later letter asked that Ben and Alice "please respond immediately [to me] about everything that happens because your mother doesn't yet know about anything." Meanwhile his mother addressed her own letter, written in Yiddish, to "My dear darlings, Alice and Benny," which expressed hope that "they should live happy and healthy together." With customary and repeated wishes for everyone's good health, she affirmed for all that "we should continue to make a living, and not need doctors."[87] With these notes from his devoted parents, Ben must have felt overwhelming shame, especially when his aging father felt compelled to offer funds to his grown son "so that money will not be an issue."[88]

With Alice's mother and sister in Ottawa to help manage the Edelson household, the children were instructed to carry on as usual. Teenager Lillian, for example, did not miss a single day at Lisgar High School, and at the urging of her aunt, who wanted her to feel her best, even wore her prettiest party dress on the day after the shooting.[89] Thanks to Samuel and Dina, who regularly worked at their father's store both before and after school, Edelson Jewellers remained open. Although the Horwitzes must have deemed Edelson's "business as usual" approach offensive, the ever-pragmatic Ben likely sensed that any interruption in service could mean the demise of his business. It could also be interpreted as an admission of guilt. So each morning, Samuel and Lemieux opened the store, and supervised its staff.[90]

But for the frightened older Edelson children to carry on like nothing happened was easier said than done. Lillian's best friend Adelene found Lillian at school "crying her eyes out." She sobbed, "My father's in jail because he killed my mother's boyfriend!" Upon hearing the shocking news, Adelene wondered why a distraught Lillian bothered to show up for classes at all.[91] Ben would be in jail for nearly two months, leaving the children to celebrate Chanukah that December without him. And their mother would suffer a breakdown, virtually holed up in her room for almost as long. Moreover, the relentless press about the case made the children's life anything but normal. On one occasion, newspaper reporters pushed their way into the house, past eldest son Samuel, and began opening drawers, searching for anything incriminating. He ordered them out, but they barely took notice of him.[92]

And life hardly seemed ordinary when the older children visited their father at the Nicholas Street Jail. Family members were limited to fifteen-minute visits at two small windows located in a gloomy metal stairwell.[93] At times, the children brought him lunch from the local deli. Lillian would report on her good grades at school, and Ben would cry.[94] Far from supporting, nurturing, and protecting his children, as was his fatherly duty, he was missing out on their lives, and forcing them to see him locked up in this terrible place. By all accounts, however, his behaviour was exemplary: the jail's punishment register includes no entries for Ben Edelson.[95] The *Citizen* reported that he mostly read, and exercised in the courtyard when permitted, although it also relayed that he "sits in moody silence,"[96] his morose disposition partly attributable, no doubt, to the persistent absence of Alice.

Ben and Alice journeyed over several countries, ran fledgling businesses, and raised seven children only to find themselves in the winter of 1931 facing the unimaginable – everything they had worked for in peril. With Ben's arrest, his freedom, reputation, privacy, and family life were all under threat. And Alice, far from showing herself the devoted wife during his two-month incarceration, was suffering a breakdown and avoiding all contact with her demoralized husband. The respectability that the Edelsons had enjoyed in Ottawa's Jewish community could never be the same, but Ben would be able to rebound in a way that Alice never could.

Opposite
Lowertown, Ottawa (ward III), 1931. From top, left to right: Ottawa
General Hospital where Horwitz died; Edelson Jewellers; Nicholas
Street Jail; Horwitz home; Edelson home; site of the initial confrontation
between Edelson and Horwitz on the night of the shooting.
City of Ottawa Archives

CITY ⟨φ⟩ OTTAWA

KEY MAP
SHOWING
WARD BOUNDARIES

CITY LIMIT ___.___.___
WARD BOUNDARY _____

REFERENCE

II	...BY ...	WARD
VI	....CAPITAL	" "
VII	....CENTRAL	" "
IX	...DALHOUSIE	" "
X	....ELMDALE	" "
II	....OTTAWA	" "
I	....RIDEAU	" "
V	....RIVERDALE	" "
IV	...ST. GEORGE'S	" "
XI	....VICTORIA	" "
VIII	...WELLINGTON	" "

COPYRIGHT '93

Corry Block (next to Union Station), turn of the century – future site of
Edelson Jewellers. City of Ottawa Archives, accession 10 T 97,
Alan Rayburn Collection

Edelson Jewellers, 24 Rideau Street (and Richard's Drug Store,
20 Rideau Street – site of the former Chateau Pharmacy and the future,
expanded Edelson Jewellers), 1930s or 40s. Collection of Sharon Edelson

Edelson sign, 1930s or 40s. Collection of the Canada Science
and Technology Museum

The window of Edelson Jewellers, 1920s. Collection of Sharon Edelson

Jack Horwitz, Victim of Shooting, and His Wife

Above is a recent photograph of the young Ottawa jeweler, Jack Horwitz, whose death is being investigated today. The picture of Mrs. Horwitz was taken in the gown which she wore on her wedding day.

The front page of *The Ottawa Evening Journal*,
25 November 1931.

E DEPT.

Ottawa Police Department, Detective Jean Tissot (middle row, fifth from left); Detective-Sergeant Aubrey MacDonald (middle row, eighteenth from right), 1932. City of Ottawa Archives, CA1245

EFFECTIVE ADD

Defended Life of Ben Edelson

Moses Doctor (left) and Royden A. Hughes, his law partner, who presented a brilliant defence in the murder trial of the Ottawa man who was acquitted by a jury on Saturday night.

but an ordinary voice that this was made.

In Human Triangles.

charge. No matter what your verdict may be, you will be able to feel that there has been a most able d'

Edelson lawyer Moses Doctor (left), January 1932.
The Ottawa Evening Citizen

Moses Doctor (second row from top, second from left),
Rideau Street Synagogue Choir, 1928. Ottawa Jewish Archives, 5-083

E. T. Essery, K.C., LL.B.   W. H. Bartram   F. P. Betts, K. C.

J. M. McEvoy, B. A.   Jared Vining, B. A.

F. E. Perrin, B. A.   G. N. Weekes   Hume Elliot, K. C.

Justice John Millar McEvoy (middle row, left), about 1912.
From *History of the Bar of the County of Middlesex*, Judge David
John Hughes and T.H. Purdom (London, Ontario?: n.p.: 1912)

די האַרווין-עדעלסאָן טראַ-
געדיע האָט אויפגעשוידערט ניט נאָר
די קליינע אידישע קהילה פון אטאווא,
נאָר עס האָט אָנגעמאכט א רושם איבער'ן
גאַנצען לאַנד.

עס איז ניט קיין געוועהנליכער מאָרד.
עס איז א טראַגעדיע, וואָס וואַקסט ארויס
פון מענשליכע שוואַכקייטען און לײדענ-
שאַפטען. ווי עס שײנט איז דאָ אַ פאַרמישט
אַ דריטע פערזאָן, אַ פרוי, און עס גילט
דאָ דער באַוואוסטער ,,פראַנצויזישער כלל
פון ,,שערשע לאַ פאם'' — זוד די פרוי.
די דאָזיגע דריטע פערזאָן קאָן אפשר
איצט אויף זיך ציהען דעם צאָרן פון דעם
פּראָפעסיאָנעלען מאָראַליסט, אַדער דעם
שמייכעל פון דעם האָפנונגסלאָזען ציני-
קער נאָר אין גרונט גענומען איז זי אפשר
די פּאַטעטישסטע פיגור אין דעם טראַ-
געדיע דריי-עק. איהר לעבען איז ווי עס
נישען אויס געווען לויטער אימפולס, ווי
ווײזט אויס אין מיטען פון א שטורמדיגען ים,
אַ שיף אין מיטען פון אַ שטורמדיגען ים,
וואָס געהט ארום פון קאָנטראָל און
שוועבט נאָר אין דער ריכטונג צו וועל-
כער עס טרײבען זי די כוואַליעם.
ס'איז אַ טראַגעדיע דורך און דורד.
כאָטש פון אויבען אויף גענומען זעהט עס
אויס, אז מען ווייס, ווער ס'איז שולדיג.

An article in the Yiddish press blaming Alice: "it appears there is a
third party, a woman ... she is the most pitiful figure in the tragic triangle.
Her life was pure impulse without control ... It is an utter tragedy, but ...
it appears that the guilty person is known."
Collection of Sharon Edelson

Ben on acquittal day, 16 January 1932.
This portrait is by the noted photographer
Jules Alexandre Castonguay.
Collection of Sharon Edelson

Widow Yetta, with Anita, back in Montreal with her parents, 1932.
Collection of Steven Chernove

The Fenster family: Yetta, Anita, and Max, around 1934.
Collection of Steven Chernove

Ben and Alice on vacation in Quebec,
summer 1932. Collection of
Sharon Edelson

Alice and Ben in their garden, 1935.
Collection of Sharon Edelson

Alice and Ben, late 1930s.
Collection of Sharon Edelson

Middle-class Jewish female respectability: Alice (far right) in Pioneer Women, sending bedding to Israel, 1948. Ottawa Jewish Archives, 4-026, Na'amat Pioneer Women, Ottawa Council Fonds, Photograph by Marvin Flatt

Alice (far left) in Hadassah, early 1960s. Collection of Sharon Edelson

Ben and Alice's 50th wedding anniversary
party, 1962. Collection of Sharon Edelson

Alice and Ben, late 1960s or early 70s.
Collection of Sharon Edelson

Ben's "Address Book" in which Ben cites "Jack's Accident" on the
upper right-hand page. Collection of Sharon Edelson

Top
Jewish Memorial Gardens, Bank Street
(old Jewish Cemetery), tombstone
of Jack Horwitz: "A memorial to a
dear brother/who was plucked in the
youth of his life/A tender fragrant
young flower/whose thread [or wick]
of life/was suddenly disconnected"
(translated from Hebrew).
Collection of Sharon Edelson

Left
Jewish Memorial Gardens, Bank Street
(old Jewish Cemetery), tombstones
of Ben and Alice Edelson. Collection
of Sharon Edelson

4

"Her life was pure impulse without control": Trial by Jewry, Community Anxiety, and the Spurning of Alice

The Ottawa Jewish community comprised an interconnected and unabashedly tight network of relatives and friends who lived, worked, prayed, and played together. In this close community practically everyone knew everyone else, or knew people who did.[1] As chronicler Max Bookman noted, "it was possible to have a personal acquaintance with almost every family or at least with the different *mishpochas* (family clans) in the community. As a result, such occasions as a *bar mitzvah*, a wedding, some other happy event or some unhappy occurrence was for all intents and purposes shared by the entire Jewish community."[2] This connectedness helped shape significant aspects of the Edelson/Horwitz case. It also made the incident all the more scandalous as the case breached shared religious, ethical, and cultural values, highlighted the waning status of Jewish masculinity and family life, and exposed Alice's subversion of proper Jewish womanhood, all of which made her a perfect scapegoat.

The closeness of the Jewish community manifested itself in a variety of ways. Certain families had been well known, for example, for inviting new immigrants to stay in their homes until they got on their feet.[3] Friends often visited with each other in their living rooms, on their verandahs, and at *shul*, or as they walked through Lowertown on a Sabbath afternoon.[4] Especially in Lowertown, "wherever you went, you felt very, very comfortable, and you felt safe and trusted."[5] This physical and psychological bubble helps explain why Norman Levine's father and his fellow peddlers behaved in a less respectable fashion when they hocked their wares in the fancier neighbourhoods outside Lowertown. Levine surmised that "they knew that once away from Lowertown they might as well have been in a foreign country."[6]

This sense of community was fostered by religious practice, most notably prayer in the synagogue. Although in Judaism it is allowable to pray alone, group prayer is always preferable. Accordingly, daily, Sabbath, and festival congregational services, and certain prayers, including the *kaddish* (the mourner's prayer), require a *minyan* (traditionally a quorum of at least ten Jewish men). This public practice underscored the importance of belonging to, and obligating oneself to, a group, a philosophy that spilled over into the social and cultural functions of the various synagogues, and of other community institutions.

Unlike synagogues in many other cities, even those smaller in size, Ottawa's four synagogues often offered shared programs. Beginning in 1923–24, for example, they collectively managed Ottawa's Talmud Torah, extra-curricular Jewish studies for children who attended public school. In 1919, the Talmud Torah Board purchased the former George Street Public School, where classes, as well as other religious, social, and cultural events, including weddings, were held.[7] With its classrooms, social hall, stage, and kitchen, it served as "the first multi-purpose community centre" for the Jews of Ottawa.[8] In 1928, all the synagogues also united in establishing and running the Young People's League, a social and cultural group which would continue for the next twenty-five years.[9]

As most of the immigrant Jews in Ottawa hailed from Eastern Europe and the Orthodox tradition, all of Ottawa's *shuls* were Orthodox. Generally, Jewish Ottawa regarded German Jews as overly assimilated, and their brand of liberal Reform Judaism as "diluted and *goyish*" (Gentile-like). When German Jews in 1920s Ottawa looked to establish a Reform temple there, the project faltered. This was partly due to their small numbers, and partly to "local public opinion" which "reflected the strong inherent orthodox Judaism of Jewish Ottawa and in particular of its leadership." "In fact," noted Max Bookman in his 1963 study of the history of Ottawa Jews, "the reputation enjoyed by Jewish Ottawa was that on the North American continent it was a stronghold of a modern Orthodox Judaism."[10] Ottawa Jews would increasingly modify their religious observance in order to accommodate the mores of the dominant culture, but there is no overestimating the attachment of Ottawa Jews to Judaism and to each other in the early 1930s.[11]

Informing the Jewish community of relevant news and events was *The Ottawa Hebrew News*. The newspaper was founded in 1928 by fledgling journalist Bookman who, by the late 1930s, claimed an impressive subscription rate for his paper of 763 households.[12]

Jewish unity was also served by the nearby public schools. Virtually all of Ottawa's Jewish children, whether from Lowertown or Sandy Hill, followed the same path as they grew up: they attended York Street School in Lowertown from kindergarten to grade eight, and then Lisgar Collegiate downtown if they planned to attend University.[13] As few Protestants lived in the vicinity of the elementary school, and the Catholic children attended Catholic schools, York Street School was overwhelmingly Jewish.[14] The school was also host to Brownies and Girl Guides and Cubs and Boy Scouts whose children and young leaders were predominantly Jewish. Leaders in the late 1930s included Edelson daughters Lillian and Vivian.[15]

In the 1920s and 30s, the Yiddish language also connected Ottawa Jews. In 1931, over 80 per cent could speak both English and Yiddish.[16] In December 1921, for example, Rabbi Berger gave his Friday night lecture in Yiddish.[17] Similarly, New York speaker Chaim Greenberg delivered his lecture "in the Yiddish tongue" at the Yehoash Folk Shule (Jewish People's School) banquet at the Chateau Laurier on the night of the shooting.[18] Founded by Labour Zionists in 1925, the Yiddish-centred Yehoash Folke Shule claimed an impressive one hundred students before it disbanded in 1936.[19] Yiddish was also the language of the Young Jewish People's Association, a popular organization that provided social and cultural activities between 1931 and 1934 to new immigrant Jewish youth in Ottawa.[20]

The religious and cultural identity and tight network of Ottawa Jews framed the shooting incident. On 23 November, for example, the anonymous phone-caller who tipped off Edelson to the continued affair between Jack and Alice sounded, according to him, like "an elderly Jewish woman" speaking in "broken English."[21] That night, Ben and Alice attended a joint meeting of the Ottawa Lodge of B'nai Brith and its Ladies Auxiliary, where Ben "took a very active part in the discussion," and was elected chair of the ticket-selling committee for an upcoming event.[22] On the afternoon of 24 November, Alice Edelson attended her weekly Hadassah chapter tea.[23] That very night, Alice and Jack traversed the familiar streets of Lowertown, hoping to go unrecognized amidst their family and friends. And before being called to the hospital, Jack's lawyer Sam Berger was giving a talk at the Talmud Torah Hall to the Young People's League of Synagogues of Ottawa.[24]

After the shooting, it did not take long for false rumours to spread about the nature of the incident. Because the *Yehoash Folke Shule* held a banquet for the Jewish community at the Château Laurier that evening, the Chateau Pharmacy, where Lemieux sought help for Horwitz, was confused with the hotel. As a result, many believed that an Edelson/Horwitz confrontation played out at the dinner prior to the attack at the Edelson store. Still others assumed a shooting occurred at the hotel.[25]

The strength of the Jewish community was especially palpable in this case when most of the three hundred people who attended Jack Horwitz's funeral were "of the victim's own faith."[26] Included in the Horwitz cortège were his childhood friends, lawyers Sam Berger and Moses Doctor, even though both men represented adversaries of the Horwitz brothers: Berger acting on behalf of Yetta and Doctor defending Ben.[27]

Jewish identity and networks in Ottawa also helped define the lives and interaction of the shooting's principal characters. Moses Doctor's Jewish identity and activism were so much a part of him that, on the occasion of his premature death in 1934, the *Journal* recognized that "he found time, despite a growing practice, to interest himself in the affairs of his own people and of his community."[28] The papers noted his membership in a variety of Jewish groups, and his teaching of Hebrew, "a language to which he devoted himself with the zest of reverence as well as aptitude."[29] They also listed Doctor's many friends and acquaintances who

attended the funeral, and declared that they comprised "delega-
tions from practically every Jewish organization in the city."[30] The
Journal reported that "he was always close to his own people, and
was loved by them all," adding that he "had brought distinction
to his race."[31]

Jack Horwitz, too, was "especially prominent in Jewish circles." He took an "active and keen interest in all matters pertaining to his faith," participating in the life of his synagogue,
and quietly donating to Jewish causes.[32] As a young man, he had
also belonged to several Jewish organizations, most notably the
Young Men's Hebrew Association (YMHA).[33] In 1921 and 1922,
he had distinguished himself as both a YMHA leader and athlete.
The association published its own newspaper entitled *The Booster*
for which Jack was one of three reporters, and treasurer. It not
only publicized and promoted YMHA events and other Jewish
philanthropic and educational work, but featured stories of
outstanding Ottawa Jews and their contributions to the city and
Jewish life.[34]

Ben and Alice Edelson were also defined by their participation
in the Jewish community. Although Ben regularly worked in the
store on the Sabbath, a widespread practice by ambitious Jewish
business owners in 1930s Ottawa,[35] the family generally observed
the laws of *kashruth*, enjoyed a fine Sabbath dinner on Friday
night, celebrated all the holidays, and attended synagogue as often
as possible.[36] And, as outlined in Chapter 2, they were involved in
a variety of Jewish organizations and causes.

The Horwitzes and the Edelsons would have crossed paths quite
regularly at community and lifecycle events. In the early 1920s, for
example, Jack, along with his brother Philip, was an avid and
accomplished bowler in the YMHA league, playing alongside Ben
Edelson.[37] And in 1925, when Jack's eldest sister Sarah married
Jack Ralph of Montreal in an elegant wedding at the Rideau Street
Synagogue, the bride's matron of honour was Alice, one of the
groom's ushers was Ben (along with Jack), and the flower girl was
Edelson daughter Vivian.[38]

How Jack and Alice met is not known, but they probably encountered one another through their families' business dealings

and physical proximity as part of a thriving ethnic economy. The second location of Edelson Jewellers, where the Edelson family also lived temporarily after moving to Ottawa in 1920, was at 158 Nelson Street in Lowertown, a building owned by Jack's father Max. And practically next door, at 154, lived Max Horwitz's family, including grown son Jack.[39] Because Ben and Jack were in the jewellery business, a *Toronto Daily Star* article suggested that Edelson and Horwitz, in addition to competing for Alice's affections, had been "rival jewelers."[40] But there is no evidence to indicate that any professional antagonism existed.[41]

That Jack and Alice each opted for a Jewish lover was no accident. Certainly proximity and convenience facilitated this choice, but Jewish law and culture reinforced it. According to *Halachah* (Jewish law), Jews were to marry fellow Jews, and dating and courtship rituals were practice and preparation for meeting this expectation. Even unobservant Jews most often complied, if not for religious reasons than for the familiarity of a shared background, for the approval of parents, or for the purpose of bearing/ raising Jewish children. Romance between a Jew and Gentile was deemed unsuitable, and was the source of community lamentation and family heartbreak. Grief especially reverberated when the non-Jew was the woman, which, according to *Halachah*, would necessarily render future children not Jewish. Even extra-marital affairs were expected to stay within the community. Adultery on its own was bad enough, and there were those Jewish husbands who kept non-Jewish mistresses, but a long-term, serious affair involving a non-Jewish lover would have made the liaison even more unseemly (albeit easier to dismiss as insignificant).

The Jewish cast of characters meant that the Jewish press covered the unusual murder case. Reaction to it was mixed. Unfortunately, the *Ottawa Jewish Bulletin* did not exist until 1937, so local coverage is not possible to gauge.[42] Throughout November and December 1931, and January 1932, however, Montreal's *Canadian Jewish Chronicle,* which dubbed itself "the first and foremost Anglo-Jewish Weekly in Canada," offered two stories about the incident. The first, which appeared just two days afterwards, declared "Ottawa Community Stunned by Mysterious

Shooting," immediately establishing the incident's Montreal connection by identifying Jack's wife as "Yetta Rosen, of Montreal."
The second story, which appeared at the start of December, simply
featured two photographs, one of Jack and the other of Ben, under
the headline "Principals In Ottawa's Mysterious Shooting Affray,"
and provided no update on the case.[43] Certainly, a newspaper
invested in advancing the cause of Canadian Jewry would not
want to highlight the sordid details of this crime, a reason that it
was featured only twice, and never profiled until at least page
eight.

One newspaper which featured it more regularly was the
Keneder Adler (*Jewish Daily Eagle*), a Yiddish paper also published in Montreal. Founded in 1908, the eight-page publication
was regarded as "Canada's most influential Yiddish daily" due
to its high circulation and its prominent and erudite editors and
writers.[44] More literary and journalistically rigorous than *The
Canadian Jewish Chronicle*, the *Keneder Adler* consistently ran
stories about the case on its front page. Its coverage, however,
largely reiterated facts from the Ottawa press, and it offered no
editorial commentary.[45]

A lone, unidentified Yiddish article found among Ben Edelson's
personal papers after his death suggests the disdain which the
larger Jewish community generally held for Alice, contempt which
would be echoed by Ottawa's Jewish community. The Yiddish editorial asserted that:

> the Edelson/Horwitz shooting is not a typical murder. It is a
> tragedy that grows out of human weaknesses and impulses.
> On the surface, it appears there is a third party, a woman,
> and it is appropriate to use the known French expression
> "cherchez la femme." This particular third person can now
> draw the ire of the professional moralist or the smile of the
> hopeless cynic, but basically she is the most pitiful figure
> in the tragic triangle. Her life was pure impulse without
> control like a ship on a turbulent sea that is tossed by the
> waves. It is an utter tragedy, but on the surface it appears
> that the guilty person is known.[46]

Alice alone, lustful, unrestrained, and selfish, is blamed for the shooting. Despite use of the word "murder," the article makes no direct reference to the two men.

Although it "shook up the whole town," the tragedy jolted Ottawa's Jews in particular.[47] As one Jewish newspaper indicated, "The Horwitz-Edelson tragedy has … shocked the tiny Jewish community of Ottawa."[48] Not only did it claim as its own the calamity's leading figures, it seemed both fascinated and shocked by the case's violation of Jewish values.

The case subverted ideas connected to some essential religious precepts. First, it challenged the sanctity of Jews, who, as "the chosen people," were selected for their social righteousness by God to enter a covenant with Him, and to be the moral beacon to other nations. (A more modern, less elitist interpretation of this principle references Jews as "the choosing people" who, unlike other nations, embraced the responsibility of this sacred obligation.) The case also undermined tenets grounded in Jewish Law, especially the *Torah*'s (and the *Talmud*'s) myriad dictates related to ethics ("to ensure moral treatment of others") and holiness ("to elevate human actions from animal-like to God-like").[49] These two categories of law are very much interconnected, as an immoral act, such as murder or adultery, "is always an unholy act as well." Indeed, a Jew who disregards the sacrosanct laws related to the ethical treatment of others, no matter how extensively he/she adheres to Jewish practice and ritual, cannot be deemed an observant or religious Jew.[50]

The case also highlighted the concept of *chillul Hashem*. Linking the unethical with the unholy as described above, a *chillul Hashem* literally means the desecrating of God's name, but colloquially refers to any public or blatant misconduct by a Jew. The transgression dishonours not only the sinner him/herself, but the entire Jewish people, and, by extension, the Torah and God.[51] Thus, a *chillul Hashem* is a source of collective lamentation in the Jewish community.[52] The disgrace is reflected in the eyes of both Jews and non-Jews alike, and, as such, the argument goes, is fodder for anti-Semitism."[53] Ben's *chillul Hashem*, with its associated violence, infighting, and jealousy, had the potential to feed into established notions of Jews as cunning and crafty. Many Jews must have worried about how the case would look to Anglo-Protestant Ottawans, many of whom already held negative perceptions of Jews. In fact, given that Jews were being scapegoated internationally for causing the Depression, and nearby Toronto and Montreal were hotbeds of anti-Semitic fervour, the community must have believed that there couldn't have been a worse time for this *chillul Hashem*.

Historian Michael Stanislawski reminds his readers, however, that it would be naive to imagine the faithful adherence by all Jews historically to these various religious precepts:

> the assumption that all Jews in the past based their everyday life and their actions on authoritative Jewish law or on shifting rabbinical interpretations of that law, is an ahistoric retrojection, a romanticization of Jewish life in the past that confuses the prescriptive and the descriptive – what Jews were commanded to do and what they actually did – as well as the historical evidence at our disposal.[54]

Clearly, Jack and Alice's adultery and Ben's shooting of Jack underscore this point.[55]

Nonetheless, murder committed by Jews was exceedingly rare. This, despite the findings touted by various government and privately commissioned studies in the early twentieth century that asserted a direct correlation between the increase in immigrants and in crime, and which labeled Jewish immigrants as especially amoral and greedy, and inclined toward criminality.[56] In fact, despite some infamous Jewish gangsters in the United States, relative to Canadians of all origins Jews participated in crime in much lower numbers. Indeed, in Ottawa in 1931, arrested criminals from Galicia, Lithuania, Poland, Romania, and Russia, countries where most immigrant Jews originated, numbered sixty-nine in total, twenty-four fewer than arrested criminals from England alone, and over a thousand fewer than those born in Canada.[57]

Jews particularly avoided "offences against the person, against property with or without violence, and against sex morals," crimes which Jews viewed as especially reprehensible.[58]

In Ottawa, however, possibly due to intensifying anxiety and need caused by the hardships of the Depression, there had actually been a dramatic increase in the number of arrests between 1930 and 1931 (from 1,530 to 1,944), and a rise in crime rates generally.[59] As the *Journal* reported, "it was a busy and eventful year for the city constabulary."[60] According to one letter to the editor in January of 1932, "this usually tranquil community has become infested by thugs of all descriptions."[61] Indeed, this problem inspired newspaper editorials and regular letters to the editor, in which Ottawans not only bemoaned their city's criminal element, but posited various reasons for and solutions to the problem.[62] Still, the majority of arrests were not for violent crimes but for petty offenses: "Breach of the Liquor Control Act," "Disorderly Conduct," and drunkenness, theft, and vagrancy. The most pressing problem in the 1930s was gambling, and police sought to curtail the vice by raiding the city's gambling houses.[63]

Murder was relatively uncommon in Canadian cities during this time, and Ottawa was no exception. Ottawa's first unsolved murder of the century did not occur until September 1913, when a noted bookie was robbed and killed, probably by fellow gamblers (the true name of victim "Charles Robinson" was Abe Rubenstein, a Jew). With the induction of the new chief of police Emile Joliat in August of 1931, and the new sheriff of Carleton County (with the unfortunate name Samuel Crooks) the following November, incidents of serious violent crime in Ottawa dropped even lower. In 1931, in addition to one arrest for manslaughter, there were only two arrests for murder: Ben Edelson and William Seabrooke.[64]

Although the Edelson and Seabrooke murder charges were the only ones that year, Ottawans nevertheless felt inundated with news about murder. The shootings happened only two weeks apart, and, as with the Edelson case, the press covered the continuing Seabrooke drama extensively. The papers tracked his man-hunt, his trial in May 1932, his guilty verdict and death sentence, his appeal and retrial, and finally his 1933 hanging.[65]

Moreover, the unfolding trials of two previous sensational murders were very much in the news. On 25 November, a day after the Edelson shooting, a jury in L'Orignal, Ontario in the eastern townships began hearing the case of an eighteen-year-old former Ottawa nursemaid who was accused of matricide, her mother's bloody body found brutally cut and stabbed the preceding May.[66] Less than two months later, Austin Cassidy was on trial in neighbouring Hull, Quebec, for the October 1930 shooting of William Bertram "Bert" Marshall of Ottawa.[67] The press reported in detail on his jailhouse hunger strike, drug overdose, and self-inflicted stabbing.[68]

For the Jewish community, that Ben Edelson could in any way be like these criminals was dreadful and shocking enough, but other aspects of the case were also confounding. Almost unfathomable was that Ben could have killed a fellow Jew. Indeed, a headline in the *Keneder Adler* highlighted this angle of the story, hinting at its rarity: "Prominent Ottawa Jew Shot; Another Jew Arrested."[69] The immigrant Jews of Ottawa would have been very familiar with Jews as the victims of the bloody pogroms of Eastern Europe. And in 1920s and 30s Ottawa, many Jewish children and teens suffered at the hands of French Canadian boys who terrorized them as they walked to and from school.[70] As well, reports of abuses and violence against Polish Jews regularly appeared in the Jewish press. At the root of these demonstrations of violence was anti-Semitism expressed by members of the dominant culture or other minority groups. Jews were used to this antagonism toward them by "outsiders," but especially in the face of this type of hostility, never would they expect one Jew to turn on another – they certainly hadn't fled the pogroms of Russia for this. Instead, Jews looked to each other for protection and comfort, and had formed a variety of institutions and organizations in Canadian urban centres to entrench this type of support.

The incarceration of Jews, especially for violent crimes, was also rare, and struck the community as quite strange. A colourful story

involving Moses Bilsky, the first Jewish resident of Ottawa, illustrates this point. Some time at the turn of the twentieth century,
Bilsky discovered that there was a lone Jew confined at the Nicholas Street Jail. With the High Holidays approaching, he insisted to
the warden that he hand him the key to the inmate's cell. Bilsky
explained "that no Jew should be in jail over the High Holy Days."
He unlocked the cell and escorted the Jewish inmate to the Bilsky
home. One police officer later remembered that if the jail ever happened to house a Jewish inmate, Bilsky would always try to get
him released "irrespective of innocence or guilt."[71] That the warden sanctioned this informal and potentially dangerous practice
not only speaks to Bilsky's influence, but to the rarity of Jewish
prisoners.

In contrast to the public nature of crime and punishment, privacy was a cherished feature of middle-class life, and indiscretions
and family conflicts were to be handled behind closed doors.[72] In
significant ways, privacy was "class and gender bound – the rich
could afford more privacy than the poor, and men could afford
more than women."[73] But when sexual transgression by men in
the middle and upper classes was discovered, the publicity around
it (although not the punishment for it) was intense. As female sexual misconduct was even more damaging to reputations, women
had a special interest in keeping their sex lives private.[74] Sex was
a provocative issue, despite the fact that within traditional Judaism, sex within the bonds of matrimony, especially for the purpose of procreation, was not to be stigmatized, but celebrated and
enjoyed.[75] Shockingly, however, the Edelson/Horwitz case revealed
the intimacy of a couple who were married to other people, and
who engaged in sexual relations for pleasure over procreation.

This focus on sex highlighted the uncomfortable and potentially
dangerous image of Jewish men as sexually potent. For the Jewish
community in the 1920s and '30s, this representation of the Jewish man, with its emphasis on the physical body, did not seem consistent with his spiritual commitments, professional ambitions,
and bookish persona.[76] Moreover in a climate of anti-Semitism,
"non-Anglo-Saxon men" like Jack "who achieved sexual notoriety

helped entrench dominant sentiments about the sexual depravity
and 'otherness' of marginalized men."[77]

Of course, the shooting itself was entirely incongruent with the
image of the studious and physically weak Jewish man. Unlike in
other ethnic groups, masculinity in Jewish culture was not affirmed through guns and violence, but through education, study,
and professional success. Conflicts such as that between Edelson
and Horwitz were to be resolved, as with the Horwitz family conference in 1929, by means of prudence and civility.[78] Although
physical bravado and athletic achievement increasingly played a
part in defining masculine identity, most immigrant Jewish parents still perceived physicality as far less significant (and certainly
more hazardous) than intellectual prowess.[79]

For both men and women, gender role fulfillment necessitated
marriage. Traditional Judaism viewed marriage as "socially,
morally, and religiously ideal," as "a prerequisite to spiritual fulfillment," and even as "a religious duty."[80] The marital home was
to be the cornerstone of religious and cultural life, the daily site
of gendered practice, ritual, and traditions.[81] So, although women
were not allowed to participate directly in synagogue life, and
experienced a variety of legal and educational barriers, "within
the European Jewish family structure, women were the undis-
puted rulers of the household."[82] As the "queen" of the home, the
woman was to transmit her Jewish values and knowledge to her
many children, modeling moral and honourable behaviour, and
earning the admiration and respect of her benevolent and equally
responsible and righteous husband.[83] Indeed, the great rabbis
espoused that he "who dwells without a wife dwells without joy,
without blessing, without good, and without happiness."[84] Adultery (defined by Jewish law as sexual intercourse between a wife
and another man, and not by a husband and another woman) was
a sin – an affront to the husband, the hallowed covenant of marriage, and to God.[85]

As Ben and Alice settled into family life, their marriage appeared troubled. Guests could hardly help but notice, for instance,
that Ben routinely left social gatherings early (he went to bed at

10:00 each night), and Alice loved to stay late, a habit that came to symbolize her dubious reputation, as well as her obvious differences from her husband.[86] As Dina recalled, "my mother would never leave a party voluntarily," and Ben "always went home without her."[87]

Ben was known to be stern, "negative," and "easy to anger." His generally cold and exacting demeanor made him a man difficult to like.[88] Even his eulogy hints at a demanding personality: the rabbi referred to his "patriarchal presence, the feeling that he was in command and was making his own decisions," and to his "strong sense of propriety" that "brought his children the idea of what life could be and should be." In addressing Ben's grown children, the rabbi noted that "he was always worried about how you looked, he was worried about manners, he wanted you to be not only presentable, but wanted you to have the discipline that he had in his own life."[89] By all accounts, Ben was strict with his children, especially the boys.[90] But he could be stern with Dina too, particularly because she worked at the store. When she arranged a window display, for example, he habitually criticized and corrected her efforts.[91]

In contrast, Alice was social, extroverted, and fun-loving.[92] Thanks to Alice who "loved people," "loved company," and "kept an open door," the large Friel Street house was "everybody's meeting place."[93] Adelene Hyman remembered it as a "free-spirited house."[94] If friends saw a light on, they didn't hesitate to drop in unannounced. Indeed, Alice's girlfriends congregated there to indulge in cigarette smoking, away from the scrutiny of their disapproving husbands. In short, her family and close friends adored her, and she created a warm and inviting atmosphere on Friel Street where "everybody was welcome."[95]

Apart from these fundamental personality differences, one cause of Alice's marital discontent and subsequent affair could have been her early marriage. Alice met and married Ben when she was a budding teenager, experiencing little life as a young single woman. This sudden transition from girlhood to wifely domesticity might not have fazed some women, but given Alice's vivacious spirit, it might have happened before she felt emotionally prepared, not only at the eager insistence of a lovesick Ben, but also at the urging of her pragmatic, widowed mother. And despite her exceptional skills as a milliner, she would have had to abandon any serious career aspirations after her wedding day.

In addition to this early marriage were young Alice's many and successive pregnancies. Between 1913 and 1919, Alice gave birth to four children, each two years apart. Starting in 1924, she would have three more children, two years, then one year apart. Alice's only extended break from childbirth before her last baby was the five-year period between 1919 and 1924. Numerous factors could account for this gap, including the Edelson move and adjustment to Ottawa, medical issues experienced by Alice or Ben, successful mutual or independent attempts at birth control, or serious marriage difficulties that kept Ben and Alice divided.[96] Whatever the reason, that the start of Alice and Jack's affair coincided with the end of the five-year hiatus helps explain why rumours abounded about the paternity of at least one of her subsequent children.

Alice was no doubt keenly aware that each new child intensified her reliance on Ben, and further defined the parameters of her life. As a young, spirited woman, her marriage to a more mature and, by all accounts, stern and dominating man, and her frequent pregnancies (which opposed the trend of dropping fertility rates and family size among Canadian, and particularly Jewish, women in the early twentieth century[97]), might have early on made her feel stifled, and old beyond her years. Certainly, there were women enduring similar circumstances who resolved to suffer stoically in silence, but in 1924, Alice opted for a different path.

After the shooting, with her affair widely publicized, Alice's image within the larger Jewish community was severely compromised. Although she had been respected as a proficient household manager and dedicated volunteer, the community, not surprisingly, judged her by reflecting on her life and character in the years leading up to the incident, and on the ways that she contravened ideas about the virtuous role of the Jewish wife and mother.

Her exceptional beauty had always been problematic in that regard. In the new era of silver screen idols, the petite, striking, dark-haired Alice looked every bit the glamorous movie star. According to her daughter Lillian, her stunning appearance inspired resentment by women in the Jewish community because she was more attractive than most of them. Lillian recalled that "she was like a fashion model because she wore these gorgeous clothes from New York a year ahead of anything that was shown here, and she had a kind of star quality. She walked into a room, and she had a group right away – she didn't have to do anything but stand there."[98]

Perceived as a *femme fatale*, she also provoked the ire of women who believed that, encouraged by their captivated husbands, she was overly bubbly, flirtatious, and coy.[99] Although the 1920s was popularly depicted as a decade of sexual emancipation and permissiveness, particularly with the advent of female suffrage, sexologists, and a thriving amusements culture, acceptance of female sexuality remained limited. Women's sexuality was still perceived as reactive to the central (and often irrepressible) actions of men, and was expected to be restrained, and confined to heterosexual, monogamous marriages. Women like Alice who were seen as pursuing or inviting sex outside the boundaries of their marriage were deemed depraved and promiscuous. Indeed, as Joan Sangster points out, the moral and legal distinction between the promiscuous woman and the prostitute was not always clear. Not only were these women consistently viewed as "abnormal," but as a menace to the sanctity of home and country.[100] For the women of the Jewish community, Alice's affair with Jack Horwitz confirmed their worst fears about her flirtatious ways, and about the susceptibility of their own husbands.

This condemnation of "loose" women intensified when they had children. While young, poor unwed mothers occupied the attention of social reformers and the courts, some of whom recommended sterilization,[101] married, middle-class women who were suspected of bearing another man's child were an object of community scrutiny. The possibility that Alice might be raising children conceived by someone other than her husband was proof of her blatant immorality, and of the community's declining values.

Suspicion of Alice might have been exacerbated by the view of her as especially young. Thirty-five years old in November of

1931, she seemed a youthful mother of seven children. The six-year age difference between Ben and Alice was not unusual, but given Ben's sober disposition and her cheerfulness, many had the impression that there existed a major age disparity between them. Mary Goldberg, for example, remembered that Alice was "a very young, beautiful woman – much younger than her husband ... and that she was "young and fun-loving, and her husband was very serious – more like a father I guess."[102]

Even more than the sacred image of the wife, the Jewish mother, as represented by the Biblical matriarchs, exemplified a selfless devotion to family, community, and religion, especially within the mythologized *shtetl* family.[103] In the face of Eastern European anti-Semitism, exile, poverty, and pogroms, the dutiful woman persevered, fiercely preserving, nurturing, and protecting her family and Jewish values, even when immigrating to North America. Here, she still "remained the emotional 'heart of the family,'" a position which served to entrench in the new world the romantic and reverential image of *shtetl* Jewish motherhood.[104]

By the 1920s and 30s, new depictions of the Jewish mother in American popular culture reinforced this iconic and sentimental image.[105] Songs like Sophie Tucker's 1925 signature ballad *My Yiddishe Mama* and films like the 1927 melodrama *The Jazz Singer* feature loving, old-world mothers "frozen in time," and the grateful children who needed and cherished them.[106] Indeed, because families were smaller by the 1920s, and Jewish mothers generally did not perform paid work, they were able to dedicate more time and effort to fewer children, which contributed to their depiction as "self-sacrificing and devoted, lavishing attention on their children." This focus included a preoccupation with their children's schooling, health, food consumption, nutrition, and safety.[107] All of these notions led one 1925 observer to comment that, unlike parents in other immigrant groups, "a Jewish mother, especially if European born, lives exclusively for her child."[108]

Clearly, Alice lived for more than just her children, and the community presumed that her self-indulgent affair with Jack robbed them of her energy, attention, and time. Mary Goldberg, for example, recalling that the Edelson children once visited her husband's beauty salon with lice in their hair, blamed their apparent neglect on Alice's adultery: "She was too busy running around with Jack, I guess. So she never had time for the kids."[109] Alice's affair not only sullied her reputation as a wife but as a mother as well, during a time when expectations about Jewish motherhood were notably high.

Of course, Jack did not conform to the image of the virtuous Jewish husband and father either. But this representation held less sway than that of the dedicated wife and martyred mother, and greater expectations for female morality helped protect his good name. But Jewish masculinity was becoming less secure and the deceased Jack, the betrayed and jailed Ben, and especially the seemingly self-serving Alice, reminded men of their declining status. North American modernity and burgeoning anti-Semitism were depriving them of their traditional authority, making them feel docile and redundant. Meanwhile their wives enjoyed a new sense of empowerment in the home, an unsettling and humiliating shift for husbands who were often now depicted in popular culture as feckless, henpecked, and anxious.[110] They were seen as assuming the traditional traits of women – they were weak, passive, and hysterical. This new image stunned those men who had achieved the masculine badge of professional success.[111]

One way they could counter this popular depreciation was through Zionist resettlement in Palestine. After all, the Zionist was everything his brother in the Diaspora wasn't: strong, physical, and tough.[112] The "Muscular Jewry" that Zionism promoted left little chance that women, limited to their role as "helpmates" in an undeveloped land, would rival them.[113] But most North American Jews before the Holocaust did not become active Zionists in Palestine, let alone ideological Zionists at home, and relied on other ways to relieve their disempowerment, and assert their manhood.[114]

Another strategy was to transfer their sense of angst and self-loathing onto Jewish women. Jewish men ridiculed their women, promoting new cultural images of them that emphasized their particularly feminine flaws. As Paula Hyman notes, "the characteristics that they mocked could be presented as female, rather than as

Jewish, qualities," which precluded men from being caught in the net of ethnic "otherness."[115] Thanks in large part to male authors, playwrights, screenwriters, and comics, portrayals of the Jewish mother as shrewish, manipulative, and materialistic would prevail after World War II.[116]

Clearly, the early twentieth-century North American Jewish family suffered from a variety of problems. They included issues related to modernity, assimilation, and anti-Semitism that often resulted in male dissatisfaction and, ultimately, in male desertion and divorce.[117] The cultural glorification of Jewish wifehood and motherhood combined with the backlash against women by emasculated Jewish men (all against the backdrop of the Depression as described in Chapter 5) provided the perfect storm for community hostility against Alice, as well as for deepening family fractures. That Alice's close girlfriends helped her cover up and continue her affair suggests not only their loyalty, but also a subversive repudiation of traditional notions of marriage and motherhood, if only vicariously, through Alice. Indeed, for her, they risked their own reputations.

Social and family problems were a source of concern for Jewish communities who measured their welfare by, among other things, the health of the family. In Ottawa, where the Jewish community was small and interrelated, the breakdown of one family could mean the collapse of others, and could detrimentally affect religious, institutional, and economic life which was organized around, and necessitated, intact family units and businesses. Historian Joyce Antler notes that because this attention to family has been "so central to Jewish life, anxieties concerning its well-being have tended to target the mother,"[118] and Alice was certainly no exception. As an adulterous wife and a supposedly negligent mother, she threatened not only her family, but the vigor and continuity of her entire community. With Alice as a common foe, the community could avoid splitting into anti Ben Edelson/anti Jack Horwitz camps, a divide that would make it especially vulnerable in a climate of anti-Semitism.

Notwithstanding her adultery, Alice Edelson sought, in many ways, a life of convention, and generally conformed to both Jewish and mainstream gender expectations. She was a capable household manager and cook, sought to help her husband build career success, was a valued worker in the family business, bore and raised children, and was a tireless volunteer. Moreover, her children adored her. But these achievements were overshadowed, for the community, by her reckless decision to feed her own pleasure and assert her autonomy. Like the rebellious flappers of the post-suffrage era, she pursued personal and sexual freedom, defiance that her "masculine" chain-smoking also suggested.[119] But flappers were generally young and single, and their blithe lifestyle was expected to end upon marriage. The fashionable, flirty, and already very-married Alice had taken things too far.

Alice and Yetta, despite their shared stations in life as the smart and resourceful Jewish wives of jewellers, could be profiled as a study in contrasts. Alice was deemed a perpetrator; Yetta a victim. As Alice became more vilified, she grew weak, fragile, and secluded; as Yetta was ever more pitied, she proved increasingly strong, sturdy, and resilient (martyrdom, a comfortable role for Jewish women, agreed with Yetta, perhaps because she sensed that she would never be down for long.). Alice sought privacy and stayed silent; Yetta sought public sympathy and desired a voice. The presence of Alice was mysterious and ethereal; the presence of Yetta was clear and forceful. The contrasting circumstances, attitudes, and perceptions of Alice and Yetta generally reflect the polarized image of women in the early twentieth century as evil or virtuous.[120] Yetta was clearly on the side of good as compared to Alice, who, according to community standards, undercut not only her own marriage, fidelity, and commitment, but those of Jack – making Yetta and daughter Anita her innocent prey.

Despite their many differences, however, Alice and Yetta in some ways suffered similar fates. Both were the victims of gender stereotypes that called for women to be abidingly moral and giving. Indeed, both Alice and Yetta were variously accused of selfish behaviour: Alice was reviled for her adulterous affair, for causing Jack's death, and for failing to support Ben as he faced his trial and jail time; Yetta was maligned for taking money from her husband's store and for claiming her fair share of his will. Because of the desire by these women to nurture and protect themselves rather than others, both their reputations were severely compromised: Alice lost her friends, and Yetta, her family.

Gossiping about the affair and shooting, and Alice in particular, became the community's favourite guilty pleasure. That there were no witnesses to the shooting other than the jailed Ben, the ailing Alice, and the dead Jack, made it even more mysterious, and subject to much conjecture and scrutiny. Adelene Hyman recollected that "there was so much gossip! I knew tongues were wagging."[121] Suzie Gellman remembered that in the Jewish community "no one talked of anything else for days and months."[122] Ten-year-old Suzie woke up the day after the shooting to find her parents discussing the incident, and the phone "ringing off the hook." Her mother's girlfriends were anxious to share in the news, and as the phone calls continued throughout the day, the women methodically reviewed the chronology of events, the known cast of characters, and all of the other gripping and sordid details.[123] Much of the talk turned to the fate of the Edelson marriage. Many assumed that in the face of such tragedy and public humiliation, there was no way a husband could forgive a wife, take her back, and ever trust her again.[124]

Alice's treatment of Ben after the shooting was given particular scrutiny, promoted by unfavourable press coverage. After describing Ben's gloomy lot in jail, the *Citizen* emphasized Alice's neglect of her husband by pointing out that she "has not seen her husband since he left the store following the arrival of Dr. Danby, as she went to the hospital with Horwitz and was not home when Edelson was arrested and taken to the police station."[125] This point was underscored in a *Citizen* subtitle that announced Ben "Did Not See Wife Since."[126] Alice had abandoned her husband in his time of need, an offense made worse by his obvious devotion to her, and his sacrificed freedom. Despite her traumatic experience witnessing a shooting, losing her lover, and enduring her husband's incarceration and trial, her predicament garnered little compassion.

After the shooting, Ben and Alice were ostracized by the Ottawa Jewish community. According to Adelene Hyman, who, as a loyal chum to Lillian, visited the Edelson home each day following the incident, this process began almost immediately.[127] Although their very close friends stood faithfully by them, the wider social circle of more prominent Jewish families discarded the Edelsons: "they weren't invited to the big dos anymore," and friends dropped in less often.[128] Hyman observed no adult friends at the house when she visited, and was "astounded" that the family seemed deserted by the community: "instead of being supportive and kind, it was standoffish."[129] Suzie Gellman recalled "I don't know if too many people felt sorry for Ben."[130] Even local Jewish comedians were making fun of the case.[131] Daughter Dina maintained that business at Edelson Jewellers never suffered, but there is a good chance that she was referencing the many non-Jewish customers who continued to frequent the store.[132]

At the King Edward *shul*, some disapproving congregants insisted that the Edelsons resign their membership. Department store magnate A.J. Freiman, who had served as president of the synagogue for a straight twenty-six years (1903–1929) might have been the most vocal. After the trial, he informed Ben that he was no longer welcome at Adath Jeshurun, to which an indignant Ben retorted that he should be free to worship where he chooses, and that Freiman had no right to be self-righteous given his own marital indiscretions.[133] Despite Ben's arguments, it seems that Freiman and others at some point got their way: membership and seat holder records from 1948 indicate that, by this time, the Edelsons were attending the Rideau Street *shul*.[134]

The Edelson children were not immune to the disaffection of the Jewish community. According to Adelene Hyman, parents didn't want their children associating with the Edelson kids because they feared the family's depravity "would rub off on them."[135] Perhaps due in part to the looser attitude toward male sexual behaviour, to boys' less judgmental approach toward their male friends, or to the eugenic notion that female sexual immorality was a hereditary trait, the older Edelson girls got the worst of this: either their invitations to teen parties were revoked by scared parents, or they were not befriended at all.[136] Lillian remembered that people "weren't hurling epithets at us," but "we were dropped."[137]

If the community didn't feel compassion for the betrayed Ben and his innocent children, they felt even less sympathy for Alice. She was especially spurned by women, who were "nasty," perhaps fearful of the prospect that she could lure their own husbands away.[138] Estelle Abelson remembered that her mother Edith, a humble woman of modest means, befriended Alice after she was shunned by her more well-heeled peers.[139] One of them even dared to "spit at her, and called her names."[140] With this general repudiation, the once unfettered Alice "didn't have the same kind of life [after the shooting]."[141] The community could at least justify in Ben's case that "Alice drove him to it."[142] But Alice had no excuses, and bore the full wrath of the community. Suzie Gellman remembered that "not too many people felt sorry for her because they felt that she caused it all."[143] On the one hand, the Jewish community was not surprised to hear of Alice's adulterous affair given her flirtatious ways; on the other hand, it was more appalled by her disreputable behaviour than by the shooting itself.[144] For Alice, this community denunciation was "devastating."[145]

Even with the rarity and stigma of divorce in the 1930s, Ottawa Jews marveled that Ben stayed married to Alice.[146] Alice betrayed her marriage, "drove" Ben to shoot Jack, retreated from her family following the shooting, "abandoned" her husband as he languished in jail and endured a humiliating trial, and pushed him toward the gallows. Few would have blamed him for initiating a divorce, especially as it was more acceptable in Judaism than in other religions.[147] Mary Goldberg remembered that "we were shocked when he took her back."[148] As Goldberg's words indicate, the community generally believed that it was Ben, not Alice, who had the upper hand in determining the fate of the marriage. The more romantic of the group believed that "he took her back" because he must have adored her, and that this love transcended the misery that she wrought; the more cynical believed he needed a mother for his seven children whom he never could have raised on his own. Either way, after the havoc that she "caused," the community generally viewed Alice as fortunate to remain Ben Edelson's wife.

In reflecting upon Alice staying with Ben, Mary Goldberg concluded, "I guess she had to."[149] Certainly, if Ben had forsaken Alice, her professional and personal options would have been slim. As a former milliner, Alice possessed a marketable trade, but a divorce, especially in the midst of the Depression, could have left her penniless, too poor to establish her own shop, or to survive in a factory on minimum wage. The influence that Jewish women were perceived as wielding in the home did not translate into political and economic power outside of it. Acquiring financial security through a second marriage was also unlikely. Although beautiful, as a woman in her thirties, the mother of seven children, and with her infidelity widely known, Alice's chances of finding an eligible Jewish man were limited at best, and virtually impossible in tiny Ottawa. Most of all, with Ben likely retaining custody of the children due to his wife's immorality, Alice could have been severed from them. Having shot a man, and as a custodial parent of seven children, Ben's opportunity to remarry might not have been much better than hers, but for some struggling Jewish spinster or widow (like Alice's mother Chaya who married a widowed father of eight), his reputation as a successful merchant would have trumped all else.

For the Jews of Ottawa, a group that was vibrant, interdependent, and insular, the Jewish community "was the only community."[150] Due to this intimacy, and the ways it was reflected in the Edelson/Horwitz case, the community gossiped about it incessantly. On the one hand, it stirred up sensitive issues related to middle-class Jewish identity, womanhood, manhood, and family life, issues that highlighted the widening cracks of contemporary Jewish life. On the other, it reminded members how relatively fortunate they really were: men could feel thankful for their less glamorous, but loyal wives, and women could feel morally superior to a "harlot" who was the cause of the tragedy.

5

"In a court of British justice, sympathy has no place": Trial by Jury, Respectability and Honour, and the Acquittal of Ben

Ben Edelson's three-day murder trial began on Thursday 14 January, at 9:35 am, at the Ottawa winter assizes of the Ontario Supreme Court at the Carleton County Courthouse. Both the Crown and the defence sought to demonstrate that he was the victim of his wife's adultery. From the perspective of the Crown, his victimization inspired intense humiliation and a longstanding rage which fuelled a plan for murder; from the perspective of the defence, it revealed a sympathetic and otherwise honourable man caught up in a tragic accident. When the trial commenced, Ben was noticeably anxious. Dressed in a blue suit, white shirt, and black and red striped tie, he "wore a strained expression on his features as the judge ... took his seat on the bench."[1] Seeking to elude the scrutiny of the swarm of spectators, he "hid himself from view as much as possible from his seat in the dock, except when he consulted his counsel."[2] But on the trial's last day, and after a parade of witnesses, Ben took the stand, and provided its most gripping, articulate, and persuasive testimony. On Saturday 16 January 1932, at 10:40 pm, after deliberating for less than eighty minutes, the jury found Ben Edelson not guilty of murder.

In the face of compelling evidence against him, it would hardly be surprising if Ben had been found guilty but, as this chapter argues, jurors viewed the shooting as justifiable because of his middle-class respectability combined with the "unwritten law." In the midst of a Depression that demoralized men both professionally and personally, the all-male jury could sympathize with a reputable man who killed his wife's lover to protect the interests of his family and restore his dignity. Whether provoked or pre-meditated, the shooting was understandable and warranted. And in the Depression, when women were blamed for many of men's ills, the jury excused Ben's transgression by effectively scapegoat-ing Alice.

The Law and the Courtroom

Under the 1927 *Revised Statutes*, the Criminal Code defined homicide as either "culpable" or "not culpable." Toronto prose-cutor Peter White KC, with the help of inquest and preliminary-hearing prosecutor J.A. Ritchie, sought to argue that Ben Edelson's actions in the death of Jack Horwitz comprised culpable homi-cide – that is, death by means of an unlawful act. An unlawful act meant Ben brandished the gun to harm, coerce, intimidate, or threaten Jack. Culpable homicide could be judged as either mur-der or manslaughter. As prosecutor, White sought to convict Edel-son of murder, the most serious of the homicide charges.[3] The jury therefore had the options of agreeing with White, choosing to find Edelson guilty of the lesser charge of manslaughter, or finding that no crime at all had been committed.

The charge of murder was characterized primarily by the exis-tence of violent intention on the part of the accused, a notion but-tressed by, but not necessitated by, the presence of premeditation. It was White's task to prove intention beyond a reasonable doubt, although the act of brandishing a gun, which arguably was "known to the offender to be likely to cause death, and is reckless" could itself constitute a finding of murder.[4] Murder, a capital offense, garnered the death penalty.[5]

The lesser crime of manslaughter could incorporate, among other defences, provocation. The *Criminal Code* defined provo-cation as a scenario in which "the person who causes death does so in the heat of passion." Provocation was "any wrongful act or insult, of such a nature as to be sufficient to deprive an ordinary person of the power of self-control" if the perpetrator "acts upon it on the sudden, and before there has been time for his passion to cool."[6] Provocation was often described as a "crime of passion," although this term had no legal status in Canadian law. As the spontaneous nature of provocation necessarily precluded premeditation, this verdict traditionally garnered a sentence less severe than the death penalty.[7]

Presiding over the courtroom was sixty-eight-year-old Mr Justice John Millar McEvoy,[8] who, when outlining lesser possible findings to the jury, would specifically instruct the members to reject the provocation defence: "The old story is that a man comes home and finds his neighbour with his wife. He draws a sword and kills both of them. That is a case of sudden provocation. Apparently Edelson was not provoked. His own story is that he was in possession of all his faculties. I think you should hold him to that statement."[9] The judge certainly believed that the case did not meet the legal definition of provocation (or insanity/temporary insanity if it had been argued[10]), and moved to prevent Ben's verdict from being reduced to a manslaughter charge based on these grounds.

The jury could also arrive at a finding of "justifiable" or "excusable" homicide.[11] This verdict suggested that the homicide met none of the criteria above, and could lead to an acquittal. The jury would have to buy into an accident or self-defence theory, or, as will be argued later, an honour-killing scenario.

Doctor chiefly advanced an "accident" theory. He did so presumably because the evidence made it a tenable defence, which, if successful, unlike a "provocation" defence, would guarantee an acquittal. With Ben as the only witness to the incident, the jury would not be exposed to first-hand testimony that could refute the argument that the shooting had been an accident.[12] Moreover, as will be discussed later, this defence offered an expedient way for a jury to acquit Edelson, even if it believed he purposefully committed murder.

For this reason, jury selection was crucial. According to the newspapers, Doctor challenged the inclusion of fourteen of the first panel of twenty jurors and four of the second panel of twenty. White disputed only three.[13] For both the defence and Crown, a limited number of these objections might have been peremptory, meaning that the lawyers did not need to give a reason (such as inability or ineligibility) for excusing a would-be juror. Certainly, Doctor would have been cognizant of the undue pre-trial publicity which could have biased the views of potential jurors.[14] He also would have been vigilant about their possible anti-Semitism. Mostly, he would have wanted jurors cut from the same cloth as Edelson – men who were respectable small-business owners, with a traditional view of marriage and the sanctity of family. Selected juryman James H. Laishley, for example, ran the Ottawa Tire Company and was an avid hunter (thus, had no aversion to guns), and, like Ben, was known as "straight-laced" and a "strict man."[15] "So," remembered Doctor's partner Roydon Hughes, "he was a good man to have on the jury for us."[16] But, as this chapter will claim, Doctor's preferred jurors also had to be just heretical enough to accept that there were times when a man had to take the law into his own hands. White would have rejected those who opposed capital punishment (as this could have precluded them finding Edelson guilty), and those who claimed that, under some circumstances, one man had the right to slay another.[17] Because, in White's words, "this case has received a great deal of publicity," jury members were officially sequestered for the duration of the three-day trial.[18]

Due in part to this publicity, the trial attracted great fascination. The *Journal* observed that "No murder trial in the history of the Ottawa courthouse has evoked such tense interest, or been attended by such crowds throughout its duration. From first to last the courtroom was packed with spectators, scores standing for hours, and many unable to gain admission."[19] Indeed, on the second day, with the break for lunch at 12:45 pm, "about a hundred spectators took their seats immediately to wait the resumption of the trial at 2 p.m. All day, the courtroom was packed to suffocation."[20] By the last day of the trial on 16 January, "the seats in the court room were filled" even before court convened.[21] Crowds in the hallways "begged with the sheriff's officers for admission"; even "newspaper men were appealed to by would-be spectators."[22] By the afternoon, when Edelson was set to take the stand, "crowds stormed the courthouse and sheriff's officers had all they could do to keep order."[23] As the *Journal* reported, Edelson testified before "a packed courtroom, with scores of people standing."[24]

The Prosecution

Born into a prominent Pembroke, Ontario, family in 1872, prosecution lawyer Peter White was a renowned legal veteran.[25] He was lauded for his brilliance and his "outstanding qualities,"[26] and, in the years surrounding the Edelson trial, was involved in several high-profile political cases.[27] Doctor had only praise for the prosecutor. In a polite nod to White in his closing address, Doctor would acknowledge that White "bears a reputation for his profound knowledge of the law, equalled [*sic*] by few and surpassed by none."[28]

Much of the trial procedure and testimony of the case was tedious and measured, involving technical legal disputes.[29] On the first morning, "progress was slow."[30] One point of contention was the testimony of prosecution witness Dr Danby. Danby had always maintained that no one at the scene had ever articulated the cause of Jack's injury, but at the trial he testified to hearing the words, "He was shot." [31] Because Danby did not know who made the statement or to whom, because he gave testimony that he never offered up before, and/or because the judge surmised that the Crown was employing Danby's testimony as *proof that Horwitz was shot* rather than *as proof that a bystander stated* that Horwitz was shot, the judge ruled Danby's remark as hearsay, making it inadmissible – a victory for Doctor.[32] When Danby reinserted the statement in his testimony a short while later, it "roused the judge and Crown Counsel to considerable protest, and some argument," so much so that after a relentless Danby again mentioned the barred comment, the angry judge told him to "quit talking."[33]

Lorenzo Lemieux also caused a stir at the trial when he introduced new testimony. As at the coroner's inquest, he was "very nervous and ill at ease," and as a result, "almost drove Mr. White to distraction." [34] For the first time, he stated that as he and Edelson drove through Lowertown on the night of the shooting, Edelson donned dark glasses. He noted that "he had never known Edelson to wear glasses before." He also testified that Edelson had a cut under his eye after the shooting rather than the bruise he described at the preliminary hearing. After a meeting among the judge and two lawyers to debate the admissibility of the new evidence, the judge ruled that it would be allowed, and that Lemieux could continue his testimony. Although he reiterated Horwitz's incriminating comment that Lemieux's boss was a murderer, White did not fare well when Lemieux also told of seeing a gun in the store years before the shooting, underscoring the point that Edelson did not acquire the weapon for the sole purpose of harming Horwitz.[35]

The second day of the trial proved far more productive. Ten Crown witnesses testified until about 4:00 pm.[36] Most of them addressed issues relating to Horwitz's clothing, which had been contaminated as evidence when it was transported in a bundle from the hospital to the undertakers before reaching the hands of police.[37] The more riveting witnesses that day promised to be Jack's brother Charles, Jack's brother-in-law Harry Hertz, and Jack's lawyer Sam Berger, all of whom had spoken with the victim in the hours before his death.

The testimony of these three men was the object of much legal wrangling. At issue was whether or not Jack believed he was dying when his conversations with them took place. If the court determined that Jack was uttering a dying declaration, the evidence was allowed; if it did not, the evidence was barred.[38] The rationale for this was based on the Christian expectation that a man who believed he was dying would not lie, lest he jeopardize divine salvation. Otherwise his statements were no more reliable than anyone else's; moreover the death of the witness (that is, his inability to testify) made any conversation with him before he died hearsay, and therefore inadmissible.

The judge repeatedly retired the jury as the lawyers thrashed out the issue, and ultimately ruled that evidence related to all three of these conversations would be prohibited.[39] This ruling was a crushing blow to White, and a significant victory for Doctor. Without the jury present, Charles, inciting "a sensation" in the courtroom, stated that Jack had said to him "Ben shot me. I'm all

in, Charlie. Mr. Berger has just made out my will."[40] Although
this testimony more than suggested Jack's fatalistic mood, the
judge deemed that Jack still "had a hope of life when he made the
statement" (perhaps because he used the colloquial "I'm all in"
rather than the more explicit "I'm going to die"), and barred the
conversation from being entered into evidence.[41] The judge made
the same ruling when both Harry Hertz and Sam Berger took the
stand to relay their final talks with Jack about the cause of his injury.[42] The judge's decision regarding Berger was especially curious. After all, Jack summoned Berger to his bedside to draw up his
will, a clear indication that Jack believed he was dying. To White's
delight, even Doctor conceded this point.[43]

By the second day of the trial, word was out that the case would
go to the jury the next day. The *Citizen* reported that "the court
is anxious to wind up the trial by the weekend."[44] Confirmation
came that Friday night when Judge McEvoy announced that the
trial would conclude on Saturday.[45] Perhaps this tight schedule
was owing to "one of the heaviest dockets in the history of the
local Supreme Court of Ontario,"[46] or to McEvoy's ill health,
which would be grave enough to force him to withdraw from a
trial just a week following the Edelson verdict.[47]

The last day of the trial was destined to be the most electrify-
ing. The anticipated police testimony contributed to this excitement. Doctor was looking for police corroboration of a bruise
or cut under Ben's eye, an injury that would cast Horwitz as the
aggressor, and thus the architect of his own demise. But Police
Sergeant Hector Levigne testified that he observed no mark below
Edelson's eye on the morning of 25 November after Ben was arrested.[48] Ben would later testify to the existence of the cut, caused,
he believed, by Horwitz's ring, although he noted, perhaps to save
face, that the cut "was not much of one."[49]

Prosecution firearms expert Charles H. Howe also reported
how he and fellow officers conducted various ballistics experiments with the defendant's bullets and gun in the police station
basement.[50] Howe provided evidence that the bullets retrieved
from Horwitz's body and the store wall matched those fired in the
tests from Edelson's automatic. White then distributed the fired

bullets and some magnifying glasses to jury members so they could note the incriminating evidence for themselves.[51]

Howe also testified that more recent experiments showed that as no powder-burn marks were evident on Horwitz's overcoat (notably at his cuff, presumably next to the fired gun), the gun would have had to have been fired from at least five inches away, challenging a potential self-defence scenario (there was no report of gunpowder burns on Horwitz's hand or wrist).[52] Defence witness and firearms expert Sherman Hardisty would testify, however, that any powder marks left on Horwitz's clothes after the shooting might have been erased through their "excessive handling."[53] Another possibility was that the grey gunpowder traces were imperceptible on Horwitz's grey coat.[54] Finally, Howe, responding to White's question about whether the gun could "go off accidentally," affirmed "not unless the trigger is pressed."[55] Hardisty would assert, though, that the gun "was not of modern type and that it fired easily," meaning that older guns possessed slack triggers.[56] Even prosecution witness Detective-Sergeant MacDonald had to concede that because the gun was an automatic, it discharged more easily than a regular revolver.[57]

Another compelling witness on the trial's last day was Jack's widow Yetta. As she took the stand, "dressed in deep mourning," her face obscured by a veil, "an air of suppressed excitement pervaded the courtroom."[58] In hushed tones, she "told a pathetic story of domestic troubles."[59] For the most part, she reiterated her testimony from the coroner's inquest and preliminary hearing, recounting her meeting with Ben at Union Station, the family conference at her father-in-law's home three years before, her persistent phone calls from Ben, the saga of Alice in the coal bin, and her husband's assertion that "Mrs. Edelson would not leave him alone," and that she "was always after him."[60]

For newspaper readers, Yetta's reference to the 1929 family meeting must have been explosive. For the first and only time, a newspaper reported her testimony that Jack might have fathered one or more of Alice's three younger children.[61] Curiously, according to the *Journal* story, prosecutor White did not dwell on the issue, but quickly changed the subject. He could have argued convincingly that even if Ben only suspected his wife of having borne another man's child, he had a powerful motivation for murder. White, however, never pitched this theory, possibly because it was a sordid and culturally delicate topic, or because it could evoke tremendous sympathy for Edelson, facilitating an acquittal.

Jack's brother, Philip Horwitz, also testified that day about the family conference. Like Yetta, he recalled a discussion surrounding the paternity of the younger Edelson children. But unlike his sister-in-law, he testified to hearing another conversation – one that was potentially ruinous for the accused. Philip recollected his father Max Horwitz say that he had heard rumours that Jack had been paying Ben Edelson. The reason for the deal was not explicitly stated, but the presumption was that Edelson had blackmailed or accepted money from Jack Horwitz in exchange for tolerating, condoning, or keeping silent about the affair (and perhaps the paternity matter, for which Ben might have solicited child-support payments). Philip also stated that although denying at first that he had paid off Ben, Jack later confessed that he had, and that Max had ordered his son to terminate the arrangement.[62] If the story were true, it demonstrated not only Ben's unsavory character in serving up his wife for profit, but also his knowledge of the affair several years earlier than he had claimed.[63] It also indicated Ben's collusion with Jack Horwitz in the kind of financial arrangement that often surfaced with sex-crime cases, and was "frowned on" by the courts.[64] Although highly provocative, Philip's testimony was undercut in two significant ways: by his vague and clumsy responses which clearly frustrated the judge; and by Ben, who insisted that prior to the family meeting, he had never discussed such matters or received compensation.[65]

The Defence

In defending Ben, Moses Doctor, assisted by his law partner Roydon Hughes, did not need to "prove" anything. He simply needed to raise reasonable doubt about the prosecutor's case for murder. Although primarily presenting an accident defence, at various

points in the trial Doctor alluded to a variety of possible shooting
scenarios in which Ben would not have been culpable. To further
his cause, Doctor called two defence witnesses: firearms expert
Sherman Hardisty, who proved a relatively minor witness, and
the accused, Ben Edelson.

Ben "appeared calm and collected" as the last day of the trial
commenced, but Doctor's decision to have him testify on his own
behalf provided the highlight of the proceedings.[66] His name had
been absent from the list of defence witnesses that Doctor first
gave the judge, but he clearly had a change of heart.[67] After all,
during the 1929 rape trial against MP Louis Auger, Doctor put his
client on the stand, and he was subsequently acquitted. Doctor
must have reasoned that Edelson, like Auger, would make a convincing witness: he was calm, persuasive, articulate, and smart.[68]
He no doubt believed, as well, that the Crown had produced compelling evidence, establishing beyond a reasonable doubt that
Edelson had the opportunity, motive, and means to murder. Doctor simply had no choice but to put Edelson on the stand to challenge these presumptions.

Ben's testimony would not only undermine the prosecution's
case, but would serve to humanize him. This would help Doctor
achieve several goals, showing that Edelson and the jurymen were
more similar than different (Doctor later pleaded with the jury to
"do for him what you would expect for yourselves."[69]), that he
constituted no threat to citizens like them, and that this transgression was an anomaly in his life and not indicative of his true
character.[70] This strategy was intended to evoke jury admiration,
sympathy, and empathy, thereby resulting in an acquittal. Doctor
questioned Edelson for one hour and forty minutes and after a
short recess, he was crossed-examined by Peter White for about
the same amount of time.[71]

As it turned out, Doctor was right: Ben Edelson proved an excellent witness. The Citizen reported that in the three hours he
endured on the stand, "not once did he waver as he related what
he knew." It noted that he conveyed the entire story of his domestic problems and the shooting "frankly and without hesitation."[72] The Journal, too, observed that "Edelson made a deep

impression by his manner of giving his evidence. He was clear and collected throughout his long ordeal."[73] It also noted that when he took repeated drinks of water, "his hand was quite steady each time he raised the glass," suggestive of his conviction and honesty.[74]

Doctor generally sought to demonstrate Ben's law-abiding nature. After his store was vacated following the shooting, for example, Ben neither fled town nor went underground. He quietly locked up, met with his lawyer, picked up his car from Lemieux's father's house, drove home, and waited to be arrested.[75] Attempting to undermine the prosecution's suggestion that Ben held Jack against his will, Doctor also asked Edelson why he locked the front door to the jewellery store after the trio stepped inside. Edelson testified this was his usual practice when he stayed in the store after closing, and that he believed this was a city by-law.[76] Doctor also asked Ben where he obtained the gun. He stated that he had possessed the gun for ten years, long before the shooting. He had purchased the .32 caliber automatic (sometimes dubbed "a ladies' gun" for its small, concealable, and compact design[77]) for ten dollars from a second-hand store in Montreal, and received it by mail along with bullets and instructions. In the interest of following the law, he later asked a detective in Ottawa if he required a permit to own the gun. He was told that as long as he didn't carry it on his person, he did not need a permit, although he certainly would have obtained one if legally necessary.[78]

Ben made it clear that he only "innocently" brandished the gun on the night of the shooting. He testified that he said to Jack, "I love Alice and the children too much to put Alice out on the street. I am ready to forgive her once more and will take her back if you will promise to leave her alone." It was only after this appeal, Ben said, that he retrieved the gun, simply "to put more emphasis on my words."[79] He knew the gun held bullets, but pulled back on the "action bar" only "to show Jack that it was loaded." As he did this, a live cartridge fell to the floor, a matter of course, but seemingly a startling occurrence for Ben. Doctor showed that Ben actually knew little about the workings of a gun because, as Ben explained, he "never had occasion to touch it before."[80] But White later extracted from Edelson that when he pulled the gun from the work bench, he knew not only that it was loaded but that the safety catch was off, an indication that he had previously handled the gun, that he had at least some knowledge of how it worked, and that he had readied it in a plan to shoot Horwitz.[81]

Ben's experience with guns, in fact, was more extensive than he let on. According to the recollections decades later of his daughter Lillian, he had actually taken shooting lessons at one time, and, at a veterinarian's suggestion, had shot as an act of mercy one of his dogs suffering from a terminal skin condition. The vet had sent over a police officer to perform the grisly deed, but Ben did it himself in "just one shot."[82] In his defence, Lillian stated that "my father knew how to shoot ... If my father intended to shoot him [Jack], there wouldn't have been those two [sic] bullets in the wall."[83] Thus, the image of a mild-mannered Ben who felt discomfort with guns contradicted the reality of a more rugged Ben who had finesse with firearms.

Doctor also endeavoured to show that, after the shooting, Ben aided Jack as much as possible. It was Ben who helped the injured man to the floor; who asked Jack how he felt; who retrieved the glass of water that Alice had ministered; who first instructed Lemieux to call a doctor; who told Lemieux to drive, not walk, to the Regent Theatre to alert Charles for whom Jack was asking (never mind that Lemieux's testimony at the December inquest contradicted almost all of these points.[84]); and who guided the ambulance workers into the store. Moreover, Ben immediately returned the gun to the workbench, when he could have otherwise fired again to ensure Jack's demise.[85] Even Jack had responded to Ben's kindness: according to Ben, as Jack lay bleeding on the floor, he "put his hand in mine and said 'Ben, don't worry. It's going to be alright,'" and uttered in Yiddish, "'it is the will of God,'"[86] a statement suggesting that, far from blaming Ben, Jack perceived the shooting as divine retribution for the illicit affair.

Ben also testified to trying to secure the integrity of the crime scene. When he observed Lemieux attempting to pick up items off the floor, he said "don't touch anything. The police will want that for evidence when they arrive." Indeed, when Edelson was left alone at the store after the shooting, he had every opportunity to compromise the crime scene, which it seems he did not do. And when he noticed two teenage girls peering through the glass door, he covered it with paper only after help arrived (presumably to ensure privacy), not before (which could have served to thwart aid or conceal aspects of the incident).[87]

He neither exploited nor created opportunities to deliberately harm Jack Horwitz. Doctor, for example, asked Edelson to compare the pedestrian and vehicular traffic on Rideau Street, where the shooting took place, with that on Myrand Street, where earlier in the evening the two men had clashed. Edelson responded that Rideau Street was "considered the busiest block in the city," whereas Myrand was "just a side-street facing an empty lot" with "hardly any lights." Doctor's question suggested that if Edelson had really wanted to get away with murder, he could have injured Jack on a remote back street when he had the chance rather than on a busy thoroughfare. White later countered that Edelson didn't try to murder Horwitz on Myrand Street only because he didn't have his gun with him. Doctor and Edelson also emphasized that it was Horwitz's idea for the trio to talk at the Edelson store. This point was crucial, as Ben could not be seen as luring Jack to his shop, especially when he knew it concealed a loaded weapon. In fact, White would try to ensnare Edelson when he stated "You decided to go to the store on Rideau Street?" A vigilant Edelson responded, "No. Mr. Horwitz suggested that."[88] Edelson later reiterated that "they coaxed me to go to the store."[89] If anything, Doctor and Edelson implied, it was Horwitz who, in proposing a meeting, grabbing Ben's wrists, reaching for the gun, and threatening to shoot, both facilitated and escalated the brawl.[90]

Most importantly, Doctor wanted to show that Ben had no proof of an affair, only suspicions. Doctor asked "Had you any knowledge before the 24th of any meetings between your wife and Horwitz?" Ben replied "None whatever."[91] Indeed, Edelson testified that when he and Lemieux followed Alice in the car that night, he was not aware that it belonged to Jack, nor that he was the driver, until just before it stopped on Myrand Street and Ben recognized the license plate.[92] With this line of questioning, Doctor tried to demonstrate that there was no premeditation for murder.

Cross-Examination

In his cross-examination, White pressed Ben on his earlier testimony that the situation could be solved in one of two ways: "one was divorce. What was the other? You did not tell us that. The other one was 'I'll shoot you if you don't leave my wife alone.'" Shockingly, and in what should have been a pivotal moment in the trial, Edelson agreed with the prosecution's interpretation of his criminal intentions. White then asked Ben, given Jack threatened to leave the store if he (Ben) telephoned Yetta, why he didn't just do so and have Jack leave. Ben replied that he "wanted to hear what [Jack] had to say" and that if he had "been aware of what was going to happen," he "certainly would have let him go." White also inquired that if Jack reacted to the divorce discussion by pledging that he and Alice were finished, "why didn't it [Jack's word] settle it. Couldn't he have gone away then?" At the risk of undermining his earlier testimony that the Horwitz family conference yielded no results, Edelson replied, "Well, I didn't believe he was through with her. He had promised three years ago to leave her alone, but he did not keep his word. I wanted to make sure." White jumped in: "You did make sure, didn't you?"[93]

White desired to demonstrate that Edelson knew about the affair before 24 November, and so had plenty of time to become enraged, and even plot a murder. White pointed to the family meeting three years prior when, according to Yetta's testimony, the relationship was openly acknowledged. Ben reiterated that the affair had been consistently denied.[94] White also attempted to show that Edelson knew of Alice's planned rendezvous with Jack the night of the 24th, but Ben maintained that he did not know for certain what was going to happen that night – only that "my wife knew that I was engaged at a bridge club on Tuesday night and this was the only night we were not together. It was my first opportunity of watching her."[95] White did demonstrate, though, that by the time the trio stepped into the store, "You knew your wife was going out with Jack Horwitz. She knew it and Horwitz knew it … The fact was nobody denied it." Edelson had no choice but to agree.[96]

Even if Ben were telling the truth that he had no prior knowledge of the affair, White must have recognized that this final admission was significant. It allowed for premeditation time between Ben arriving at the store and eventually pulling the trigger. In law, there is no specific time criterion that premeditation must meet: it requires only enough time "to deliberate calmly," which could translate into mere moments before the crime takes place.[97] Indeed, at several points in his cross-examination, White, seeking to establish that Ben had planned the shooting all along and was not suddenly provoked, asked "May I take it that up to this time you had control of yourself? ... I mean that whatever was the cause of this shot, it was not in anger." Ben agreed that he was "not in anger."[98] "Well," declared a smug White, "that settles that."[99]

White also focused on incriminating words at the crime scene. He first referenced Alice's threat, "You will pay for this." Ben insisted that Alice's comment was directed to Lemieux, whom she resented for driving her husband that night. White suggested that her remark could have been meant for Edelson in response to the harm he inflicted on Jack, but Ben stated that he heard Alice utter Lemieux's name. White then questioned Edelson's insistence that he didn't hear Jack say to Lemieux, "You did not think your boss was a murderer." How could he plainly hear Alice's comment but not Jack's? Ben maintained that Alice had "yelled out at the top of her voice."[100] Looking to refute this fact, White later re-called witness Lemieux who, in responding to White's question about the tone of her voice, stated with certainty that "she did not scream."[101]

Perhaps the most striking part of White's cross-examination was when he had Ben reenact the shooting. Ben stepped down from the witness box, and stood in front of White's desk. Together, they erected a pile of books to replicate the height of the jewellery showcase behind which Edelson was positioned at the time of the incident. Edelson then recreated the scuffle, with White "acting the part of Horwitz." Ben described Jack grabbing his arm, striking Alice to the floor, hitting him below his eye, and twisting his wrist.[102] Then, stated Ben, with his finger away from the trigger, the gun went off.[103] "Put me in the position of Horwitz," White insisted, and Edelson did so, shifting White's body.[104]

The *Journal* reported that when White and Edelson conducted the reenactment, "the scene was tense drama."[105]

Edelson's detailed testimony seemed to clarify events for both sides. Even White stated that "the story told by Edelson more or less removed the importance of some of the evidence given previous to the accused man taking the witness stand."[106] The judge also remarked to the jury that "some of the more intricate matters of law which looked to be important at the opening of the trial seem to have been eliminated by the prisoner going into the box and telling you what the happenings were."[107] Ben's testimony served two significant functions for the court: first, it confirmed that the fatal bullet was fired from his gun, precluding other possible sources; second, given Ben's insistence that he had not been enraged or out of control on the night of the shooting, it ensured that the provocation defence could not be left with the jury. Ben himself later recognized the value of taking the stand on his own behalf: "I agree that my own evidence had a great deal to do with my acquittal. I went on the witness stand and told just what happened."[108]

White's Closing Argument

Due to the persuasive nature of Edelson's eyewitness account, White's closing address took aim at his testimony: "He tells a story, which on the face of it, is an impossibility."[109] White especially challenged Ben's reenactment in the courtroom, questioning how the bullet diagonally traversed Jack's body from left to right if the men were standing face to face, and how the bullet entered at the level of Jack's abdomen if Ben's elbow rested on the higher display case.[110] The credibility of Ben's version of events regarding the shooting was crucial, for as the judge later pointed out to the jury, "if Edelson is not telling a true story of the struggle then you will find great difficulty in accepting any other parts of his story. If you find the struggle did not take place as he said it did, then you cannot accept much of his evidence."[111] White warned the jury that "if you bring in a verdict of not guilty you have to take this man's story holus' bolus, swallow it hook, line and sinker. The story bears upon its face its own refutation."[112] As White himself knew, however, and as this chapter will contend, a sympathetic jury could, in fact, advance a "not guilty" verdict while wholly believing in a defendant's guilt.

Judge McEvoy too cast doubt on the veracity of Ben's testimony. He remarked to the jury that it was not obliged to believe Edelson's version of events – after all, "if a man is on trial for his life, there is always the temptation to defend himself even if it means perjury."[113] Just four months later, a different judge, presiding over a Horwitz family insurance case, would make a similar claim about the veracity of Ben's testimony, expressing misgivings about the undue credibility and latitude that it was afforded: "it is unfortunate that the only evidence in this case as to the facts is that of Ben Edelson, a most [self] interested witness, whose evidence, if I had been trying the murder case, would have been most closely scrutinized."[114] What White and the judges might have detected were the discrepancies that emerged in Ben's careful attempt to conceal his wife's role in the shooting.

Although Doctor did not directly address the concept of reasonable doubt – a curious omission by the defence in a criminal trial – White clearly had it on his mind. He maintained that "only when a juror can put his finger on reasonable doubt can he satisfy his own mind that there is reasonable doubt." To preclude that possibility, he offered a simple, logical train of thought: "Is there any doubt about the fact that this man is dead? Also is there any doubt he died as a result of a bullet wound ... Is there any doubt that bullet was shot out of a gun? Is there any doubt it was at that time in the hands of Edelson? Is there any doubt he ascertained that it was loaded?"[115]

In the end, although White was a seasoned prosecutor, he proved no match for Doctor. True, Doctor had only to raise reasonable doubt during the trial, but White certainly proved less than aggressive in his overall prosecution. He failed to reveal Edelson as a fiend, and neglected to pursue sinister motivations for murder, such as revenge for the alleged illegitimacy of at least one of his children. Surprisingly, he also skirted the immorality and misbehaviour of Alice, whose longstanding betrayal was at the core of her husband's alleged rage and premeditation.[116] Presumably, White sought to underplay this disloyalty so as not to evoke jury sympathy for Ben, but the tactic backfired. As well, in contrast to Doctor's explicit request for an acquittal, White's prosecution of the accused vacillated between emphasizing manslaughter and murder.[117] This strategy might have confused or exasperated the jury. On the Monday morning after the trial, lawyers at the courthouse were "praising the brilliant defence conducted by Moses Doctor" who was "the recipient of many congratulations from his colleagues."[118]

The Acquittal: Middle-Class Respectability and the Unwritten Law

Aside from the courtroom performances and personas of White and Doctor, there are three possible reasons that jury members found Edelson not guilty: one, they were convinced by Doctor's argument that the shooting was an accident (although the jury had to render irrelevant the aggressive mindset of both Jack and Ben, and the history of hostility between them); or two, they were unconvinced by the Crown's argument that the shooting was intentional and premeditated, and deserving of penalty; or three, they believed neither theory, viewing the shooting as the justifiable effort by a respectable man to safeguard his honour and property according to the unwritten law.

Ben's middle-class standing proved crucial in his acquittal by a jury who was composed of other middle-class men, and who likely identified with the accused. Presumably consisting of white, Anglo-Protestants, and two or three French Canadians,[119] half the jury was composed of farmers and the other half of city-dwellers. Although the occupations of the six urban men were riddled with class ambiguities – one being a merchant, the others tradesmen – they generally represented the middling and lower-middling classes.[120] All of the jurors could undoubtedly identify with Ben's strong work ethic and admire the success he came by independently and honestly. The skilled or semi-skilled workers could especially relate to Ben's adeptness and artistry in working with his hands, and the farmers and the merchant to him owning his own enterprise. And the jury no doubt internalized the fact that the shooting took place not in some foreboding back alley but in a prime commercial area – the site of both entrepreneurial and consumer respectability. In the courtroom, a man's morality was assessed according to his industriousness and professional success, and Ben Edelson's life and work epitomized both.[121]

The jury also might have respected Edelson's achievements as compared to those of Horwitz, who attained his success with the resources and help of his father, also a jeweller. Unlike Edelson, who struggled for everything he had, it appeared that the Canadian-born Horwitz had lived a more charmed life. This privilege might not have sat well with Depression-era jurors who might have perceived Horwitz as a spoiled brat, one with a corresponding sense of entitlement to another man's wife.

In addition to running a successful business, Ben, the jury learned, claimed title to a large house and property. As historian Lara Campbell asserts, in the Depression, when owning a home was vulnerable to high unemployment, "home ownership was a clear sign of moral worth ... the most visible symbol of hard work and thrift – the moral qualities one needed to possess in order to be considered a good citizen." It was "the pinnacle of respectability."[122]

Another facet of Edelson's middle-class respectability was his efforts at assimilation as compared with those by other immigrants. Indeed, knowing that "racism was deeply encoded in the language and meanings of criminal responsibility," Doctor took care, upon Ben assuming the stand, to confirm his status as "a naturalized British subject."[123] The predominantly Anglo-Protestant jury would have appreciated that, unlike many immigrants, Edelson was a fluent English-speaking Canadian (and former American). And although he wasn't Christian, he was reverential and God-fearing. Ben's neighbourhood of Lowertown was insular and Jewish to be sure, but it was a serviceable enclave that allowed for steady upward mobility, and eventual migration to more prosperous, integrated areas. Unlike far too many "foreign" agitators and idle poor who abused the laws of their new land and proved a burden on its system, Edelson had followed the rules. He even performed volunteer work. Had Edelson been a greenhorn, without the civic, middle-class, masculine, badges of ownership and citizenship, the jury would certainly have been less willing to view him as deserving of acquittal.

Reaction to Moses Doctor's death just two years later revealed the admiration a Jewish man could earn for his successful integration into the dominant culture. The *Citizen* reported that at his funeral, "Jewish citizens of the Capital together with many Gentiles joined in common sorrow."[124] The *Journal* commented on "the remarkable gathering of persons of all classes and creeds," and observed "the general loss felt in the community, not only among the Jewish people but by all classes associated with the lawyer."[125] The papers listed the scores of prominent figures from Ottawa's legal and political establishment, including Ottawa mayor P.J. Nolan, and assorted judges, magistrates, lawyers, and aldermen.[126] Rabbi Freedman of the United Synagogues of Ottawa, who officiated at the funeral, noted that "he was making such a mark for himself amongst all people, irrespective of race, creed or nationality."[127] For Anglos and Jews respectively, Doctor personified the successful middle-class Jew who did not seek to usurp Gentile authority or try to "pass," but who, like members of all minority groups worthy of "admiration," strove to conform to and access Anglo-Protestant influence.

The trial only fleetingly alluded to the Jewish background of the leading actors. Dr Shapiro, for example, an attending physician when Jack was dying, was asked in court by prosecutor Peter White if he were "of the same religion" as Horwitz. When Shapiro answered yes, White asked him if there were "any such things as last rites in your religion." Shapiro replied that he did not think so, to which opposing counsel Moses Doctor responded "I take strong objection to such a line of questioning. There certainly is such a thing." White sarcastically responded "my learned friend better take off his gown and get into the witness box."[128] Inquiring as to how Edelson could have possibly remembered Horwitz's license plate number on the night of the shooting, White also glibly asked Ben if he also knew the date of the High Holidays in the previous October.[129] Moreover, Moses Doctor asked him if he and Horwitz conversed in English as opposed to Yiddish in the moments after the shooting.[130] Despite these incidental remarks, the press cited no anti-Semitic comments, or even references to Judaism, by the judge or gentile witnesses.

Perhaps most surprisingly, Edelson's violence was never tied to racist assumptions in the courtroom about Jewish manhood. Black and non-Anglo immigrant murder defendants were inevitably deemed inherently belligerent and brutish,[131] but physical aggression as a masculine Jewish trait was never raised by the prosecution. The absence of this argument might have been due to the equally odious stereotype that Jewish men were weak, but more likely was due to class privilege from which even some "reputable" black defendants had benefitted.[132]

Edelson's status as a family man also worked in his favour. As Kimberly White argues, "strong social ideals and legal sanctions around conjugality and marriage during this period helped charge the moral undercurrents of legal decisions in domestic murder cases."[133] Especially for a middle-class man, a wife and children were held up as signposts that he was lovable, financially accountable, emotionally stable, and entrenched in the community.[134] Most of the jurors would have been husbands and fathers themselves, who would have appreciated Ben's sense of familial responsibility and sacrifice.[135] One of these jurors was surely sixty-three-year-old Ferdinand Lauzon, a French Catholic who by the age of forty-two was married with ten children.[136]

Bachelorhood, in fact, was seen as a liability during the Depression, as unemployed, itinerant, single men "caused the greatest worry to those in authority." They were regarded as "a menace to law and order."[137] Ottawa police chief Joliat openly blamed these "undesirables" for the rising rate of robberies in the city.[138] One of them was twenty-two year-old William George Seabrooke, who was arrested for murder only two weeks after Ben, and was a jobless, unmarried vagrant accused of robbing a gas station in Lowertown, shooting the attendant, and fleeing the scene.[139]

When police began their investigation, they did not search out a "family man," but immediately suspected "a dope fiend or a homicidal maniac," and interrogated "criminals recently released from prison and a number of other underworld characters of Ottawa and Hull."[140] In 1933, after languishing five months in jail awaiting trial, Seabrooke was ultimately found guilty and hanged at the Nicholas Street Jail.[141]

At a time when many demoralized men turned to crime, or drank too much, beat their wives, refused to find work, or deserted their families, Ben Edelson, by contrast, was the model of decency, family devotion, and financial dependability.[142] He wasn't intoxicated when he shot Horwitz, a rare occurrence when men killed other men.[143] If Ben had been convicted, his children would have become a financial burden on the state, a repugnant outcome for jurymen during a period of great suffering with too many families already on scanty government relief.

Even more critical to Ben's acquittal than his middle-class propriety, however, was the jury's reliance on the "unwritten law." This was the belief that there existed certain basic, unalienable, and universal rights premised on moral imperatives upon which certain dictates of the law, the state, culture, or custom should have no bearing. A product of both historical convention and male bravado, this law asserted that an incensed husband, father, or brother, in order to safeguard his family and community (and his own honour), could justifiably kill a man who sexually seduced his female kin.[144] Accordingly, a homicide could be both premeditated (as opposed to provoked) and justifiable, and deserving of acquittal. In other words, even if the jury believed that Edelson committed murder – that he intended, even planned all along, to kill Horwitz – they could also believe that his actions were completely warranted.

The unwritten law was premised on white, middle-class gender roles and expectations. First, it recognized that women were the property of men, and expected men to safeguard women, who were innocent, frail and vulnerable. Second, it expected sexual purity among single women and spousal fidelity among wives, traits which made women deserving of this male protection. Third, it assumed that men should not trespass on the property of others, especially by morally and sexually defiling their women. Fourth, it placed male humiliation, anger, and retribution at the centre of its concerns (as opposed to women's welfare, desires, and agency), and affirmed that men could kill with impunity if it meant ridding their family and community of a sexual predator. The unwritten law was plainly gendered, serving the exclusive protection of the male murderer.[145]

The unwritten law was utilized in some form or another in many nineteenth-century trials, and with winning results. As criminologists Rosemary Gartner and Jim Phillips point out, "although not generally a formal part of the law, in practice the doctrine had allowed dozens of men to escape murder convictions."[146] Shockingly, even Mr Justice McEvoy, in his one-hour charge to the jury, acknowledged this fact. He pointed out that there were times when "the law might excuse a man for killing another who had been going with his wife."[147] Indeed, there were other cases against jealous husbands in which judges "gave credence to the notion that the 'protection of the home' could justify murder."[148] That Judge McEvoy raised this provocative point suggests that the ideals of the unwritten law hung heavy in the courtroom.

Defence counsel could not advance the unwritten law as it was not an official defence in the British legal tradition; nonetheless its power lay in its implicit and stealthy presence.[149] Edelson himself never even alluded to the unwritten law: he never expressed satisfaction that Horwitz was dead, or represented him as a threat to the women of the community. He never even labeled Alice as a seduced or wronged woman.[150] Making these points might have only served to buttress the prosecution's case that he himself was a lawless vigilante.[151] Instead it was up to Doctor, "under the guise" of the accident scenario (or really any scenario in which Ben was not culpable), to evoke compassion and pity for a dedicated husband who had been robbed of his manly honour.[152] As Doctor suspected, "the narrative of the disloyal wife and the devoted, hardworking husband was a powerful one that could, in some cases, lead to a lighter sentence."[153] In fact, it's possible that Doctor always assumed jurors would not be fooled by the accident scenario, and that he offered it only as a legal loophole for them to acquit Edelson based on the unwritten law.[154]

White often revealed his awareness of the unwritten law, and of a jury vulnerable to its influence. He emphasized to the jury that judgment based on sympathy for Edelson was neither appropriate nor just.[155] If sympathy were a factor, which it shouldn't be, claimed White, then "there was a widow and fatherless child to consider."[156] He noted that "in a court of British justice, sympathy has no place," and warned the jury that "your judgment cannot be rendered in a true sense of duty if you are going to be swayed by prejudice or sympathy."[157]

A notable example of the unwritten law at work is the 1906 Mitchell/ Creffield case. George Washington Mitchell shot and killed Franz Edmund Creffield in Seattle. Mitchell had been tracking the self-proclaimed preacher for several weeks before he unceremoniously shot him in the head. Mitchell sought to avenge the sexual molestation of at least one of his two sisters by Creffield, who headed a fanatical Oregon religious sect of which they were members. After the shooting, popular opinion, prominent citizens, the Oregon and Seattle press, and even the police defended Mitchell's actions, as Creffield was guilty of seducing numerous women and had been hunted by many aggrieved men. Mitchell was acquitted, less because of his deft insanity defence than because of the unwritten law.[158]

The verdict in a 1937 Ottawa murder case is also suggestive of the unwritten law. In many ways, the case bore an uncanny resemblance to the Edelson/Horwitz incident. In September of 1936, forty-six-year-old Michael Augustino was tracking the whereabouts of thirty-six-year-old Mary, his wife of twenty years and the mother of their seven children. He eventually discovered her with her longtime lover, Michael McCluskey, a man whom Mary had promised her husband several years earlier she would no longer see. When Augustino insisted that his wife return home, the two men began to brawl. In fear for his life, Augustino pulled out a pen knife and began stabbing McCluskey. A frenzied Mary threw herself between the men to stop the attack, and her husband stabbed her in the heart. Like the Edelson/Horwitz case, this murder case saw the accused take the stand in his own defence, and, after defence testimony asserting an accident scenario, ended with his acquittal.[159]

In the Augustino case, even the working-class and ethnic identity of the accused did not effect a conviction, suggesting the supremacy of the gendered aspects of the unwritten law. Michael Augustino worked in a paper factory, and, unlike Edelson, who was never referenced in the press as a Jew, was consistently identified in the papers as an "Italian mill worker."[160] The stabbing took place in the centre of the working-class Italian neighbourhood where the Augustino family lived.[161] The immigrant background of Augustino, however, took a back seat to his decency and devotion to family, and his wife's blatantly immoral behaviour.[162] The defence counsel asserted that he was clearly the "wronged husband."[163] Despite Augustino's obvious rage about the affair, his brandishing of a weapon, his purposeful assault of McKluskey, and his desertion of the scene as his wife lay bleeding to death, he was acquitted. With the announcement of the verdict, scores of supporters and courtroom spectators "cheered, and clapped their hands and stamped their feet."[164] This euphoric response, like that following the Edelson verdict, was not unusual in trials that featured the unwritten law.[165] That it was his wife who died rather than a cunning male predator did not dampen the sense of vindication that the courtroom felt Augustino deserved.[166]

Although the unwritten law was rooted in Victorian culture and by the first decades of the twentieth century seemed old-fashioned to some,[167] it had resonance during the Depression. In these years, the economic volatility of the country translated into male feelings of vulnerability, anxiety, and fear. Any more uncertainty was simply too much to bear. As Michiel Horn notes in his book *The Dirty Thirties*, "What middle-class Canadians were deprived of was not necessarily income or position, but security. And for them, this may have been the most disturbing loss of all."[168] For the jury, Jack and Alice's adultery understandably struck at the very core of Ben's sense of security.

By virtue of the unwritten law, men who killed could be seen as "the best of masculine virtue," especially in contrast to the vulgar, uncivilized characteristics of the sadistic sexual perpetrator.[169] Men who killed to protect their women embodied a strong, decent, disciplined, and determined character.[170] Far from betraying their gender by being hyper aggressive, they used only selective violence, conforming appropriately to masculine conduct.[171] As Angus McLaren demonstrates, men "were repeatedly instructed by the courts and the press that in some situations their recourse to violence would not only be condoned but applauded."[172] In fact, Ben had exhibited restraint in refraining from assaulting Jack years before he did, or from killing his adulterous wife (which as evident in the Augustino case, could also be excused).[173] The jurors might have found all of these dignified but accessible qualities of masculinity reassuring in otherwise humiliating and emasculating times.

As White feared, the possibility certainly existed that sympathy for Edelson motivated an acquittal by a jury who in fact believed that he was guilty of premeditated murder, and stealthily instituted the unwritten law to exonerate. The jury might have been especially moved when, after referencing his twenty-year marriage to Alice, Ben cried on the stand.[174] The primitive, seemingly uncomplicated unwritten law allowed the jury's sympathy for Edelson, as well as its contempt for Horwitz, to eclipse the convoluted rules and nuanced definitions of legal codes and statutes. In the end, the unwritten law inspired the jurors to serve basic street justice instead. Perhaps they simply believed that Horwitz had it coming.[175] Indeed, Roydon Hughes recalled later hearing that jury foreman Laishley had presumed from the start that Edelson was not guilty, and that he had been "against Horwitz" because he was "interfering with another man's wife."[176] The jury, Hughes later concluded, "thought that Horwitz should have been shot for hanging around Edelson's wife."[177] All of this meant that the prosecution never stood a chance: incriminating testimony against Ben had little impact on a jury who wasn't being told anything it hadn't already forgiven.

Although Doctor argued that it was not his goal "to wax elo-
quent and appeal for an acquittal on the grounds of sympathy,"
he did exactly that. An overarching theme in his fifty-minute
closing argument was Ben's love for his wife.[178] He took every opportunity to evoke compassion for Edelson, despite the fact that
it was entirely irrelevant to an accident (or self-defence) scenario.
Doctor exalted Ben "as a loving husband and father" who "was
willing to forgive [Alice] everything and continued giving her the
love he had always given her ... here we have a man whose love
for his wife and children is so sacred that he would take her from
her paramour and forget all that had happened." "It all amounts
to this," concluded Doctor, "he cared too much for this woman.
He loved his children." Doctor's words to the jury were so moving that "there were many people in the court unashamedly dry-
ing their eyes," and "many women wept."[179] Thanks in large part
to Doctor, there seemed no shortage of sympathy for Ben.

In contrast to a requisite of the unwritten law, however, Doctor,
in his examination and closing argument, seldom maligned the
seducer/murder victim. Aside from Horwitz being a childhood
chum, he was a widely respected businessman with established
credibility. Moreover, his transgressions could be used by the prosecution to convey Edelson's motivation for murder. Thus, Doctor
never emphasized the principles of respectable male behaviour
that should have guided Jack: chivalry and sexual restraint[180] –
both of which were undercut by his persistent lying and cheating,
his betrayal of Yetta, his lust for Alice, and his possible paternity
of at least one Edelson child.

Instead, at those rare and awkward times when Jack's misconduct had to be mentioned, Doctor simply blamed it on Alice. In
his closing argument, for example, he dubbed Jack "as this man
who had wrecked [Edelson's] home" and stated that "he was misleading" Alice "for his own purposes," but then he promptly
added "or was she misleading him?" Doctor explained that Alice
was older than Jack, suggesting that she was a Svengali, and
obscuring the fact that she was merely one year older than he
was.[181] He impugned Alice for Jack's misdeeds when he claimed

that Horwitz grabbed for the gun because he "had been goaded on by a hysterical woman."[182] For the unwritten law to play out, and for the sake of his client, Doctor was forced to pursue this tactic. After all, unlike the Mitchell/Creffield case, in which the male murder victim could be cast as a predator and the women his helpless prey, Jack was a model citizen and Alice was no innocent who yearned for protection. So Doctor used Alice's immorality instead of Jack's to incite sympathy for a husband who simply desired to defend and preserve his family. And the strategy paid off.

Doctor had practice in slandering the reputation of women during trial, attacking their moral and sexual standing, and placing blame squarely on their shoulders. In the 1929 rape case against MP Louis Auger, for example, he had tarnished the character of the man's seventeen-year-old accuser as well as that of her aunt, whom Doctor claimed orchestrated the rape accusation. He lamented the "wiles of women" and declared that "from time immemorial women had been guilty of machinations against men."[183] Whether or not Doctor actually believed his own assertion is difficult to know, but his insistence on the manipulative and scheming character of women proved credible enough for a jury of men to acquit his client. There was no reason to think that this strategy wouldn't work with the Edelson jury too.

Doctor took many opportunities during the trial to make Alice Edelson look bad. He asked Edelson, if immediately after the shooting, he saw anything was "going on between Horwitz and Mrs. Edelson." Edelson replied, "Yes. I saw her kissing him and heard her say she would do all she could for him." After Ben stated that his wife accompanied Jack in the ambulance, Doctor asked "Did you see her again that night and have you seen her since?" Edelson shockingly replied that he hadn't.[184] These questions elucidated little about the incident, but succeeded in making Alice appear a selfish woman, and a heartless and negligent wife.

In his closing argument, Doctor essentially blamed Alice for the entire tragedy, and made inflammatory comments about her character. He dramatically referred to Alice as "the woman who forgot her marriage vows" and who "was false to her husband and children." Pitting Alice the lustful adulteress against Yetta the innocent wife, and casting Alice as the destroyer of families, Doctor affirmed that "if this woman had disregarded her paramour that night there would not be a widow sitting in this courtroom today. There would not be a fatherless child."[185] In emphasizing Edelson's forgiving attitude toward "his wife who had betrayed him," Doctor directly challenged the all-male jury to "think of taking this woman home!" declaring "perhaps you or I would not have felt the same way if our wives had been running around with other men" – "you and I might think she should be out on the street."[186] Doctor asked "Do you think for a moment the man who would forgive this base woman is a murderer? I say no."[187] Doctor made himself perfectly clear when he named the victims of "the love triangle" and his list excluded Alice Edelson.[188]

Doctor's closing argument drew tremendous accolades. It "was described by many eminent lawyers who crowded the courtroom on Saturday as one of the most brilliant and effective ever heard in a local court." Even his adversary Peter White praised it "for its originality and directness."[189] The *Citizen* reported that "the appeal to the jury of Moses Doctor was impassioned throughout," and that because it was so captivating, "not a sound [in the courtroom] could be heard."[190]

Yet, White, in his closing argument, remarked on the defence counsel's contradictory and hypocritical approach to Alice. On the one hand, Doctor emphasized Ben's chivalrous dedication to his wife; on the other hand, he and Ben blamed her for the entire ordeal. White stated that "one would wonder at the consistency of the accused's expressions of tremendous affection for his wife which were so ably professed for him by my learned friend. I have no doubt human nature has not changed since the Garden of Eden when Adam, after being turned out, said 'the woman gave to me, and I did eat.'" Comparing Ben to a calculating and culpable Adam (rather than submitting to the customary Eve-bashing), White himself never attacked Alice's reputation, except when he observed philosophically that "in all these human triangles there must be at least one woman."[191]

Alice's moral reputation was fodder for the defence in the same way as that of a female victim prosecuting a sexual assault case.

Notions of respectability for women incorporated a number of elements, "but in the courtroom, sex was at the center."[192] Flirting, participating in an illicit sexual relationship, and bearing an illegitimate child all undercut the credibility of female accusers.[193] As the "perpetrator" of these behaviours Alice, like other "designing women," was seen as purposefully manipulating and exploiting men for her own gain.[194] Like a sexual assault case in which "probing a woman's sexual past or current moral character" was a tactic used by men in the courtroom, the Edelson trial made Alice the target of her husband and his lawyer – "prominent men with obvious social credentials" whose status helped guarantee that their negative impressions of her would be readily believed.[195] In sexual assault cases, shame was a "potent weapon of humiliation" for women. For the woman who brought charges against her male perpetrator, his conviction might have been worth the indignity, but not for Alice, whose sexual life was laid bare in the courtroom, who was so thoroughly denied agency there, and for whom there was no vindication or reward. Alice's absence as a courtroom observer might not have been attributable to indifference, anger, or even illness, but to the promise of utter humiliation in a trial that deliberately sought to disgrace her. By staying away, she protected herself in a fashion that was completely within her control.

Even if Alice had wanted to defend her character, however, she would have been denied the chance to do so, as she was not permitted to testify for the prosecution. Although she was the only surviving witness, as the spouse of the accused she was ruled an "incompetent witness." This status was grounded in theological assumptions entrenched in centuries-old British common law that maintained a husband and wife were united as one person (in reality, with her subsumed by him); a spouse shared interest in the outcome of proceedings (and was thus motivated to lie); and marriage was a singular and sacred relationship which should not be undermined, and which was deserving of protection (although the husband's crime, especially if perpetrated against her family, was usually enough to jeopardize the marriage).[196] By extension, under statutes of marital privilege, even if Alice could testify due to an exempted circumstance such as permanent separation or divorce, she was not compellable to disclose any communication made to her by her husband during their marriage. This meant that if Ben had articulated his desire or intention to kill Horwitz, she was not obligated to reveal it.[197]

While some have argued that the notion of spousal incompetency (still on the books) preserves marital harmony, and spares the spouse (and the courtroom and society) of a "repugnant" scenario, the concept is highly problematic.[198] First, the rules of spousal incompetency have the potential to subvert justice, especially as in Alice's case when a wife is the lone witness to her husband's crime. As well, they preclude (and thus don't protect) personal relationships that when compared to marriage are arguably of equal or greater significance (and could also motivate a witness to lie). Moreover, they are inherently sexist. As the overwhelming majority of crimes are perpetrated by men, the rules of spousal incompetency explicitly deny the sovereignty of women, and have been used to suppress their influence, credibility, and speech, while safeguarding the actions and reputation of men: they forbid a wife from testifying against her husband even if she wants to.[199]

Whether Alice could have testified *on behalf* of her husband is another question. According to British law, spouses were not deemed competent to testify for each other. This rule was also grounded in assumptions of marital oneness and shared interest.[200] But in Canada in 1906, this rule was amended so that a spouse was declared a competent witness for the defence.[201] Alice, therefore, could have testified for Ben if she were willing. Not surprisingly, and the cause of some confusion, the amendment does not specify whether the spouse could be compelled to testify if she were unwilling, as Alice might have been in light of her probable resentment toward Ben for killing, or at least endangering, Jack.[202]

If Doctor felt that her testimony could have helped Ben's cause, it is possible that Alice might have been compelled to testify, with any confidences that Ben shared with Alice still protected by the rules of marital privilege.[203] But given her almost certain antagonism toward Ben, her divided loyalties to her family and Jack, her

frail emotional state, and the perceived immorality which undermined her credibility, Doctor clearly decided against it. Moreover,
he knew that putting Alice on the stand meant that the prosecution was entitled to cross-examine, risking the deliberate or
unwitting disclosure by Alice of hitherto hidden evidence against
Ben. As far as the defence was concerned, the fewer the witnesses
the better. Ben, too, might have insisted that Alice not take the
stand, fearful of the trauma that testifying would cause her, and of
her implicating herself as she described the shooting. Undoubtedly, if Alice had taken the stand, her character would have been
assassinated from both sides, with Doctor sacrificing her to gain
jury sympathy for Ben and the Crown demonizing her to show
that her loose and lascivious ways could drive a man to murder.

    In the end, with or without Alice's testimony, the jury might
have acquitted Ben simply because it believed that it was Alice
Edelson, and neither her husband nor paramour, who was ultimately to blame for the entire mess. Indeed, if there existed an illicit relationship between a man and a woman, "the woman was
far more likely to be a target of moral censure. More was expected
of her: she was required to act both as the moral guardian of her
own character and as a brake on the unbridled sexuality of the
male."[204] If Alice had only assumed her feminine obligation as a
moral custodian and civilizer of men, and convincingly rebuffed
Jack, Ben would not have been forced to threaten him and he
would still be alive. Although the female agency embedded in this
social more contradicts the female passivity in the unwritten law,
the jury, especially after Doctor's indictment of Alice as a substi-
tute for Jack, was almost certainly unaware of the incongruity.
The jury might have simply reasoned that all roads led to Alice: it
was Alice's sexual immorality that precipitated the shooting, and
Ben, like Jack, was a victim.

    This indictment of Alice was in keeping with the general cli-
mate of female scapegoating during the Depression. Amid high
jobless rates among men, and rising paid-labour participation by
women, anxiety existed about the erosion of traditional gender
roles, particularly women's dwindling dependence on men.[205]
Women in the workforce were consistently accused of "stealing"

men's jobs, and of denying men the right to be the breadwinners of their families. In doing so, women were perceived as robbing men not only of their paychecks but of their masculinity, leaving them demoralized and hopeless. This charge also permeated the home where women's traditional influence, once promoted by middle-class culture, was now blamed for their families' financial troubles, and was now seen to undermine men's authority over their children and household.[206] Behaviour like Alice's was just another way that women served to undercut men's dignity and self-esteem in these hard times, and highlighted wives' lack of appreciation and gratitude. While earnest men struggled for survival, and for the preservation of their families, "frivolous" women like Alice were seen as tearing men down and their families apart.

On the Sunday night after the Saturday acquittal, a *Journal* reporter visited Ben Edelson at his home. The reporter was greeted by Edelson "calmly smoking a Sherlock Holmes pipe with an air of complacency and well-being." Ben invited the journalist into the dining room where he "talked as freely as a New Year's Eve host at a surprise party." He admitted that the verdict was more than he had hoped for, and was "glad the jury took the view they did."[207] For Ben, whether he was found not guilty by way of an accident theory or jury sympathy really didn't matter.

The newspapers seldom published photographs related to the case, but on the Monday after the verdict, the *Journal* printed an exceedingly flattering photograph of Ben. Before then, the rare picture of him had always been the same one: an odd, unbecoming, and unrecognizable profile shot with eyes downcast and head tilted back, presumably his mug shot.[208] This time, thanks to prominent Ottawa photographer Jules Alexandre Castonguay, who produced the elegant portrait,[209] Ben looked every bit the matinee idol – handsome, confident, mischievous, and debonair. Wearing a dark, striped three-piece suit, light shirt, and faintly checked tie, he confronted the camera with a glint in his eye and a slight smile. The caption read "Picture of a Free Man."[210]

At first, the Jewish community, sympathetic to Ben's long ordeal, was pleased and relieved by his acquittal. In fact, although county police chief Charles McCarthy cautioned spectators, many of whom were Edelson friends and family, against overt expressions when the verdict was read, initial reaction to the "not guilty" verdict was so jubilant, the judge "became annoyed calling for order."[211] When the judge formally discharged Ben, "that appeared to be the signal for resumption of the demonstration," and when he left the dock, he was "acclaimed by the throng," and "besieged by friends and relatives."[212] The *Citizen* reported that with this outpouring, "the courtroom witnessed a scene which will go down in history as one of the most impressive in a Supreme Court sitting here.[213] Once downstairs, "men and women alike ... slapped him affectionately on the back, wrung his hands and embraced him. He was practically carried bodily from the courthouse."[214] Ben's acquittal meant not only the exoneration of one man, but of every honourable "family man," and indeed of the entire Jewish community.

The *Citizen* also reported that after the verdict, Moses Doctor "shared with his client the acclaim of the crowd." One man, a close friend of Ben, even "placed a resounding kiss upon the flushed cheek of the lawyer." When the exhausted Doctor attempted to leave the building after his eleven-hour ordeal in court, he "again was met with wellwishers who simply refused to let him go." Only with the assistance of police was he able to flee secretly through the courthouse basement, and then quickly drive home.[215]

In the first day or two following the trial, friends and acquaintances could not have been happier about Ben's exoneration. He was "besieged with calls from friends and others congratulating him on his acquittal."[216] On Sunday night, the Edelson home was filled with visitors, and "lightness, brightness, the laughter of children, and talk of women."[217] When he returned to work on Monday, less than forty-eight hours following the acquittal, he "was showered with congratulations by his many friends, who made personal calls while others telephoned him."[218] One man at the store declared, "You are the most popular man in town, Ben."[219] In fact, when Edelson entered his B'nai Brith lodge meeting that Monday night, members gave him a "striking ovation." Vice-president Robert Edelstein also "extended the lodge's wishes for his success in the future."[220]

Still, the Jewish community was flabbergasted that Ben eluded punishment. Perhaps most shocked was Yetta Horwitz, who, after the verdict was read, sat in stunned silence as the courtroom cleared.[221] One woman remembered, "We were all astounded Ben got off."[222] Others recall that the Jewish community was simply "amazed," and thought the acquittal "strange."[223]

The Jewish community was stunned because, except for Edelson's own family, it never really viewed the shooting as an accident or even as self-defence.[224] Interviews in 2006 with community members who resided in Ottawa at the time of the tragedy reveal they believed that Edelson was provoked – that he killed Jack Horwitz in a fit of jealous rage: Francine Shaffer referred to a "crime of passion," declaring that term "a perfect name for it." It was "obvious," she said, "we knew it wasn't an accident"[225]; Suzie Gellman agreed that the community viewed the shooting as "a crime of passion": "I don't think anyone thought it was an accident"[226]; and Lionel Metrick insisted the gun "didn't accidentally go off. He let him have it!" Metrick stated that Edelson, angered over the affair, and fearful that Alice wanted a divorce to marry Jack, "settled it with a bullet – like in the movies."[227] For those who knew that the gun went off twice, the general opinion was that an accident might account for the first shot but it couldn't explain the second. Ben's stern personality helped fuel the notion that the shooting was surely intentional – a man so cold and unwavering surely had the potential to kill, especially if he felt cornered. Never mind that this portrayal of a shrewd Ben ran contrary to that of him as out of control, a formal condition of provocation.

While there were some who believed that Edelson planned the shooting, the Jewish community generally did not subscribe to either notion: that it was premeditated or justifiable. Although the jury might have subscribed to the unwritten law, the Jewish community would have resisted entertaining the thought that Ben did anything but succumb to a sudden and uncontrollable rage.[228] It could not accept the idea of a Jew killing anyone, let alone the possibility of a premeditated shooting targeting a fellow Jew – and it trusted that Ben felt this way too. Not surprisingly, after the initial relief, jubilation, and then shock of Ottawa Jews upon hearing of the acquittal, resentment set in: Jack Horwitz was dead, and that Ben went unpunished for taking a human life, no matter what the reason, was simply incomprehensible.[229]

On Monday 18 January, Ben issued an official statement to the press. He graciously thanked jail personnel for their "fair treatment," the press "who so accurately and fairly reported the proceedings," court house officials, and his defence counsel. He stated "I think I have had a very fair trial and am naturally pleased at the outcome," and concluded with "I feel justly satisfied that twelve of my peers have vindicated my innocence."[230]

In contrast, Alice Edelson, maligned throughout the proceedings, and tried by the even nastier court of public opinion, would never really know absolution. A *Journal* reporter noted that while female family and friends were visiting Ben to share in the joy of his acquittal, "if Mrs. Edelson ... was at home, she was not to be seen," suggesting at once her shame and her indifference to her husband's victory.[231] And not even Ben could muster up the effort to put a positive spin on his future with her. When a journalist asked him about the fate of his "domestic affairs," Ben replied that he was "not ready to make any statement concerning them."[232]

6

"A sudden silence fell":
The Legacy of the Case

In Ottawa's old Jewish cemetery, the Edelson and Horwitz plots, just steps apart, reveal both nothing and everything about the 1931 tragedy. Jack Horwitz's headstone refers to him only as a "dear brother," making no mention of his roles as a husband and a father. And neither his wife Yetta nor daughter Anita rests beside him. Beneath the impressive monument that marks the Edelson plot, Alice's modest stone declares her a "beloved wife and mother." Of course, no one expects an epitaph to reflect the intricacies of one's complex life on earth, but these words do more than render invisible the circumstances of 24 November 1931: many would say they distort and even mock them. These inscriptions, however, are just part of an enduring effort by the Edelson and Horwitz families to detract attention from the tragedy, and to uphold their good name. In the face of the media and gossiping frenzy that surrounded the Edelson/Horwitz murder case, a conspiracy of silence by the families and their lawyers existed almost from the very beginning. But despite everyone's best efforts to hush up the case, the Jewish community would surreptitiously discuss and remember it for decades, especially the unsavoury role of Alice Edelson.

Attempting to obscure a tragedy and even erase it from memory is not a strategy emblematic of the Jews. They are often dubbed a "people of memory" because of their adherence to commemorative holidays and rituals, and their cultural emphasis on both joyful and bleak historical milestones, such as the birth of the state of Israel and the Holocaust, respectively.[1] In fact, much of the academic scholarship that proliferated in the 1990s around issues of memory related to Jews and the Holocaust.[2] These studies often asserted that survivors, unlike many amnesiac victims of childhood maltreatment, for example, suffered from an "excess of memory." They felt compelled to share their stories (as the flood of survivor memoirs over the last five decades testifies), and to commemorate as a group their shared past.[3]

Studies of memory generally "give central place to trauma" as the experience "worth talking about – worth remembering," but they necessarily identify the connected concept of "forgetting."[4] The past is a "treacherous burden," one which "would crush us" if forgetting did not allow us to "continuously divest ourselves of its weight."[5] Accordingly, in response to being "overwhelmed by memories," some Holocaust survivors demonstrated "numbing, detachment, or suppression."[6] The dynamic of this process is complex. As Lawrence J. Kirmayer points out, "the distinction between forget, repress, ignore and dissociate is not simply an arbitrary choice of metaphor. Each is a phenomenologically distinct form of not remembering."[7] For survivors of trauma, this "not remembering" is mired in the fear of pain, reprisal, victimhood, survival, remaining in the past, or burdening children.

In other words, forgetting is not necessarily a fortuitous act (nor a neurological lapse), but is "as much an active process as remembering."[8] Some authors have employed the term "intentional forgetting" to indicate that some types of forgetting "serve our goals and needs," and are "in response to explicit or implicit cues to forget, initiated either by ourselves or others."[9] Put another way, "it is easy to forget when there is a tacit agreement not to remember."[10]

For the Edelsons and Horwitzes, a tacit agreement certainly existed, facilitated by, and manufacturing, silence about the shooting. Indeed, for family memories to persist and assume meaning, there must be talk, essential for family memory "construction, reconstruction, and repair."[11] "It is not enough," notes one memory scholar, "that a photo album exist or a few pieces of memorabilia be passed from one generation to the next. Rather ... family memories ... must be repeatedly and actively reinforced with continuous interaction between an older generation that wishes to transmit memories and a younger one that is present and willing to receive them."[12] With a conspiracy of silence, as existed in the Edelson and Horwitz families, the potential for individual memory is "severely strained," and the ordeal subsequently undergoes revision in the collective memory, or gets banished altogether.[13]

Both families ensured that silence was quickly and firmly entrenched. Initially a response to shock and form of legal self-protection, it quickly became a gatekeeper for privacy and normalcy. Almost immediately after the shooting, Moses Doctor advised Edelson to return home, await the police, and say nothing of the incident. With the exception of conversations with his lawyer and his rabbi, Edelson "followed out this advice faithfully," and after being arrested and detained Wednesday morning, upheld a "stony silence."[14] By Friday, Edelson had "not yet broken the silence he imposed upon himself since the time of his arrest."[15] Alice Edelson also remained quiet. She was said to have sat in "stolid silence" at the hospital and at Charles Horwitz's house, and, except for her outburst when arriving home Wednesday morning, wouldn't be heard from for weeks.[16]

Initially, the dispute over ownership of Jack's two stores was widely publicized, with both sides offering detailed statements of their cause to the press, but by Sunday, 29 November, "a sudden silence fell ... upon all the participants." The Horwitz brothers, as well as their lawyers, "decided against any further explanation of what they termed to be the administration of their private affairs." Ben Goldfield, lawyer for Charles Horwitz and Harry Hertz, declared, "I have no further statements to make. It is strictly a family affair and I can see no reason why the public should be interested in it." Yetta Horwitz's lawyer T.A. Beament, who managed the case after Sam Berger's resignation, simply stated "my client's business is their business and not public business."[17] In fact, it was Berger who, several days earlier, had refused to make any more comments to the press, affirming that the business wrangling was of "a purely personal and private nature, and he did not think the public would be interested."[18] Berger, of course, could not have been more wrong.

On Monday, 18 January 1932, the *Journal* declared in a front page headline that Edelson "Resumes Life as if Nothing Had Happened." The paper emphasized that Edelson, already back at work, "was busy serving customers," and "showed no signs of the great strain to which he had been subjected during his trial." Edelson insisted that "everything is going on as if nothing had happened," and when asked by a reporter of his future plans, he stated that "business would go on in the store as usual," and that "he desired the whole affair to be dropped."[19] Adelene Hyman, who visited her friend Lillian at the house throughout the ordeal, remembered that the moment Ben was acquitted it was simply "business as usual" for the family. Reiterating and reinforcing this point, Hyman wryly recollected of Alice, "same thing, same hats."[20]

The normalcy that Ben and Alice Edelson so desperately sought is evident in an astonishing photograph of the couple in July 1932. It features them on vacation in Quebec, and shows no sign of their turbulent year. In bathing suits, and with Ben holding his trademark pipe, the smiling pair seems eerily cheerful, relaxed, and devoted as they frolic arm-in-arm.[21]

Several incidents occurred in the two years after the shooting, however, which revived the case. Surprisingly, there was no civil action against Ben by Yetta or the Horwitz siblings for the wrongful death of Jack Horwitz, but the surviving Horwitz brothers filed a provocative insurance claim. This was followed by a nasty feud between members of the Edelson and Horwitz families, and by the mysterious death of Moses Doctor.

After the fatal shooting, Jack's beneficiaries sought to collect $2,500 on a company insurance policy, one that Jack had purchased to protect his jewellery business from loss due to bodily injury. The Loyal Protective Insurance Company informed his family, however, that it would not honour their claim. It argued that he sustained his injury while engaging in a fight, and therefore bore some responsibility for his own bodily harm, disqualifying him from meeting the conditions for payment.

Jack's beneficiaries took the insurance company to court. The plaintiffs in the case, represented by T.A. Beament, presumably acting for Yetta Horwitz, and Ben Goldfield, acting for Charles and Philip Horwitz, argued that Jack's participation in the brawl was neither deliberate nor aggressive. They claimed that it was provoked by Edelson who brandished the gun, that Jack reasonably feared for his life, and that he acted in self-defence. They maintained furthermore – utilizing Ben's own trial testimony – that the shooting itself was an accident. The lawyers offered various definitions of the word "accident" and "accidental" and cited relevant precedent-setting cases involving resistant insurance companies, all with the purpose of demonstrating that Jack was not culpable for his own injury. On 27 May 1932, Ontario Supreme Court judge J. Logie ruled in favour of the plaintiffs: "I think, notwithstanding Edelson's evidence, that Horwitz throughout knew or thought he knew that he was fighting for his life, and the injury received in the struggle for the pistol was not received by Horwitz while he was engaged in fighting within the meaning of the policy."[22]

What is most fascinating about this insurance case is that it referenced the Edelson murder trial in odd and unexpected ways. First, as indicated by his statement above, Judge Logie believed that Horwitz had defended himself against a menacing Edelson, thereby undermining the veracity of Ben's powerful testimony; second, Judge Logie asserted openly that the murder trial had been "mishandled"[23]; and third, in their effort to label the shooting and Jack's death as an accident, the Horwitzes employed the very verdict that exonerated their foe, Edelson. Perhaps the judge ruled in favour of the Horwitzes to help compensate for what he deemed a misguided decision in the murder trial. The next day, the *Toronto Daily Star* could announce, "Slain Man's Heirs to Get Insurance."[24]

By 1932, however, beneficiary Yetta was no longer associated with Jack Horwitz Ltd. or the Horwitz family. Phillip was the president, Charles was the manager, and Harry Hertz occupied Yetta's former job as secretary-treasurer.[25] Yetta was back in Montreal, virtually disowned by the family.[26] In 1935, Yetta married bachelor Max Fenster, a furrier by trade, who had been a childhood neighbor and long-time admirer in Montreal.[27] And with that, little Anita Horwitz became Anita Fenster.[28] By the 1940s,

Yetta and Max were living in Los Angeles where she worked as a saleswoman and he owned a service station.[29]

Almost a month following the Horwitz insurance verdict, a nasty dispute between the Edelson and Horwitz families erupted which publicly revived the animosity between them. Despite their desire to move beyond the trauma of the homicide, resentment and anger got the better of them. On 15 June 1932, Ben Edelson laid charges against Jack's brother-in-law Harry Hertz for "impeding or incommoding peaceable passengers" on Rideau Street. Hertz sought to prevent passersby from entering Edelson Jewellers, inciting a quarrel between Ben and Harry outside the store spirited enough to draw a crowd and hamper traffic. The formal charge – the brainchild of Moses Doctor who was again counsel for Edelson – was typically reserved in these Depression years for panhandlers who harassed pedestrians, which prompted even the *Citizen* to brand this legal battle "an unusual case." Perhaps sensing undue embarrassment or defeat for his client, Hertz's lawyer insisted the matter be settled out of court, a possibility that Doctor promised to explore.[30]

In December of 1932, six months after the "peaceable passengers" dispute, and almost a year after Edelson's acquittal, post-trial tensions climaxed. Magistrate Glenn E. Strike noted that this antagonism "has apparently developed into a feud between these two families, and it has reached a stage where this court must stop it if at all possible." Harry Hertz and Samuel Coblentz (Alice's brother) were ordered by Magistrate Strike to keep the peace for one year, and were each fined a hefty $1,000. A week before, the two men had been charged with disorderly conduct after an evening encounter when each man claimed to be assaulted by the other and both filed charges. During the exchange, Hertz had hurled insults at Samuel's (and Alice's) sister Rose, and an incensed Samuel retaliated, hitting Hertz. Magistrate Strike admitted that he "got what was coming to him." Strike also expressed dismay at Jack's younger brother, eighteen-year-old Jacie, who, as a witness of the incident, declared that he himself had once spat in front of Ben and Alice Edelson and "would do it again." "I cannot understand young Horwitz, who appears proud of what he did," lamented the Magistrate, "it is something only a six-year-old child or an uncivilized man might do." Magistrate Strike was bewildered by the entire feud, declaring that "it is an amazing thing that in a civilized age like ours such a thing as this should occur."[31]

Although not part of the criminal proceedings, this type of abuse by the Horwitzes was leveled against the Edelson children as well. Dina remembered that "we couldn't walk on the street without a member of the Horwitz family spitting at us or yelling dirty names at us." As both of the 1932 legal cases suggest, Harry Hertz was especially hostile, spitting at a fearful Dina when she happened to walk by the Bank Street store.[32]

In fact, throughout the 1930s, Harry Hertz proved himself a rather unscrupulous character, experiencing a suspiciously high number of mishaps and legal problems.[33] In November 1933, for example, he was accused of falsifying the will of his sister's husband. Mr Justice Kingstone ruled that the "revised" will written by Hertz, one much kinder to his sister, was "nothing more than a forged document."[34] Clearly, Harry Hertz, in his pursuit of riches and control, was not intimidated by the limits of the law.

Just over a year after the brawl between Hertz and Alice's brother came the shocking death of lawyer Moses Doctor. On Tuesday, 20 March 1934, Doctor was found dead at the age of thirty-three at his rented downtown apartment.[35] At about 8:30 that night, the building's cleaning woman, responding to family concerns about his whereabouts, discovered him on the sofa, lifeless. She telephoned Dr Danby, the same doctor who had assisted at the Horwitz shooting, who arrived at the apartment to confirm his death.[36]

Despite the detailed press reports surrounding Doctor's death, it remained shrouded in mystery. After only a cursory investigation, coroner Dr Craig ruled that a formal inquest into the cause and circumstances of the young man's death would not be required, and declared that Doctor had succumbed to heart failure due to natural causes.[37] The body was quickly delivered to Gauthier funeral home in preparation for burial.[38] The newspapers also seemed to preempt suspicions about the unusual circumstances of Doctor's death, upholding his stellar reputation in the process. The *Journal* reminded its readers, for example, that in recent years, Doctor had not been well. He had undergone surgery for ulcers and, in the last few months had complained of exhaustion, even considering a hospital rest-cure.[39] Given his demanding law practice and extensive volunteer work, it was no wonder that his many obligations "taxed his constitution to the uttermost."[40]

In an effort to thwart suspicions about illicit use of his downtown apartment, the *Journal* also reassured readers that the married Doctor, who lived with his wife in Sandy Hill, made dignified use of the space.[41] The paper stated that "it was his wont, when he desired privacy to prepare his briefs, to write addresses for the numerous societies he was called upon to address, and to bury himself in the classics and legal tomes on which he was an authority, to occupy this place." The apartment had no telephone, "so that Mr. Doctor could work undisturbed." The papers were sure to inform readers that "his retreat was well-known to his family and office staff," and that he "never used the apartment at night but only for a few hours in the daytime."[42]

What the newspapers likely knew but never mentioned, however, was that Moses Doctor took his own life.[43] At his apartment that day, he overdosed on sleeping pills or ingested poison.[44] Behind closed doors, family members and friends speculated as to the reasons for his suicide. One possibility was that he was overwhelmed by massive debt (possibly incurred through unlawful means), a scenario supported by the valuation of his estate.[45] Other circulated rumours involved a clandestine affair with a married woman,[46] and lingering guilt in helping to clear Ben Edelson, a man he believed committed murder.[47] Whatever the reasons for his suicide, the tragedy left its imprint on his father Rabbi Doctor, who died just six months later, and on his beautiful young widow Rose who, uncharacteristically for the period, never remarried.[48]

The unusual handling of Doctor's death by the authorities and the media can be explained by his suicide. Because traditional Judaism prohibits an autopsy as it desecrates the human body, it is probable that Doctor's father vetoed the procedure.[49] In addition, the absence of an inquest, the vagueness of the reported cause of death, and the defensive newspaper reporting effectively served to conceal the stigma of suicide by a rising political star and an esteemed officer of the court.[50] Moreover, with suicide a sin in Judaism, the cover-up allowed Doctor to be buried in the Jewish cemetery, a crucial issue in light of his position as a Jewish leader and role model and as the son of a prominent rabbi.[51]

After the brief resurgence of murder-case gossip during the Horwitz insurance dispute, the Edelson and Horwitz/Hertz scuffles, and Doctor's untimely death, all between 1932 and 1934, the silence invoked after the shooting resumed. Lillian maintained (albeit with some hyperbole) that her father "never, never spoke about it – never."[52] Ben and Alice simply "swept the incident under the rug," and moved on with their lives.[53] Mary Goldberg, who was friends with Alice in the 1950s and 60s, remembered that she never discussed the incident and that Mary, well aware of the family silencing by then, "wouldn't ask."[54]

Ben's only written acknowledgement of the shooting appears in his little brown "Address Book." A 1923 promotional souvenir from one of his jewellery suppliers, this was really less an address book than a tiny journal. In it, Ben recorded the birth, marriage, and death dates of family members, for at least forty-two years. Some of the documented milestones, which Ben obviously logged from memory, predated 1923; others were entered concurrent with an event or added later.[55] Nevertheless, Ben did reference the shooting:

JACKS [*sic*] ACCIDENT
TUESDAY NOV. 24/31
TRIAL STARTED ON
JAN. 14. 1932, ENDED 16TH.[56]

Ben's use of the word "accident" here is telling. He does not refer to the incident as a shooting or a killing, and certainly not as a murder. Also, although he does not explicitly reference his acquittal, by using the word "accident," he absolves himself of any accountability in Jack's death. Indeed, he might have used the expression "Jack's accident" not to designate Jack as its victim, but as its perpetrator. Either way, Ben's omission of Jack's last name and of the fact and date of his death suggest his reluctance to document the event for posterity.

The Edelson children heard only minor and rare allusions to the incident within their family. In fact, Lillian did not learn of it at the time from her parents but from a "very excited" girlfriend who telephoned her and said, "Do you know your father shot somebody?"[57] During the hearings and trial, Alice's mother and sister burned many of the newspapers that came into the house so the children would be shielded from the coverage and they never discussed it among themselves or with friends.[58] This secrecy was so entrenched that seven-year-old Jack, having no idea that his father had been jailed for several months, welcomed his father home after the acquittal by innocently asking, "Hi Dad, did you have a good trip?" An incensed Ben, thinking his son was being cheeky, gave him "a little whack" across the face.[59] As Lillian simply stated, "there was never any need" to talk about the case; Dina agreed: "What for?"[60] As a result, after the acquittal, "everything went back to normal rather quickly."[61] Eli, the youngest of the Edelson children, was thirty years old before he even heard about what had happened.[62]

In later years, the topic was broached only slightly more often. Ben alluded only to the aftermath of the event, making the occasional comment about staying married to Alice. When once asked by Lillian why he remained with his wife, Ben replied, "What would you kids have done without a mother?" – an answer that may indicate either his pragmatism or his need to save face despite his inability to give up the woman he loved. Alice made only a rare reference to shoving Ben's arm during the shooting, and never spoke with her adult daughters, "woman to woman," about her adultery.[63]

As part of putting the whole episode behind them, the Edelsons seemed determined over the following decades to reaffirm their respectability. With the end of the Depression and the advent of war, Ben and Alice, and children Dina, Lillian, Vivian, Joyce, and

Eli, were able to move in 1939 to a lovely home at 509 Clarence Street at Wurtemburg.[64] It was located five blocks east of the Friel Street house, just west of the Rideau River. The wartime and post-war economic boom, including 24,000 new civil service jobs in Ottawa, facilitated a thriving trade at Edelson Jewellers.[65] Edelson's carried a huge selection of regimental crests, which military men proudly purchased for their rings and tie tacks, and which Dina had learned to solder. And with Ottawa as a departure and arrival point for many troops, both optimistic soldiers and war-weary veterans bought engagement rings with diamonds that Ben regularly imported from Holland (and later Israel). Melting down fine jewelry sold to him by customers, Ben also got permission to sell gold to the Canadian Mint.[66] With business booming, Edelson Jewellers boasted eight employees.[67]

On 25 November 1950, however, nineteen years to the day that Jack Horwitz died and Ben was arrested, a massive fire gutted the building that housed the Edelson store. "Swept by fierce flames," the store sustained $150,000 worth of damage and was the scene of eager looters "mining" for stray jewellery in the fire-hose water surging through the street.[68] Undaunted, after the clean-up and restoration Ben relocated his business from 24 Rideau to the adjacent, more expansive space at 20 Rideau in the same building, and with the help of Dina, continued to run it until his retirement.[69] In the early 1950s, the Edelson family finally left Lowertown and moved to the more upscale Fairfax Street, where they lived "a nice, quiet life."[70]

With the Edelsons ostracized by many respectable members of the Jewish community after the incident, Alice "picked herself up and looked them in the eye, and wasn't taking any of it."[71] Ben and Alice simply "went their own way" with a smaller and altered circle of friends, and Alice graciously helped them and their children in whatever way she could.[72] In the mid-1930s, for example, Alice organized a surprise birthday party for Lillian's friend Adelene, and bought her a suitcase for her travels as a teenage volunteer with B'nai Brith.[73] Mary Goldberg, who first befriended Alice in the 1950s, remembered her as "a lovely hostess," who in the 1960s made a bridal shower for Mary's daughter.[74] Ben and Alice's own children got married in quick succession in the late 1930s and early 1940s, offering the Edelsons a welcome distraction.[75]

By the 1950s and 60s, four of the seven Edelson children had children of their own, and Ben and Alice, like many Jewish seniors, reveled in their role as grandparents.[76] True to form, Ben, the patriarch of the family, was still rather "serious," expected everyone to "toe the line," and was not overly affectionate, but he quietly expressed "extreme love" for his grandchildren. On Sundays, when they would visit, they descended upon the den where Ben sat smoking his pipe, and begged him to take them for ice cream; if he relented, they piled in his mammoth Buick Roadmaster. Their grandmother was predictably playful and warm, and could be found in the kitchen, happily preparing her famous chopped herring and buns.[77]

Like most middle-class Jewish women who craved community and respectability, Alice immersed herself in volunteer work. She joined Pioneer Women (today Na'amat Canada) in the 1940s, an organization that sought to improve the lives of Jewish women and children in Palestine by raising funds for their social services and health care.[78] And as an ongoing member of the Lillian Freiman chapter, she focused throughout the 1950s and 60s on her pet cause, Hadassah. She was her chapter's chairperson for Israel bonds (daughter Lillian joked that Alice "sold more Israeli bonds than anybody in Ottawa"[79]); worked on the annual bazaars as a committee member, and by selling tickets and staffing booths; assisted with and hosted weekly teas; and donated door prizes from Edelson Jewellers.[80] She also gave anonymous donations so that underprivileged women could attend the Hadassah banquets.[81] In 1955, she was named a "Life Member," by 1967, she was first vice-president of her chapter, and in 1971, she became chapter president.[82] When Alice died in 1972, her dedication to Hadassah was duly recognized. New president Minnie Greenburg noted that "we have not only lost a Chapter President, but a great friend of Hadassah-Wizo." In her memory, Ottawa Hadassah-Wizo inscribed her name on "the Honour roll for life-long devoted service" at the Asof Harofe Hospital in Israel.[83] Still, despite the respect she earned for her charitable contributions, Alice was never able to fully regain her community standing.

Jack's seven siblings rarely alluded publicly to their brother at all. When Jacie's 1939 marriage was announced in the papers, for example, only his living siblings, as well as his late parents, were mentioned.[84] When Charles died in 1972, the Rabbi's eulogy named only his living siblings and his predeceased wife, Anne.[85] And the children of the Horwitz brothers heard little of the incident as they grew up. Philip's son Jonathan, for example, had seen photos of "the uncle who died," but he never discussed him with his brother, sisters, or cousins. Even today they know only the most basic facts: that Jack courted a woman, her husband found out, the two men scuffled, Ben shot Jack, and Jack died. Jacie's son Jack maintained that "the story I always got was he was 'shot,' never 'killed' ... he got shot and died." In contrast, Jonathan recalled that in his family, the Edelsons were known as the people who "killed" Jack. The cousins concurred, however, that in both their families, neither the word "accident" nor "murder" was ever used, perhaps to avoid either minimizing or sensationalizing the incident, respectively. As both cousins mistakenly believed that the shooting transpired at the Horwitz, not Edelson, store, Ben's liability, in either scenario, had been somewhat diminished.[86]

Although there wasn't much interaction between the Edelsons and Horwitzes in the decades that followed the shooting, it was inevitable that in Ottawa's small Jewish community, the two families would cross paths. Various members lived in the same neighbourhoods, volunteered in the same Jewish groups, attended the same life cycle events, and patronized each other's businesses.[87] Overall, Jack Horwitz's nephews, who grew up thirty to forty years after the shooting, never had the sense that the families feuded with, or even avoided, one another.[88]

Steven Chernove, son of Anita, Jack and Yetta Horwitz's only child, also knows very little about the case. Steven first learned the story of his grandfather's adultery and death when he was in his twenties in the 1980s. The story was affirmed a few years later by Yetta when she stated that her first husband had been killed, and that she had been disowned by the Horwitz family. Aside from that one episode, Yetta never spoke to Steven about her life in Ottawa. He remembered that there was always a "shroud of silence" surrounding his family history. He always sensed in his childhood that his family withheld information, and that he was "out of the loop." This silence not only revolved around the shooting of his grandfather Jack Horwitz, but also around the life and premature death of his mother Anita.[89]

It wasn't just the families involved who kept silent. Ottawa Jews, despite their vigorous gossip initially and their private conversations for decades to come, were always publicly discreet about the case (rarely, for example, did Ottawa Jews grant interviews to the press in the days and weeks after the shooting), and collective memory about it diminished. The focus of much academic memory literature, collective memory is a group's shared history articulated and commemorated in the public sphere.[90] Often preoccupied with issues of distinguishing and affirming group identity, it strives for a unified and uncomplicated historical narrative, and is mediated through contemporary media, museums, monuments, and books, and through shared perceptions of what a group deems desirable, moral, and just. Collective memory is often in the business of harvesting and utilizing historical information for a current need (for the purpose of nationalism, for example), and is often the manifestation of a communal sense of obligation to mark the past. But the Edelson/Horwitz murder case was never memorialized through any cultural medium (except through the 1930s press), nor summoned to provide material for a "usable past." Nor did it ever inspire a moral obligation in the Jewish community to remember, presenting no ethical risk, in fact, if it forgot.[91] Indeed, unlike those historical episodes that are "deserving" of collective memory, this case confirmed that collective "forgetting" was far more honourable,[92] reminding us of the extent to which a harrowing and even politically "useful" event can be so easily "forgotten, suppressed, or mythologized until unrecognizable."[93]

Indeed, memoirs written over the last several decades by Ottawa Jews have not referenced the case. Lawrence Freiman's 1978 autobiography, *Don't Fall Off the Rocking Horse*, vividly recalls the year 1931. At twenty-two, he left Harvard Business School in June of that year to help run the struggling family department store at 73 Rideau Street, a block away from Edelson Jewellers. But Freiman makes no mention of the shooting at all.[94] Similarly Alice's stepsister, Bess Schecter, in her 1995 book, *My Memoirs*, recalls 1931 as a "splendid" time due to her courtship and wedding, and is quiet about the scandal.[95] Judge Abe Lieff also excludes the case from his 1991 memoir, *Gathering Rosebuds*, even though he was good friends with Edelson's lawyer, Moses Doctor.[96]

Unlike Freiman, Schecter, and Lieff, Adelene Hyman never penned a memoir, but she too went out of her way to "forget" the case, despite having good reason to remember it. In 1931, she was best friends with Lillian Edelson, heard Lillian sob that her father killed a man, and frequented the Edelsons' Friel Street home throughout the ordeal. But even when the ninety-one-year-old Hyman visited with the older Dina Edelson in 2008, and they reminisced together about the 1930s, the apple trees behind the Edelson's Friel Street house was the preferred topic of conversation. Hyman never brought up the shooting with Dina, a subject that was still painful for them both.[97]

All of this "forgetting" helps explain the dearth of information about the incident in the Ottawa Jewish Archives. Like most community archives, it seeks to extol local history, and has necessarily relied on members to build up their collections marking homegrown achievements. So when Shirley Berman, a volunteer with the Ottawa Jewish Historical Society in the early 1970s, and founder of the Ottawa Jewish Archives later that decade, sought specifically to amass material related to the shooting, she "was discouraged by everyone who lived through it." Berman recalled that "mum was the word about this affair ... I never could get anyone to divulge anything." "When I tried to wrench information out of the community," she notes, "it was as if it never happened."[98] Berman believed that "still remembering the pogroms, and the anti-Semitism of their past lives," Ottawa's immigrant Jews generally possessed a *"shah shtill"* mentality, a Yiddish expression literally meaning "hush, still," and emblematic of the community's reluctance to draw negative attention to itself for fear of discrimination and harassment.[99]

The absence of archival information helps explain why even a relatively recent book about the Ottawa Jewish community ignores the incident, but this scarcity of sources is just part of the story. The truth is that the authors and editors of *A Common Thread: A History of the Jews of Ottawa* (2009) deliberately omitted most dark episodes in Ottawa's Jewish history. Like nearly all general local histories, especially those published and funded by community associations, leaders, and proud members, *A Common Thread* highlights the successes of the community without overtly referencing its quarrels and scandals. Thus, although the book devotes an entire chapter to the 1930s and 40s, the Edelson/Horwitz murder case never gets mentioned.[100]

Nonetheless, there are those in the Ottawa Jewish community who remember the Edelson/Horwitz shooting in very particular ways. Suzie Gellman recollects it as one of three "sensational" tragedies in the late 1920s and 1930s that haunted her as a child. The other two events were the horrific discovery of an American girl found dismembered in a suitcase, and the kidnapping and murder of the Lindbergh baby.[101] As a child, she found the Edelson/Horwitz incident the most shocking of the three. Its physical proximity, its known actors, and its connection to the Jewish community all made their imprint. Not surprisingly, Gellman's memory of the animated discussions surrounding the shooting overshadow her recall of events related to the trial whose procedural and legal considerations would have been of no interest to a little girl at the time. For Gellman, "the incident was everything!"[102]

Virtually all those I interviewed recounted the event as a shared experience. Instead of speaking in the first-person singular, they consistently employed the term "we," unwittingly using it to reference the Jewish community. They also used the generic term "community" in the same way, assuming they held common perceptions and possessed a united voice about the event.[103]

That Edelson was found not guilty in a court of law should have vindicated him in the eyes of Ottawa's Jewish community, but it hasn't. The view of the case by the community has been consistent with its initial reaction that the shooting was not an accident, but a crime of passion. As such, like many accused before him, Edelson has always been associated with guilt to some extent, and his exoneration questioned.[104] Indeed, one prospective bride was cautioned by her family against marrying a man whose "grandfather killed someone," advice that reveals an overriding impression of Ben's sinister character.[105]

But it is Alice Edelson who is still seen as the chief villain in the case, and the person ultimately to blame for Horwitz's death.[106] Lionel Metrick stated in 2006 that "of course she was responsible." If she were "a woman of valour," she would have told Jack Horwitz "to go fly a kite."[107] Some of the nieces and nephews of Jack Horwitz were even told growing up in the 1950s and 60s that Alice had once been a prostitute in New York, a story made more plausible perhaps by the scores of brothels on the Lower East Side where Alice was raised, and by Philip's allegation that Ben had received money from Jack. Certainly, the general impression was that Alice possessed corrupt morals and was experienced in enticing otherwise decent men.[108] Moses Doctor was partly responsible for this reputation because "in order to get Ben off," Doctor "had to drag her name in the mud to make it like she was a terrible person ... he had to blacken her name."[109]

But even as a cautionary tale for young women, the case was not worth collectively rehashing. Unlike the adulteress in a typical Victorian saga who is brutally killed, or dies homeless, deserted, or insane, Alice would live out her life within the community as a comfortable, middle-class wife. At best, the story was more a cautionary tale for men like Jack Horwitz who dared trespass on another man's wife. But lessons in sexual morality have generally been reserved for potentially defiant women, not actively audacious men. Despite all that Alice lost, including Jack, she was seen as having won the ultimate prize: Ben's apparent forgiveness, and his permission for her to "come back." Alice's return to married life was never perceived as her decision, but his. Protected and privileged as Ben's wife, she was supposed to be grateful, especially in contrast to Yetta, the marginalized and vulnerable widow.

Interestingly, despite their condemnation of Alice – and despite her public "confession" the morning that Jack died – the community has never subscribed to the theory that she was in any way culpable in the actual shooting of Jack. It has also never espoused the notion that she deliberately shot Jack, although such a theory could have been supported by Ben's testimony that an unrelenting Jack coerced her to recommence the affair and threatened to expose it.

In contrast to the Jewish community's contempt for her, Jack Horwitz's reputation has remained relatively intact. For example, Lionel Metrick remembered him as "a very dear fellow" and "a beloved individual."[110] Abetting his relatively unblemished reputation is the fact that his marital status has been consistently overlooked. While all those interviewed remembered Alice's infidelity, many didn't know or recall whether her paramour Jack was married or not.[111] Indeed, his adult nephews assumed that Jack was a carefree bachelor engaged in one of several brief affairs with beautiful women.[112] Of those others who did recollect his marriage, none remembered his wife's name, nor that she and Jack shared a daughter.[113] Jack's nephews never knew about the existence of their cousin Anita.[114]

The most damaging rumour that has circulated quietly but consistently for decades is Jack Horwitz's role as the biological father of at least one of Alice's seven children.[115] The rumour, which likely took root with Yetta's testimony at the trial, has inspired some observers over the years to assert the "strong resemblance" of certain Edelsons to Jack and other members of the Horwitz clan.[116] The story has also caused some to reflect on the children's first names, one or more of which might have been selected by Alice, they surmise, to pay honour to Jack, and to spite Ben.[117] Certainly, at least one of the Edelson children has pondered his/her lineage in relation to the incident.[118] Whether this gossip would have circulated in the absence of the shooting is difficult to know, but it seems to have served the dual purpose of further discrediting Alice, and of illustrating the lesson that transgressions long since over can have a profound and lasting impact.

The people I spoke to also do not want the case remembered as a typical occurrence of their community. They emphasize that it was a rare event, and that most Ottawa Jews were moral and law-abiding citizens. Sid Kronick noted the rarity of a gun "in a Jewish shop" (despite the fact that jewellers, especially diamond merchants like Ben, routinely kept guns in their stores[119]) and, along with Lionel Metrick, insisted the shooting "was an unusual episode."[120] Francis Shaffer reiterated that the case was "unusual for a Jewish community," and that unsavory events like this were more common in the Gentile community.[121] Suzie Gellman agreed that "you somehow don't think of these terrible crimes happening in the Jewish community because Jewish people are peaceful – they want peace. They're not fighters. You don't think of the Jewish people as looking for trouble. You just don't."[122]

For all of these reasons, many in the Jewish community did not grant me interviews. One irritated woman claimed that in 1931, the case was barely noticed at all. Others sought to protect the Edelson and Horwitz families, both the memory of those who are dead, and the standing of those alive. One Horwitz family member insisted that I write the book as a novel and change all of the names, while an Edelson family member sought legal advice about possibly vetoing the publication of this book. On both sides of the family, several people who had granted me interviews cancelled the meetings, largely due to pressure from relatives.[123]

In the 1970s, 80s, and 90s, the tendency of family and community members to either recall or "forget" the case was likely prompted by the deaths of its central figures. On 28 December 1972, when she was seventy-six years old, Alice fell unconscious while watching television, likely suffering a stroke. Ben came home from the store and found her slumped lifeless on the couch, her cigarette burning a hole in the sofa. She passed away in hospital a short time later.[124] The eighty-two-year-old widower would live for almost another two decades, remaining with daughter Dina in their Fairfax Street house for several years, and then moving into Hillel Lodge, Ottawa's Jewish home for seniors, for just over eight more. But Ben would suffer one final tragedy: in 1988, his youngest daughter Shirley, who had always been sickly, died in Florida of liver disease at sixty-two years of age. Nine months later, Ben died on 12 October 1988 at the age of ninety-eight.[125]

Jack Horwitz's widow Yetta made a life for herself in Los Angeles. She became a drapery saleswoman at Sears, raised her only child, Anita, and then enjoyed her role as a doting grandmother.[126] After her husband Max Fenster died in 1974, she remained a widow for the next twenty-four years, dying in 1998 at ninety-eight.[127]

Yetta's daughter Anita Horwitz Fenster stepped into the archetypal life of post-war, middle-class womanhood. She attended UCLA and, in 1948, married college sweetheart Robert Chernove, who became a successful insurance agent, eventually owning his own firm.[128] Anita became a mother to two boys, and an active volunteer in her college sorority alumnae society and in the Los Angeles City Panhellenic Association.[129] In 1963, as a way to revitalize their troubled marriage, Robert took Anita to Mexico, where she suddenly fell ill and died at the age of thirty-seven.[130] Enduring another huge loss and never fond of Robert, Yetta blamed her son-in-law for Anita's untimely death, and was dismayed when he married a wealthy widowed socialite only one year later.[131]

In 2005, seventeen years after Ben's death, Edelson Jewellers also met its demise. By then it was located at 222 Rideau Street, its original site at 24 Rideau having been long since demolished. Despite Dina's best efforts to keep the business alive by relocating several times, and by paying staff from her own meagre savings, Edelson Jewellers, with its dated inventory, fell victim to the popularity of the Rideau Centre mall, to increasing crime in the area, to the diminished reputation of local shops, and ultimately, to Dina's advanced age.[132] After more than eight decades as an Ottawa fixture, the business was liquidated. Edelson Jewellers – an immigrant dream, a family business, a Jewish success story, and the relic of a tragedy – was gone.

In 1942, Eva Bilsky, a daughter of one of Ottawa's first Jewish residents, Moses Bilsky, wrote a children's book entitled *What Happened After?* The book, written under the pseudonym "Aunt Eva," speculates what became of famous fairy tale characters after

readers got told they lived "happily (or unhappily) ever after."
Aunt Eva knew what we all know: that life following a heady adventure is often just as compelling as the adventure itself. That Ben
and Alice stayed together for the next forty years until her death,
that they lived a regular middle-class life, that family members
long honoured a code of silence, that the Ottawa Jewish community never really exonerated Ben, and that Alice continued for
decades as the target of scorn all demonstrate that "what happened after" claims its own brand of intrigue, both crafting and
erasing memory.

Conclusion

Although accomplished and productive, the Edelson and Horwitz families were by no means remarkable. It was only one extraordinary night in November 1931 that distinguished them from the tens of thousands of other immigrant and Canadian-born Jews in the 1930s. As this book has argued, this murder case was unusual, and serves as a valuable tool in exploring issues of gender, ethnicity, and class, particularly the ways in which a man's middle-class status and a woman's perceived immorality could help to excuse his misconduct and indict hers.

Although the Jewish community was shocked by the actions of Ben, it reserved the lion's share of its contempt for Alice. Alice's behaviour was perceived as challenging everything that Ottawa Jews held dear. It is plausible, in fact, that the cigarette-smoking, flirtatious, and adulterous Alice purposefully dissented, resisting the confines of an unyielding husband and of a conventional life in a claustrophobic community. Unlike Alice, many wives in the Depression – unemployed, deserted, or destitute – had neither the money, privacy, time, nor beauty to rebel in this way. Nor did they have the courage: Alice risked everything to maintain her relationship with Jack. Her behaviour allows us to examine the rebellion of a woman who, unlike most Jewish women the scholarship profiles, was subversive outside collective, public labour movements: Alice's revolt played out within family life, which meant that one could never be sure of what went on behind closed doors. In this way, her case had the potential to expose the misconduct of anyone. Given the community's strong religious and cultural identity,

interconnected families and businesses, tight social and institutional network, and collective ambition, her actions threatened
many facets of Jewish life. These included not only the sanctified
image of marriage and family, but also community solidarity, middle-class respectability, and upward mobility. Alice was a reminder
that despite the appearance of a strong work, family, and volunteer ethic, and adherence to religious laws, cracks were appearing
in the very foundation of the community.

One of these fractures was expressed through the popular image
of Jewish men as ineffectual and emasculated, an image confirmed
not only by Alice's affair, but by Ben's tolerance of it in the years
before the shooting. Ben undermined his masculine authority by
allowing Alice to carry on for so long, thereby assuming the traditionally feminine role as the long-suffering victim of a philandering spouse. Nonetheless, neither the Jewish community nor the
lawyers spoke of Ben in these terms. Instead, the Depression-era
community, courtroom, and jury were all invested in him as the
defender of his family, and focused on the manly way in which he
finally retaliated. And privately, Ben could take solace in the
chivalry with which he protected Alice, both from herself (that is,
her possible, surely ruinous plan to run off with Jack), and from
criminal charges.

For the jury, Ben possessed all the badges of male respectability
during an uncertain time. Despite pervasive anti-Semitism, and
with militant anti-Semites like Ottawa's Detective Tissot having influence in Ontario during these years, men like Ben Edelson could
be accepted as valued citizens. Ben was seen as neither a feminized
dupe nor as a criminalized brute, the pejorative perceptions commonly attached to Eastern European immigrants and others not of
the dominant culture. Instead, thanks to his upward mobility and
assimilation, he was viewed as a respectable, middle-class man.

But middle-class respectability alone did not vindicate Ben in
the courtroom: an even more powerful force was Alice's sexual
misconduct, as revealed through the lens of the unwritten law.
The unwritten law was designed to excuse and justify the actions
of a man who killed another who had transgressed against him
and his female kin. The power of this convention was stronger

than any anti-Semitism the jurors might have each harboured; instead, they banded together as men to assert their role as custodians of the family and the moral regulators of women.

In the Edelson/Horwitz case, there was another element at work. Because the unfaithful wife was as complicit as the male interloper, the unwritten law crucified Alice. The case certainly illustrates how a lone woman could be scapegoated for the inappropriate and even lethal behaviour of men: it was not she who, like Ben, brandished a loaded gun, or who, like Jack, rejected a young wife; nevertheless, Ben's lawyer, Moses Doctor was able to cast Alice as the worst offender of the lot. During the trial, the image of Alice vacillated between woman as vixen and victim, as perpetrator and property, and as heartless and hysterical. These images reflected the polarized depictions of women in the 1930s, and the pejorative way in which almost all traits associated with womanhood were perceived. The female scapegoating of the Depression, exacerbated by popular fears of the post-suffrage, "modern" woman, helped ensure that Alice was damned.

Although the unwritten law likely got Ben acquitted, we shouldn't be too quick to extol its virtues as the great equalizer among men. In an article about jury nullification in two cases involving female defendants, Carolyn Strange points out that "periodic compassionate judgments dramatize the power of the law to rectify inequalities outside the courtroom. They maintain the illusion that even the lowest citizens – women, the poor, and people of colour – are equal before the law." But these lenient verdicts, she stresses, do not "correct systemic inequality." As Strange notes, "acquittals contribute not to the correction of sexism, racism, and classism in the justice system but rather to their obfuscation."[1] Thus, although in a climate of anti-Semitism, the acquittal of the immigrant Jew Ben Edelson appeared benevolent, his generous treatment only served to reinforce entrenched notions related to both middle-class and patriarchal privilege.

This privilege underscores the arbitrary nature of the law, and the ways in which it got exercised for or against the accused. The notion of criminal responsibility was fluid and fickle. It was forever shifting and was mediated by a jury through a variety of factors, not the least of which was the sex, race/ethnicity, and class of those involved in the crime, and of the jury itself.[2] For the dominant culture, these particular factors spoke not only to the socio-economic background of an individual but to his/her moral character, which was perceived as more honed in those who were, or at least resembled, white, Anglo-Protestant, middle-class Canadians. For women especially, moral character was linked to their sexual behaviour which, even when they were not the ones on trial, got scrutinized and debated. Thus, Ben's respectability and Alice's misconduct combined to produce the perfect storm in which his culpability was nullified, and his acquittal ensured.

The Jewish community took its cues from the Edelson and Horwitz families who, in silencing the incident, saw no point in perpetuating the shame that it inspired, or burdening subsequent generations with its stigma. As such, the case demonstrates the power and expedience of collective "forgetting." Because the Edelson and Horwitz families never wanted that singular event to define who they were and what they could be, it quickly became a taboo subject. The community acquiesced in this silence, but only in public, privately reveling in the intrigue and gossip which that one night unleashed. Today, elderly family and community members still prove reluctant to speak of the incident, and when conceding to do so, still – without fail – disparage Alice.

This book could be accused of doing exactly what the Edelson and Horwitz families have so fervently resisted: publicizing the incriminating scandal. But this work is not intended as a sensationalistic recounting of these events. Instead, it serves as a reminder of the classist and sexist attitudes that governed the standards of both community and courtroom. Arguably, their treatment of Alice was no less a *shandeh*.

A Note on Sources

Both the *Ottawa Evening Citizen* and the *Ottawa Evening Journal* document the events that transpired before, during, and after the shooting using verbatim court testimony. The same holds true for the much anticipated trial in mid-January. The papers did not reprint complete testimonies, or those of every witness, but with vivid and detailed coverage transported their readers to the pews of the courtroom. This comprehensive treatment, despite various shortcomings, makes these newspapers crucial sources for information about the case, especially as the location of the original court records is unknown, other English-language newspapers and the Québec French-language press were generally silent on the case, and Yiddish press coverage is both incomplete and not easily accessed. This brief note on sources will focus on the Ottawa newspapers, and will address the English, French, and Yiddish press. It will also consider various issues related to conjecture in the book.

Although extraordinarily helpful, the extensive coverage by the Ottawa newspapers is overwhelmingly narrative and factual, and simply a reiteration of court testimony. Curiously, the newspapers offer no editorials about the shooting. Despite those about other murder cases in the news,[1] and all the fodder for moralizing, lurid, or entertaining rants, no editors or feature columnists tendered their opinions about the case. Moreover, the news articles themselves seldom incorporate personal comment or interpretation. For reasons not entirely clear, it seems that some kind of editorial gag order was in place, made more efficient by the persistent absence of bylines.

In addition, unlike other newspapers that debated celebrated cases involving "the unwritten law", the Ottawa press did not discuss its implications in the Edelson/Horwitz incident.[2] This largely generic coverage also meant that anti-Semitism, so prevalent in 1930s Ottawa, is almost undetectable, suggestive, as I have argued, of admiration for Ben's middle-class respectability, and of sympathy for his union with an adulterous wife.

Letters to the editor from readers are also absent from the papers. This stands in opposition to the general trend for readers to passionately lobby for or against the accused, and particularly in contrast to those letters which appeared in the Ottawa press condemning the October 1930 murder of William Marshall and the December 1931 murder of service-station attendant Paul Levigne.[3] Given the morality issues raised by the Edelson case, it is impossible to imagine that readers were unmoved to express either their outrage or sympathy for particular actors. The size of the crowd that attended the inquest and trials suggests that this silence should not be interpreted as a lack of popular interest. Indeed, this dearth of reader response, like the editorial silence, speaks to deliberate suppression by the Ottawa press.

Significantly, no photographs or drawings of Alice appear in the newspapers. This omission is especially curious given that she was at the centre of the conflict, the object of much public fascination, and so often described in terms of her exceptional beauty and allure. Perhaps her role as the mother of seven young children inspired compassion by the press. In contrast, one eight-year-old photograph of Yetta appears twice: a portrait of her on her wedding day.[4] The wedding portrait serves to dichotomize the two women in the scandal, casting Yetta as the respectable and hopeful bride whose future would be destroyed by a calculating adulteress.

The Archives of Ontario holds the province's historical legal records, including the extensive records of the Carleton County Supreme Court as well as the Attorney General Central Registry Criminal and Civil Files for the period 1873 to 1976; nonetheless, transcripts of the Edelson murder trial, as well as related documents, are not to be found there. The Carleton County Supreme

Court records are sporadic, and except for the odd and cursory mention of the Edelson/Horwitz case, as in the Supreme Court Registrar's criminal indictment files, it gets no coverage.[5] In the Attorney General Central Registry Criminal and Civil Files for 1873 to 1976, the Edelson/Horwitz case is not represented at all. In all probability, the court transcripts and other related papers were discarded in the 1960s by A.W. Nichol, the Executive Officer of the Office of the Attorney General. Told simply "to use his own best judgment" in culling the files for their 1964 deposit into the Archives of Ontario, he destroyed over ninety per cent of the pre-1948 collection. Although Nichol retained "virtually all the files on famous murder cases," he likely deemed the Edelson case legally and historically insignificant due to the "not guilty" verdict and acquittal, and thus to the absence of an appeal. Other casualties of Nichol's zealousness included files related to women's and native rights. Fortunately, the files spanning the years 1948 to 1967 were relocated to the Archives some time later, and were conserved in their entirety.[6]

Another obstacle in the use of Ontario government sources which make the Ottawa newspaper accounts so valuable is the *Freedom of Information and Protection of Privacy Act*. It imposes strict conditions on, among other things, records that are less than one hundred years old, and materials gifted by private donors who want aspects of their collection to remain confidential. It also imposes stringent regulations on records concerning individuals dead less than thirty years. As Ben Edelson died in 1988, certain files, such as those in the records of the Nicholas Street Jail where he was incarcerated, are not attainable.[7] Privacy restrictions also surround the 1931 census.

With the exception of the *Citizen* and *Journal*, newspapers offer only scanty reporting about the case. The English-language papers of Toronto, Montreal, Cornwall, and Renfrew ran only occasional stories. The French-language press provides even fewer sources. Montreal's *Le Devoir*, for example, is absent of any reference.[8] Only three stories appear in *L'Action catholique* and two in *La Patrie*.[9] Although *L'Action catholique* consistently deemed the event front-page worthy, its coverage, like that of *La Patrie*, is brief and descriptive, and is never augmented by editorials or letters to the editor.

Perhaps it should not be surprising that the English press outside of Ottawa, and the French-language press generally were not overly invested in the case. But given the proximity as well as the sensationalism of the case, its anti-Semitic potential, and its characters with Toronto, Montreal, and Cornwall connections, more widespread coverage would not have been unexpected.

Evidence of coverage in the Jewish press in Canada is not much better. The publication record of most of these early-twentieth-century newspapers, whether English or Yiddish, is brief and inconsistent, making existing archival collections scanty at best.[10] Issues relevant to the period of the Edelson/Horwitz case are missing from many of these collections and where they exist, most underreported the event, likely because their mandate was to highlight the achievements of the Jewish community. An exception is the *Keneder Adler* (*Jewish Daily Eagle*), which is available on microfilm, and in its entirety, at several Jewish libraries and archives, and which offers decent coverage of the case.

Most articles about the case in newspapers other than the *Citizen* and the *Journal*, whether English, French, or Yiddish, present little more information and insight. They demonstrate that reporters simply borrowed the story as presented by the Ottawa press, often reiterating facts word for word, and shedding no new light on what happened.

Although the accounts in the *Citizen* and the *Journal* include conflicting versions of events (which undermine factual reliability) and a slew of similarities (which indicate hackneyed reporting), in the absence of other primary sources, especially the court transcripts, they are invaluable, and comprise the foundation of this work. As there are so many lengthy articles, I tried to minimize confusion where I could: where a story spans several pages and is demarcated on these pages by a different version of the same title (or a different title altogether), I elected to document these articles as separate entities. As such, the endnotes do not reveal those articles which under various titles continue for more than one page.

A consideration of sources naturally raises the matter of conjecture. As suggested above, no source, either written or oral, is without its problems – in some form or another, biases, distortions, inaccuracies, and incompleteness are almost always evident, serving to render some voices silent, or to challenge "the truth" advanced by others. As a result, sources often produce more questions than answers. My sources left me reflecting on several issues: what viewpoints (for example, those of the dead Horwitz or the secluded Alice) are missing? Whose version of "the truth" (for example, the historical newspapers or the contemporary interviews) is more authentic, credible, and convincing? How does one reconcile the tension between "the truth" evidenced in documents (for example, the jury's "not guilty" verdict) and its incongruous subtext which these same documents ignored (the unwritten law)? Furthermore, how do all of these considerations inform the overall telling of the Edelson/Horwitz story, and the analytical tools of gender, ethnicity, and class?

Given these substantive lacunae and competing truths, exacerbated by the family and community shame that invoked silence, I had to rely, to some extent, on conjecture. In the name of academic honesty, scholars often mark these times for speculation by utilizing conditional terms such as "arguably," "maybe," and "perhaps" – words that can be unsettling and irritating for the reader. In light of the extensive documentation provided here, I have tried to minimize my use of such words when conjecture is warranted, in the hope that, on those occasions, the reader will trust in the knowledge and integrity of the author.

Notes

ABBREVIATIONS

AO   Archives of Ontario

BPC Meeting, Board of Police Commissioners

COA City of Ottawa Archives

IC   Individual Collections

JPL Jewish Public Library

NYPL New York Public Library

OCD *Ottawa City Directory*

OHW Ottawa Hadassah-Wizo

OJA Ottawa Jewish Archives

OSOH Osgoode Society Oral History Programme

PW   Documentation Pertaining to the Legal Career of Peter White Jr.
     [clippings]

RSA Rabbi Saul Aranov Collection

SC   Collection of Steven Chernove

SE   Collection of Sharon Edelson

INTRODUCTION

1 "Ben S. Edelson Is Acquitted on Murder Charge," *The Ottawa Evening
   Citizen*, 18 January 1932, 14. Prosecutor Peter White spoke these words
   at Ben's January trial.

2 Between 1920 and 1950, approximately 1,443 people were charged with
   murder in Canada: 40 per cent (579) were convicted of murder, 55 per
   cent of whom (319) were executed; 48 per cent were acquitted or found
   guilty of a reduced charge; and 12 percent, for reasons of "lunacy," were
   not tried. See White, *Negotiating Responsibility*, 16.

184   NOTES TO PAGE 4

3 For "mystery," see, for example, "17 are Called to the Inquest as Witnesses," *The Ottawa Evening Journal*, 1 December 1931, 4; for "sensational," see, for example, "Ben Edelson Arraigned on Charge of Murder
   and Remanded a Week," *The Ottawa Evening Journal*, 25 November
   1931, 1; "Few Persons Will be Able to Hear Case," *The Ottawa Evening
   Journal*, 1 December 1931, 1, and "Sensational Evidence Given at Horwitz Inquest," *The Ottawa Evening Journal*, 2 December 1931, 13.
4 Paula Uruburu employs the term "crime of the century" in the full title
   of her book *American Eve*. Fifty-two-year-old White was attending a
   production of *Mamzelle Champagne* atop New York City's Madison
   Square Garden, the lavish building that he himself designed. As the song
   "I Could Love a Million Girls" rang out sardonically, a frenzied Thaw
   approached White and shot him in the face. Thaw was eventually acquitted by reason of insanity and sent to an asylum for the criminally insane.
   The story of the illicit affair and notorious shooting was dramatized in
   the 1955 film *The Girl in the Red Velvet Swing*. See Lessard, *The Architect of Desire*, 10, 239–40, 69; Uruburu, *American Eve*, 331, 358.
5 See, for example, Joselit, *Our Gang*; Cohen, *Tough Jews*; Vincent, *Bodies
   and Souls*; Stanislawski, *A Murder in Lemberg*; and Kitzler, *Jewish
   Pirates of the Caribbean*.
6 In reviewing Kitlzer's book *Jewish Pirates of the Caribbean*, Adam Kirsch
   writes "there is something strange about the way American Jews, the
   most secure, prosperous, and assimilated Jews in history, keep returning
   to tales of Jewish violence and thuggery to affirm their potency ... Surely
   there are enough examples of courage in Jewish history – physical and
   moral." See Kirsch, "Edward Kitzler's history."
7 For scholarly works, see, for example, Stanislawski, *A Murder in Lemberg*. Against the backdrop of intense Orthodox opposition to increasing
   Reform influence in the Galician city of Lemberg in 1848, an Orthodox
   Jew slipped into the kitchen of forty-one-year-old Reform rabbi Abraham Kohn and poisoned the family's soup, killing the rabbi and his baby
   daughter. My thanks to colleague Anna Chichopek for bringing this
   book to my attention.
8 McLaren, "Males, Migrants, and Murder," 162. In June of 1904, for example, New York City theatre manager Morris Finkel shot his wife, Yiddish actress Emma Thomashefsky Finkel, and then killed himself. Emma
   miraculously survived the assault, but would remain disabled until her

1929 death at the age of fifty-two. The story of the Finkel shooting rocked
Jewish New York, and its theatre world, and was documented by the Jewish
press in sensational detail. The story has also been referenced in virtually
every memoir that has come out of the American Yiddish theatre. See Jones,
"Stage Killing." My thanks to librarian and Yiddish-language scholar Faith
Jones for bringing this case to my attention.

In October 2005, in Boca Raton, Florida, one Jewish man shot another
outside a synagogue during High Holiday services. The victim was dating
a former girlfriend of the shooter, and had assisted her in obtaining a re-
straining order against him. On a personal webpage that discussed the
story, one man wryly joked that he "didn't see Jew-on-Jew shootings
edging out the traditional weapon of choice, Jew on Jew *suings*, anytime
soon." While the joke distastefully generalizes about the affluent and liti-
gious character of American Jews, it also reflects the Jewish revulsion for
violence, and the rarity of Jews assaulting other Jews. Certainly, there were
those at the synagogue who simply assumed that the gunshots, disrupting
the sacred services of a crowded synagogue, indicated an anti-Semitic attack. Even knowing that this wasn't what happened, and that the shooting
was a personalized incident, the rabbi hired a security guard "to keep
watch" during the holidays. See "Synagogue Shooting Shocks," "Shooting
outside West Boca Synagogue," and King, "Rabbi: Shooting 'Isolated'
Incident."

In July 2011, a thirty-five-year-old man killed a young boy in an Orthodox Jewish community in Brooklyn. As one resident stated, "You can't possibly describe ... how upset people are this boy was murdered by a
person living in the community, who shares his religion and his neighborhood." See Gilgoff and Marrapodi, "Child's Grisly Murder." Only a hand-
ful of such killings has occurred in the United States or Canada since the
Edelson/Horwitz incident. In February of 1966, for example, a twenty-
three-year-old man in Southfield, Michigan interrupted the Rabbi's Sabbath
sermon by seizing the microphone and ranting about the "phoniness and
hypocrisy" of the synagogue. With nine hundred congregants watching, the
man then pulled a gun, and after firing two bullets into the ceiling, shot the
Rabbi, and then shot himself. The shooter died three days later; the Rabbi
died the following month. The incident was memorialized in a short story
by Joyce Carol Oates, the young man's professor, "Detroit Almanac." In
May 1981, Phoenix restaurant entrepreneur Steven Steinberg stabbed his

wife Elana twenty-six times. The jury heard both anti-Semitic and misogy-
nistic testimony that described a materialistic and demanding "Jewish
American Princess" who exerted excessive pressure on her overworked
husband to earn more money. Despite a history of pathological gambling
and anger problems, and even after lying to police about thieves attacking
Elana, Steven was held up as the true victim in the case. His lawyers,
who brazenly argued that he stabbed his wife as he sleepwalked, asserted
a temporary insanity defence. The jury agreed that Steven simply "snapped"
trying to satisfy his spoiled wife, and voted to acquit him. Like Alice
Edelson, Elana was blamed for driving her husband to kill. See Frondorf,
Death of a "Jewish American Princess," passim.

9 Stanislawski, *A Murder in Lemberg*, 1.

10 For Canadian examples, see Dubinsky, *Improper Advances*, Kramer and
Mitchell, *Walk Towards the Gallows*, Walker, *Race on Trial*, Dubinsky
and Iacovetta, "Murder, Womanly Virtue, and Motherhood," Strange,
"Wounded Womanhood and Dead Men," and McLaren, "Males,
Migrants, and Murder." Kramer and Mitchell's work, as well the first
two cited articles, highlight those rare cases in which the accused were
minority or immigrant women.

11 Dinnerstein, *The Leo Frank Case.* In 1917 Atlanta, Leo Frank was
falsely accused of murdering a girl who worked in the pencil factory that
he managed. Sentenced first to death, then to life imprisonment, Frank
was eventually lynched by an angry mob. In *The Butcher's Tale*, Smith
describes the hysteria surrounding the "ritual murder" of a Christian
boy, and reminds us of the blood-libel charges consistently leveled
against European Jewry between the thirteenth and nineteenth centuries.
See the opening maps, for example.

12 Dubinsky, *Improper Advances*, 140.

13 Ibid., 139-40.

14 Auster, *The Invention of Solitude*, 36. Auster's grandparents, Harry and
Anna, immigrated to America from Austria, and after failed business
ventures in a variety of cities, including Peterborough, Ontario, they settled in Kenosha, Wisconsin. In order to avenge Harry's adultery as well
as his spending, Anna retrieved her pistol from under her mattress and,
feeling she "was just like crazy," shot her husband several times. In April
1919, she was acquitted of the murder charge. See Auster, *The Invention*

of Solitude, 38, 41, 43, 45. Many thanks to author and poet Lil Blume for bringing this book to my attention.

15 Menkis, "Antisemitism in the Evolving Nation," 49.

16 Ibid., 41-9; Little, 'No Car, No Radio, No Liquor Permit,' 78.

17 See, for example, Abella, *A Coat of Many Colours*, 179–205, Abella and Troper, *None is Too Many*, and Levitt and Shaffir, *The Riot at Christie Pits*.

18 Levitt and Shaffir, *The Riot at Christie Pits*.

19 OJA, Rabinovich, "Isolated Actions," 1–2.

20 Arcand also did so at a Catholic church in Ottawa. Alan Abelson interview.

21 OJA, Rabinovich, "Isolated Actions," 4–5.

22 Ibid.

23 Ibid., 7; COA, Box 1 (69D04) – BPC, File – 31 May 1935, sworn statement by Herbert G. Munro, 22 May 1935.

24 The *Journal* noted simply, for example, that before testifying, Ben Edelson "was sworn under the Jewish oath." After the acquittal, it referred to Doctor as the "well known Ottawa Jewish barrister," but did so while describing the praise heaped on him by legal colleagues. The paper also observed that at Edelson's home a day after the verdict, a group of animated female family and friends "were discussing affairs in Yiddish." See "Ben Edelson Goes on the Stand and Tells How Horwitz Was Shot," *The Ottawa Evening Journal*, 18 January 1932, 13; "Edelson Back at Store Today after Acquittal," *The Ottawa Evening Journal*, 18 January 1932, 1; "Verdict More than Expected Says Edelson," *The Ottawa Evening Journal*, 18 January 1932, 13. Perhaps only the *Journal*'s description of Ben as having a "swarthy countenance" could be interpreted as pejorative. See "Ben Edelson Arraigned on Charge of Murder and Remanded a Week," *The Ottawa Evening Journal*, 25 November 1931, 3. In the French-language press, a lone reference to Ben and Jack as "bien connus de la colonie juive" ("well known in the Jewish community") appears in "Jack Horwitz Est Tué chez un Bijoutier" ["Jack Horwitz is Killed at a Jeweller's"], *L'Action catholique*, 25 Novembre 1931, 1.

25 Carolyn A. Conley notes that the term "respectability" is not easily defined, and is therefore "problematic" for historians. But, as she asserts, and as this book will demonstrate, "the importance of 'respectability'

cannot be overestimated." Its associated expectations were closely linked to issues of gender, race, and class: it generally incorporated notions of financial independence, sober living, fine speech, personal cleanliness, domestic order and tidiness, appropriate dress, and polite and lawful behaviour. As Conley points out, respectable citizens did not always conform to all of these dictates. But even if, like Ben Edelson, they broke the law, they did not necessarily sacrifice their respectability: "merely being convicted of violating the law did not render a person criminal or even non-respectable." See Conley, *The Unwritten Law*, 4–6.

26 See, for example, Troper, *The Defining Decade*

27 Dubinsky, *Improper Advances*, 112. Dubinsky is referring specifically to trials of sex crimes here, but, as will be mentioned in Chapter 6, the Edelson/Horwitz murder trial resembled a sexual assault trial in some significant ways. Carolyn A. Conley supports the point that judges and juries were swayed by the respectability of the accused, and "until and unless a man of respectable reputation proved that he had renounced society's standards on a permanent basis," they generally found him to be "deserving of mercy." See Conley, *The Unwritten Law*, 178–9.

28 Michael Mandel argues that courts determine the severity of a sentence not only by assessing the nature of the crime, but the offender as a "social being." The courts find that a lesser punishment is warranted based on the offender's "conformity to the capitalist system," that is, his class position and privilege. See Comack and Balfour, *The Power to Criminalize*, 143. Middle-class respectability did not always serve a defendant well in the courtroom, however. Constance Backhouse writes that in the rape and seduction cases of MP Louis Auger in 1929 and 1930, Auger "found his status as a middle-class, male parliamentarian to be of little protection; in the end it worked to his considerable disadvantage." See Backhouse, "Rape in the House of Commons," 41.

29 Dubinsky, *Improper Advances*, 23.

30 Roediger, *The Wages of Whiteness*, 13–14; Ignatiev, *How the Irish Became White*, 2–3.

31 Brodkin, *How Jews Became White Folks*, 36–7.

32 Dick, "A Tale of Two Cultures, 522–4. For a detailed examination on the origins of the provocation defence, see Horder, *Provocation and Responsibility*.

33 McLaren, "Males, Migrants, and Murder," 175.

34 Morton, "Jury Nullification?" Two cases involving suspected or certain
    jury nullification include those of Clara Ford (1895) and Carrie Davies
    (1910). See Strange, "Wounded Womanhood and Dead Men," 149-88.
    Relatively recent Canadian cases include *R. v. Morgentaler* [1988] 1 SCR
    30 at 78; *R. v. Latimer* [2001] SCC ISCR3; and *R. v. Krieger* [2005]
    ABCA 202. See Morton, "Jury Nullification?"

35 Morton, "Jury Nullification?"

36 McLaren, "Males, Migrants, and Murder," 174–5.

37 White, *Negotiating Responsibility*, 17.

38 Ibid., 103; Dubinsky, *Improper Advances*, 25.

39 Dubinsky, *Improper Advances*, 127.

40 Hyman, *Gender and Assimilation in Modern Jewish History*, 107.

41 Karen Dubinsky notes that for a woman victimized in a rape case, "the
    surest way to protect one's reputation was, sadly, to die." See Dubinsky,
    Improper Advances, 20.

42 Kramer and Mitchell, *Walk towards the Gallows*, 168.

43 Dubinsky, *Improper Advances*, 24.

44 Ibid., 134.

45 AllGreatQuotes.

CHAPTER ONE

1 "Parts of Bullet Found," *The Ottawa Evening Journal*, 15 January 1932,
    7.

2 "Today's Official Weather Report," *The Ottawa Evening Journal*, 15
    January 1932, 1.

3 "Widow of Horwitz on Stand in Murder Trial," *The Ottawa Evening
    Citizen*, 16 January 1932," 1; "Mrs. Horwitz Tells Story of Family
    Trouble," *The Ottawa Evening Citizen*, 16 January 1932," 10; "Ben S.
    Edelson Is Acquitted on Murder Charge," *The Ottawa Evening Citizen*,
    18 January 1932," 14.

4 "Ben S. Edelson Is Acquitted," 14.

5 Lillian Katznelson interview.

6 Dina Edelson interview.

7 "Ben S. Edelson Is Acquitted," 14.

8 Ibid.

9 Ibid.

10 Ibid.

11 "Mrs. Jack Horwitz Tells Story," 1; "Widow of Horwitz on Stand," 1;
    "Mrs. Horwitz Tells Story at Edelson Trial," *The Ottawa Evening
    Journal*, 16 January 1932, 1.

12 "Widow Relates Details of," *The Ottawa Evening Journal*, 16 January
    1932, 22. This declaration suggested that Isaac Jacob (Jack), Shirley
    (Joyce), and/or Elihu (Eli), seven, five, and four, respectively, were Jack's
    offspring.

13 "Widow Relates Details of," 22. Given that birth control, even if care-
    fully practiced, was generally unreliable in the 1920s, it is feasible that
    Alice became pregnant by Jack, especially in view of the eight-year span
    of their relationship.

14 "Lorenzo Lemieux," *The Ottawa Evening Journal*, 2 December 1931,
    14; "Ben S. Edelson Is Acquitted," 14.

15 Dina Edelson interview.

16 "Widow Relates Details of," 22.

17 "Ben Edelson Goes to Trial at Assizes Next January; New Evidence is
    Presented," *The Ottawa Evening Journal*, 16 December 1931, 15.

18 Ibid.; "Mrs. Horwitz Tells Story," 10; "Crowded Court Tense as Accused
    Tells Dramatic Story," *The Ottawa Evening Journal*, 18 January 1932, 14.

19 "Mrs. Horwitz Tells Story," 10; "Widow Relates Details of," 22.

20 "Widow Relates Details of," 22; "Ben S. Edelson Is Acquitted," 14;
    "Crowded Court Tense," 14.

21 "Ben Edelson Goes to Trial," 15; "Mrs. Horwitz Tells Story," 10; "Ben
    S. Edelson Is Acquitted," 15.

22 "Lorenzo Lemieux," 14.

23 "Ben Edelson Goes to Trial," 15.

24 "Lorenzo Lemieux," 14.

25 "Widow of Horwitz on Stand," 1; "Mrs. Horwitz Tells Story," 10.

26 Samuel Rosen, *Ontario, Canada Marriages*; Yetta Rosen, *Ontario,
    Canada Births*; Jacob Horowitz [Horwitz], *Quebec Vital and Church
    Records*. In addition to the incorrect spelling of Jack's last name, the
    records cite Yetta's first name as "Tetta."

27 Lillian Katznelson interview.

28 "Montreal Social," *Canadian Jewish Review*, 1 October 1926, 2.

29 "Ben S. Edelson Is Acquitted," 14.

30 Lillian Katznelson interview.

31 "Ben S. Edelson Is Acquitted," 14.

32 Edelson employee Lorenzo Lemieux later testified at both the coroner's inquest and the preliminary hearing that Edelson indicated the caller was the wife of Alice's would-be lover. See "Sensational Evidence Given at Horwitz Inquest,"*The Ottawa Evening Journal*, 2 December 1931, 13, and "Ben Edelson Goes to Trial," 15.

33 "Ben Edelson Found Not Guilty and Is a Free Man," *The Ottawa Evening Journal*, 18 January 1932, 13. Affirming the caller was Yetta, who herself had motivation for Jack's murder, might have only made Ben seem guiltier.

34 "Employe[e] of Ben Edelson Tells of Calling Doctor to Attend Jack Horwitz," *The Ottawa Evening Journal*, 26 November 1931, 17; "Portion of Bullet," 2.

35 "Ben Edelson Goes on the Stand and tells how Horwitz Was Shot," *The Ottawa Evening Citizen*, 18 January 1932, 13.

36 "Edelsons Still Holding Key to Fatal Shooting," *The Ottawa Evening Citizen*, 26 November 1931, 3.

37 "Ben Edelson Goes on the Stand," 13.

38 "Ben S. Edelson Is Acquitted," 14.

39 Ibid.

40 "Ottawa Jeweler Faces Trial on Capital Charge," *The Ottawa Evening Citizen*, 14 January 1932, 2; "Portion of Bullet," 2; "Ben S. Edelson Is Acquitted," 14. Lorenzo Lemieux's version of events as relayed at the coroner's inquest never indicated that Alice and Jack left the car, nor did it reference Edelson's physical attempt to detain the car. See "Sensational Evidence Given,"13.

41 "Edelsons Still Holding Key," 1, 3.

42 "Ben S. Edelson Is Acquitted," 14; "Ben Edelson Found Not Guilty," 13.

43 "Ben S. Edelson Is Acquitted," 14.

44 Ibid.; "Sensational Evidence Given," 13; "Employe[e] of Ben Edelson," 17.

45 "Ben S. Edelson Is Acquitted," 14; "Sensational Evidence Given," 13.

46 "Sensational Evidence Given," 13.

47 "Ben Edelson Goes to Trial," 15.

48 "Ben S. Edelson Is Acquitted," 15.

49 "Sensational Evidence Given," 13.

50 "Ben S. Edelson Is Acquitted," 13.

51 Ibid., 14; "Sensational Evidence Given," 13.

52 "Lorenzo Lemieux," 14; "City Police Striving to Solve Mystery of Jewelry Store Drama," *The Ottawa Evening Citizen*, 25 November 1931, 1.

53 "Ottawa Jeweler Faces Trial," 2.

54 Ibid.

55 "Sensational Evidence Given," 13; Ibid.

56 "City Police Striving," 7.

57 "Lorenzo Lemieux," 14.

58 "Ben Edelson Arraigned on Charge of Murder and Remanded a Week," *The Ottawa Evening Journal*, 25 November 1931, 3; "Ben Edelson Goes to Trial," 15.

59 "Lorenzo Lemieux," 14; "City Police Striving," 7.

60 "Ben S. Edelson Is Acquitted," 14; "Sensational Evidence Given," 13; "Lorenzo Lemieux," 14.

61 Born in Vilna, Moses Doctor immigrated to Ottawa with his family in 1901 when he was a year old. His father, Rabbi Louis Doctor, eulogized as "one of the most devout orthodox Jews in the Capital," was a notable Jewish scholar and bibliophile, and after working as a *shochet* (ritual slaughter), became the cantor and rabbi of Ottawa's Rideau Street *shul* in 1902, a position he held for thirty-two years. His presence in the community did not go unrivaled by his accomplished son. Moses Doctor participated extensively in the synagogue, and in Jewish education pursuits, social service agencies, and Zionist groups. See OJA, IC, File – Doctor, Rev. Louis, "Ottawa Talmud Torah 1st Annual Banquet," program, 1969; OJA, IC, File – Doctor, Rev. Louis, "Rev. Louis Doctor Called by Death," *The Ottawa Citizen*, 20 September 1934; OJA, RSA, Box – Untitled Manuscript on Ten Decades of Jewish Life in Ottawa, File – Decade of Immigration … Saga of the Synagogues, 2; Max Bookman, "Excerpts from A History of the Jew in Canada's Capital," in *Canadian Jewish Reference Book and Directory 1963*, edited by Dr Eli Gottesman (Montreal: Jewish Institute of Higher Research, Central Rabbinical Seminary of Canada, 1963), 399; OJA, Finding Aid, IC, File – Florence, A.L.; "Moses Doctor Young Lawyer," 13.

62 "Ben S. Edelson Is Acquitted," 14; "Sensational Evidence Given," 13, "Lorenzo Lemieux," 14.

63 "Ben S. Edelson Is Acquitted," 14.

64 Ibid., 15.

65 Lillian Katznelson interview; Dina Edelson interview. Lillian heard the first version from her mother, and Dina heard the second version from her father.

66 Dina Edelson interview.

67 "Edelsons Still Holding Key," 1.

68 "States Mrs. Edelson Kissed Dying Man," *The Toronto Daily Star*, 2 December 1931 (internet).

69 "Hope to Finish Edelson Trial Tomorrow Night," *The Ottawa Evening Citizen*, 15 January 1932, 1; "Ben Edelson Arraigned," 3.

70 "Hope to Finish," 1; "Much Progress Made with Crown Evidence before Judge McEvoy," *The Ottawa Evening Citizen*, 15 January 1932, 8.

71 See Kramer and Mitchell, *Walk towards the Gallows*, 123, 146.

72 "City Police Striving," 7.

73 Dina Edelson interview.

74 "'The Guardsman' Now Showing at Regent Contains 'Play within a Play,'" *The Ottawa Evening Citizen*, 18 November 1931, 23; Untitled, *Journal*, 24 November 1931, 21; *The Guardsman*, IMDb; "*The Guardsman*," *The New York Times* www.movies.nytimes.com; "*The Guardsman*," Classic Film Guide. Disguising himself as a Russian officer, the husband romances his wife to test her fidelity. She succumbs to the soldier's affections, claiming, only once her dismayed husband admits to the ruse, that she knew it was him all along. The 1931 movie, based on Ferenc Molnar's play of the same name, starred the married Broadway thespian couple Alfred Lunt and Lynn Fontanne.

75 "Lorenzo Lemieux," 14.

76 Ibid.

77 "Horwitz Estate Divided among Three Persons," *The Ottawa Evening Citizen*, 27 November 1931, 2; "Coroner Says Not Known if any Witnesses," *The Ottawa Evening Journal*, 25 November 1931, 3. There is some discrepancy about how Harry Hertz, working that evening at the Horwitz family store at 46 Rideau Street, found out about the shooting, and arrived at the hospital on the heels of Jack being admitted: Harry later stated that he had received a call from Yetta informing him of the incident, and that he arrived at the hospital just before 10:00 pm, but Yetta variously stated that she did not know of the incident until after 11:00 pm, until 12:00 am, and until 12:40 am.

78 "Lorenzo Lemieux," 14; "Ben Edelson Goes to Trial," 15; "Parts of Bullet Found," 7.

79 "Ben Edelson Arraigned," 3. Sam Berger, born in 1900, grew up on King Edward Avenue in Lowertown, and was the son of Rabbi Joseph David Berger and Freda Baron who had immigrated to Ottawa. As the spiritual

leader of the Rideau Street Synagogue from 1902 to 1927, and the local authority on Jewish ritual, laws of *kashruth*, and Jewish marriage and divorce, Rabbi Berger served as a role model for his activist son. Berger's work on behalf of the Jewish community as a prominent leader and generous philanthropist of numerous religious, secular, and Zionist organizations continued throughout his life. See OJA, IC, File – Berger, Samuel, "Berger, Samuel," *Who's Who in Canadian Jewry*, 330; OJA, IC, File – Young Men's Hebrew Association, *The Booster*, January 1921, 5; OJA, IC, File – Berger, Samuel, "J.N.F. Negev Dinner in Honour of Samuel Berger, Q.C.," 9 December 1968 [hereafter "J.N.F. Negev Dinner"; OJA, IC, File – Berger, Samuel, Kathryn May, "The Grand Old Man of Canadian Football," *The Ottawa Citizen*, 12 April 1992 [hereafter May, "The Grand Old Man"]; "Samuel Berger President Local Zionist Branch," *The Ottawa Evening Citizen*, 15 January 1932, 26.

80 OJA, IC, File – Berger, Samuel, "J.N.F. Negev Dinner"; OJA, IC, File – Berger, Samuel, May, "The Grand Old Man." By 1939, Berger would be appointed Queen's Counsel. He would later distinguish himself as a prominent civic leader, and as a real estate and sports-franchise mogul. He would become especially well known as part owner of the Ottawa Rough Riders and owner of the Montreal Alouettes football clubs. He was also CFL president.

81 "Ben Edelson Arraigned," 3.

82 "Much Progress Made," 8.

83 "Ben S. Edelson Named Slayer of J. Horwitz," *The Ottawa Evening Citizen*, 10 December 1931, 4.

84 "Ben Edelson Arraigned," 3; Ibid., 4; "Lorenzo Lemieux," 14.

85 "Jeweler Is Slain, but None Says How," *The Toronto Globe*; 26 November 1931 (internet); "Ben Edelson Arraigned," 3; "Ottawa Community Stunned by Mysterious Shooting," *The Canadian Jewish Chronicle*, 27 November 1931, 8.

86 "City Police Striving," 7.

87 Ibid.; "Ben S. Edelson Named Slayer," 4; "Sensational Evidence Given," 13; "Lorenzo Lemieux," 14; "Mrs. Horwitz Tells Story," 10; "Widow Relates Details of," 22.

88 "Police Court Hearing in Edelson Case Starts," *The Ottawa Evening Journal*, 15 December 1931, 1. Jack's birth registry indicates his birth

date as 10 December 1897. His death certificate, however, shows his date of birth as 20 November 1901, which would have made him thirty years old rather than thirty-four years old at the time of his death. The newspapers consistently reported that he was thirty when he died. See Jacob Horwitz, *Ontario, Canada Births* and Jacob Horwitz, *Ontario, Canada Deaths*.

89 "Ben Edelson Goes to Trial," 15.

90 Jacob Horwitz, *Ontario, Canada Deaths*. Also see "Perform Autopsy Trying to Learn Cause of Death," *The Ottawa Evening Journal*, 25 November 1931, 1.

91 "Coroner Says," 1; "Coroner Says," 3.

92 "City Police Striving," 7.

93 "Coroner Says," 1.

94 "One Store Opens Two Are Closed," *The Ottawa Evening Journal*, 25 November 1931, 1.

95 "Wife of Ben Edelson Likely to Be Called as Witness at Probe," *The Ottawa Evening Journal*, 26 November 1931, 1.

96 "City Police Striving," 7; "'My Life Is Ruined,' Mrs. Jack Horwitz Cries in Sorrow," *The Ottawa Evening Journal*, 25 November 1931, 1.

97 Ibid.; "Ottawa Jeweller Fatally Wounded Dictates His Will," *The Toronto Daily Star*, 25 November 1931 (internet)

98 Ibid.

99 Eric Slone correspondence. Slone's maternal grandfather was Charles Horwitz.

100 "'My Life Is Ruined,'" 1.

101 "City Police Striving," 7.

102 "Hundreds Pay Last Tribute to Victim of Store Tragedy," *The Ottawa Evening Citizen*, 26 November, 1931, 1; "Wife of Ben Edelson," 1.

103 "Hundreds Pay Last Tribute," 1.

104 Ibid.; "Wife of Ben Edelson," 1. Rabbi Nathan Kollin of the King Edward, assisted by Rabbi A.H. Friedman of United Synagogues of Ottawa, and Cantors Stolnitz and Rabin, officiated at the service at both the home and the cemetery. "Wife of Ben Edelson," 1; 5; "Hundreds Pay Last Tribute," 1. As misfortune would have it, another Jewish funeral was taking place that day. Max Kapinsky, however, was a member of Rideau Street Synagogue. In addition to Kapinky's eight sons, "many members

of Ottawa's Jewish community as well as a large number of other friends
paid tribute." See "Obituary: Max Kapinsky," *The Ottawa Evening Citizen*, 26 November 1931, 20.

105 "Wife of Ben Edelson," 1.

106 "Ben Edelson Arraigned," 1.

107 Ibid., 3; "City Police Striving," 7.

108 "City Police Striving," 7.

109 "Ben Edelson Arraigned," 3.

110 "Hundreds Pay Last Tribute," 1.

111 See, for example, "Jack Horwitz, Victim of Shooting, and His Wife,"
The Ottawa Evening Journal, 25 November 1931, 1.

112 "Wife of Ben," 5; "Hundreds Pay Last Tribute," 1.

113 "Wife of Ben," 5.

114 Steven Chernove telephone interview.

115 "Estate of Late J. Horwitz, All Left to Widow," *The Ottawa Evening
Citizen*, 26 November 1931, 15; "Edelsons Still Holding Key," 3;
"Widow to Get Entire Estate," *The Ottawa Evening Journal*, 8 January
1932, 22.

116 "Estate of Late J. Horwitz," 15.

117 "Horwitz Estate Divided," 1; "Horwitz Will Leaves Estate among
Three," *The Ottawa Evening Journal*, 27 November 1931, 1.

118 "Horwitz Estate Divided," 1, 2.

119 "Legal Battle over Horwitz Estate Looms," *The Ottawa Evening
Journal*, 28 November 1931, 4.

120 COA, *1931 OCD*, 269.

121 "Legal Battle," 4.

122 "Dispute over Dead Man's Estate Causes Withdrawal of Horwitz Family
Counsel," *The Ottawa Evening Citizen*, 28 November 1931, 1.

123 "Sam Berger out of Horwitz Case," *The Ottawa Evening Journal*, 28
November 1931, 1.

124 "Samuel Berger President," 26.

125 "Samuel Berger Enters Contest in St. George's," *The Ottawa Evening
Journal*, 25 November 1931, 7. The *Journal* reported that there were
eight candidates vying for only two seats in city council. *The Canadian
Jewish Chronicle,* however, profiled Max Feller as one of seven, not
eight, candidates running for alderman of St George's Ward, and referred
to him as "the only Jewish candidate for aldermanic honours in the

Capital City." See "Max Feller," *The Canadian Jewish Chronicle*,
4 December 1931, 17.

126 "Dispute over Dead Man's Estate," 1.

127 Ibid.

128 "Ottawa Community Stunned," 8.

129 After 1931, there is no record of Yetta and Anita residing at the marital
home on Stewart Street, nor in any other dwelling in the city. COA, *1932
OCD*, 768.

130 "Widow to Get Entire Estate," 22.

131 Steven Chernove telephone interview; Steven Chernove correspondence.
Steven Chernove is a son of Anita, and a grandson of Yetta; Yetta Rosen
Horwitz, *Quebec Vital and Church Records*. Thanks to Sharon Edelson
for locating this document.

132 Rebecca Horwitz, *Ontario, Canada Deaths*; Max Horwitz, *Ontario,
Canada Deaths*. Max Horwitz died of ALS nine years before baseball
player Lou Gehrig was diagnosed with the disease that would later bear
his name. The Hebrew inscription on the Horwitzes' adjoining tombstones, excerpted from a Hebrew prayer for martyrs, notes that "They
were loving and pleasant during their lives. And the two of them were
not separated in death." See Harlow, ed., *Siddur Sim Shalom* [prayer-
book], 421, line 4. Many thanks to Bill and Rose Klein for this reference.

133 "Edelsons Still Holding Key," 3.

134 "Ben Edelson Arraigned," 3; "City Police Striving," 7; "Lorenzo
Lemieux," 14.

135 "Lorenzo Lemieux," 14; "City Police Striving," 7.

136 "Much Progress Made," 8.

137 Ibid.; "Ben S. Edelson Named Slayer," 4; "Ben Edelson Arraigned," 3;
"Lorenzo Lemieux," 14.

138 "Much Progress Made," 8.

139 "Edelsons Still Holding Key," 3.

140 "Ottawa Jeweler Faces Trial," 2.

141 "Mrs. Horwitz Tells Story," 10.

142 Detective-Sergeant MacDonald, for example, later testified that he did
not remember seeing Alice at the hospital. When Harry Hertz was
asked who was in the operating room when he arrived, he said "several
nurses," despite Dr Danby's testimony that Alice, Harry, and others were
in the room together. Dr Shapiro, who tended to Horwitz starting at

11:45, encountered nurses, Charles, and Yetta, but also made no mention of seeing Alice. See "Ottawa Jeweler Faces Trial," 2; "Much
Progress Made," 8; "Portion of Bullet," 2.

143 "Horwitz Estate Divided," 2.

144 "Ben Edelson Arraigned," 3.

145 Lillian Katznelson interview. The *Journal* reported that as Alice entered
the house, she shrieked "You know what it is! You know what it is!" See
"Ben Edelson Arraigned," 3.

146 "Ben Edelson Arraigned," 1, 3; "Employe[e] of Ben Edelson," 17; Lillian
Katznelson interview; "Are Satisfied Three People Only in Store," *The
Ottawa Evening Journal*, November 30 1931, 7.

147 "Jeweler Is Slain but None Says How."

148 "Ben Edelson Arraigned," 1, 3; "Employe[e] of Ben Edelson," 17; "Are
Satisfied Three People," 7.

149 "Edelsons Still Holding Key," 1.

150 "City Police Striving," 7; "Ben Edelson Arraigned," 1; "Verdict of Coroner's Jury Finds that Jack Horwitz Was Shot by Ben Edelson," *The Ottawa Evening Journal*, 10 December 1931, 2.

151 "States Mrs. Edelson Kissed Dying Man."

152 "Mysterious Shooting at Ottawa," *The Cornwall Standard*, 26 November 1931, 8.

153 "City Police Striving," 7.

CHAPTER TWO

1 Rosenberg, *Canada's Jews*, see Table 6, p.12; Table 7, p.12; Table 10,
p. 20.

2 By the early nineteenth century, Friedrichstadt was an important site
of commerce, a trading centre for hides and furs, and manufactured a
variety of items, including cigars, soap, and chocolate. Although this
commercial significance gradually declined with the building of the
Riga-Dunaburg Railroad in 1862, the town's population steadily rose.
Rosenthal, "Friedrichstadt."

3 The children were Isidore, Israel, Samuel, Benjamin, and Rose.

4 Lillian Katznelson interview.

5 SE, picture postcard of *Noordland*, 1907, from Ben Edelson. *The Thirteenth Census of the United States: 1910-Population* incorrectly lists

Ben's year of immigration to America as 1909. Ben arrived in Liverpool on 10 July, and on 17 July set sail for America on the *Noordland*, a four-hundred-foot liner that could accommodate five hundred third-class passengers. See SE, picture postcard of *Noordland*, 1907, from Ben Edelson. Also see "S/S Noordland, Red Star"; "The ShipsList – L Archives."

6 Lillian Katznelson interview.

7 Lenarcic, "Jewellery and Silverware Industry." *The Canadian Encyclopedia HISTOR!CA.*

8 In addition to selling and repairing watches and jewelry, the shop sold Edison and Victor phonographs and parts, as well as musical instruments and supplies. SE, "Emanuel Gershuny," letter of recommendation, 24 November 1908; South River Historical and Preservation Society, "South River Population, 1880–2000."

9 South River Historical and Preservation Society, "Aftermath of the 1908 South River Fire."

10 SE, "Emanuel Gershuny," letter of recommendation, 24 November 1908.

11 NYPL, *1910/11 Jersey City, New Jersey City Directory*, 715-17. The versatile Sorenson, who in addition to being a watchmaker, jeweller, and optician (like jewellery, eyeglass frames were made of silver, and required deft hands and small tools), was a justice of the peace, and lived and worked at 25 Montgomery Street where Ben also resided. See SE, "Repair Check," A. Sorenson; Lenarcic, "Jewellery and Silverware Industry" The Canadian Encyclopedia HISTORICA; SE, Benjamin Edelson business card; NYPL, *1910/11 Jersey City, New Jersey City Directory*, 495, 181.

12 Lillian Katznelson interview with author.

13 Ibid.

14 SE, "Hulse and Playfair, Funeral Directors," statement of interment, 2 January 1973; Ibid. Lillian noted that her mother was thirteen when her parents met and sixteen when they married, which would mean that Alice was born in 1895, but no personal or official documents cite this year; SE, Canadian passport and citizenship papers, Alice Edelson, 1961.

15 Most of the Jews, composed largely of the labouring poor, were modest shop-owners and merchants, but many worked in skilled trades, including watch-making and tailoring, in service work as porters, drivers, and maids, in religious positions as rabbis and ritual slaughterers, and increasingly in professional occupations. See Rosin, "Panevezys (Ponevezh) Lithuania"; Sudarsky and Katzenelenbogen, eds. *Lite.*

16 In May of 1881, over half the town had been destroyed by fire, including eight streets with Jewish businesses and three of its ten synagogues. Over the next two years, there were several more devastating fires in which hundreds of people were left homeless and impoverished. See Rosin, "Panevezys (Ponevezh) Lithuania"; Sudarsky and Katzenelenbogen, eds. *Lite.*

17 Sharon Edelson correspondence, 16 September 2008. The children were Alice, Rose, Nathan, and Samuel. Both Ben and Alice had a sister named Rose and a brother named Samuel. They would also name their eldest child Samuel, who would marry a woman named Rose.

18 SE, Ben Edelson's "Address Book"; SE, "Certificate of Marriage Registration," 28 August 1964.

19 SE, Canadian passport and citizenship papers, Alice Edelson, 1961.

20 When Alice turned sixty-five, she refused to collect old-age pension for fear that her age would become known. Ben convinced her to accept the payments by giving her the idea to offer the money to charity. Dina Edelson interview. Alice's pride in her appearance also motivated her to dye her hair black, and to visit Goldberg's Beauty Salon, where she routinely got manicures to refurbish her long, red nails. Dina Edelson interview; Mary Goldberg interview.

21 SE, Benjamin Edelson business card, Alfred T.F. Sorenson; SE, "Repair Check," A. Sorenson.

22 SE, homesteaders postcard, Ben Edelson, New York City to Alice Coblentz, New York City, 13 June 1911.

23 SE, monogram postcard, Ben Edelson, New York City to Alice Coblentz, New York City, 24 July 1911.

24 Benjamin Edelson, *Thirteenth Census of the United States Federal Census: 1910-Population.*

25 NYPL, 1910/11 *Jersey City, New Jersey City Directory*, 181; Benjamin Edelson, *Thirteenth Census of the United States Federal Census: 1910-Population.*

26 SE, Ben Edelson's "Address Book."

27 This is not to say that the Jewish population itself declined: in Canada, it climbed from 126,196 to 156,726, and in Ontario, from 47,798 to 62,383. Rosenberg, *Canada's Jews*, see Table 6, p.12; Table 7, p.12; Table 10, p. 20.

28 Ben's daughter Lillian remembered that "he knew every working part of

a watch." He could also fix clocks, and was later commissioned to adjust the Peace Tower clock on Parliament Hill. Lillian Katznelson interview.

29 Lillian Katznelson interview. In 1915, Alice's brother and mother also came to live in Quebec. Nathan Coblentz established Nat's Auto Parts in Montreal, and Chaya Coblentz, a widow for many years, married Lachine widower Yakov Schecter in 1918. A Russian immigrant, Schecter found success as the owner of Lachine Home Furnishings, and was the father of eight children. Yakov's daughter Bess remembered that "life at home was … difficult. Chaya was always exacting; she had not adjusted well to the maternal role she had accepted." Bess recalled that "although she was a decent person, Chaya unfortunately was not someone meant to be a stepmother. She was often cross and short-tempered with the younger stepchildren which, of course, led her to bicker with my father … She seldom treated the younger children with any warmth or much consideration." Despite Chaya's new heavy responsibilities, she at least married well which was most always preferable to the looming poverty of widowhood. See OJA, "Bonds Will Honour Bess Greenberg," *Ottawa Jewish Bulletin*, 22 February 1991, 1; Greenberg, *My Memoirs*, 65, 22–4, 91, 27. For Yakov, the prospect of raising eight children alone no doubt seemed daunting, and to the shock and dismay of his family, he married Chaya a mere six months after his wife died of cancer. His twelve-year-old daughter Bess was only informed of the courtship on the day of the wedding. Chaya's daughter Rose (Alice's sister), who never married, also periodically lived with them. See Greenberg, *My Memoirs*, 22–4.

30 The exceptions here are the three cities with the greatest Jewish population, Montreal (5.95%), Toronto (7.34%), and Winnipeg (7.87%), and the city of Windsor, Ontario (3.52%) with the seventh greatest Jewish population. See Rosenberg, *Canada's Jews*, see Table 86, p.116. The percentage of Jews in Ottawa at this time has also been cited at the slightly lower 1.92 %. See Goldberg, "The Depression and War," 55.

31 COA, Fletcher, *Capital Walks*, 79–80.

32 Lillian Katznelson interview; SE, Ben Edelson's "Address Book."

33 OJA, Lo, "The Path from Peddling," 23; Lillian Katznelson interview.

34 Alan Abelson interview.

35 As a boy, Norman Levine lived on Guigues Street at King Edward, and recalled that aside from his family and the one next door, the entire street

was French Canadian. See OJA, Levine, *In Lower Town*. In 1916, The Lieff family lived on McGee Street between St Andrew and St Patrick where most of their neighbours were "friendly French Canadians." See Lieff, *Gathering Rosebuds*, 47.

36 COA, *1931 OCD*, 699.

37 The Jewish Max Berger, who lived with his wife Bella, was a furrier who used their home as his workshop; the French I. Houle, who lived with his wife Sophie and their four adult children, worked at a wholesale fine produce business. Children Grace and Yvonne clerked at Price Bakery, Emile clerked at the Department of National Revenue, and Romeo worked at the Embassy Theatre. See COA, *1931 OCD*, 699, 270.

38 OJA, Kershman, "Family, Friends, Lower Town" [side 2]. Historian and Archivist Shelley Berman coined the phrase "The *shtetl* of Lower Town"; Goldberg, "The Depression and War," 55.

39 OJA, Kershman, "Family, Friends, Lower Town" [side 1]; OJA, Kershman, "Lower Town Tour" [side 1]; Steinman, *A Jewish Odyssey*, 23.

40 OJA, Kershman, "Lower Town Tour" [side 1].

41 Ibid.; OJA, Norman Levine, *In Lower Town* (Ottawa: Commoners Publishing, 1977); OJA, Kershman, "Family, Friends, Lower Town" [side 2]; Rubin, *Those Pesky Weeds*, 45. Noted writer Norman Levine remembered that his Jewish neighbour on Murray Street peddled with "a broken-down horse pulling a shabby wagon with old mattresses, old bed-springs, bottles and sacks," and called out through the streets of Lowertown "rags, rags for sale." See OJA, Levine, *In Lower Town*, and Adelene Hyman interview. Machziki Hadath synagogue was known as "The Peddlers' Shul." See OJA, Kershman, "Family, Friends, Lower Town" [side 1].

42 OJA, Lo, "The Path from Peddling," 17.

43 OJA, Levine, *In Lower Town*.

44 OJA, Lo, "The Path from Peddling," 24, 21-2.

45 COA, *1931 OCD*, 875. Like Max Horwitz and Ben Edelson, many of these Jewish retailers had been trained in Europe as watchmakers, and were valued for their exacting skills (Lillian Katznelson interview). Max owned two successful stores, one at 177 1/2 Bank Street, and one at 46 Rideau Street. Four of his five sons entered the jewellery business, as well – Joseph in Detroit, and Charles and Phil, as well as their sister's hus-

band, Harry Hertz, working for the family business in Ottawa. Charles was also the manager of Jack's booming stores on Bank and Sparks Streets. And the potential existed for greater family involvement given that, before his death, Jack was contemplating expansion. See COA, *1931 OCD*, 269, 261; "Ben Edelson Arraigned on Charge of Murder and Remanded a Week," *The Ottawa Evening Journal*, 25 November 1931, 3; "City Police Striving to Solve Mystery of Jewelry Store Drama," *The Ottawa Evening Citizen*, 25 November 1931, 7.

The elegant 1925 wedding of Jack's sister Sarah reveals a family for whom the jewellery trade proved lucrative. The newspaper devoted a column to describing "an interesting wedding of much charm." The décor at the Rideau Street Synagogue included "quantities of ferns and cut flowers," and following the ceremony, "a largely attended reception and dance" was held at Racquet Court. The groom wore tails and white gloves, and the bride "was prettily gowned in white crepe meteor, beaded in crystal." She departed the reception for her American honeymoon wearing "a smart black velvet coat dress trimmed with Kolinsky, a seal wrap and a black satin hat." The couple gave pearl necklaces to the women in their wedding party, and gold penknives to the men. See OJA, J.C. Horwitz Collection, File 1 – Clippings, "Synagogue Is Scene of Pretty Wedding" [1925], reprinted in "Couple of the Year Celebrate 50th," *The Gazette* [Montreal], 11 January 1975. Even after the successive deaths of Max and Rebecca by 1930, the elder Horwitz children were able to secure the future of sixteen-year-old Jacie. He graduated from Queen's University in 1936, and from Osgoode Hall in 1939, becoming a prominent Ottawa lawyer. He would later become a renowned provincial court judge. See OJA, Finding Aid, Judge Jacie Charles Horwitz.

46 Lillian Katznelson interview.
47 SE, Ben Edelson's "Address Book."
48 Greenberg, *My Memoirs*, 30.
49 COA, *1931 OCD*, 774.
50 Rankin, *Meet me at the Château*, 46, 61–4, 71–2.
51 COA, *1931 OCD*, 776.
52 SE, "Benjamin Edelson Eulogy."
53 Lillian Katznelson interview; Dina Edelson interview.
54 Lionel Metrick interview.

55 Most often, they were French girls from large families who were desperate for work, and toiled for cheap wages until they got married. Lillian Katznelson interview; Dina Edelson interview.

56 OJA, Kershman, "Family, Friends, Lower Town" [side 1]. See, for example, Steinman, *A Jewish Odyssey*, 22.

57 Joseph, "Jewish Women in Canada," 190–1.

58 Lillian Katznelson interview; Sharon Edelson correspondence, 19 June 2008; Dina Edelson interview.

59 Francis Shaffer telephone interview; Suzie Gellman interview.

60 SE, "Benjamin Edelson Eulogy."

61 "Mysterious Shooting at Ottawa," *The Cornwall Standard*, 26 November 1931, 8.

62 Suzie Gellman interview.

63 With their fluctuating earnings, the immigrant Greenbergs, for example, moved between Lowertown and Sandy Hill. In 1915, Roger, a fruit peddler, and his new bride Rose lived on St Andrew Street in Lowertown; by the 1920s, when business improved they lived on Blackburn Street in Sandy Hill. But with the Depression in the 1930s, "each year seemed to herald another move, and another downward slide, both economically and socially." The Greenbergs, who by 1933 had six children, were forced to move back to the "much tougher neighbourhood" of Lowertown. OJA, IC, File – Minto, Wayne Skene, *Minto: A Tradition of Family Values: The First Fifty Years* (Canada: Tribute books, 2005), 10–11, 13. Eventually, Roger Greenberg founded Minto Construction, and created, along with his sons, a real estate and development empire.

64 Lieff, *Gathering Rosebuds*, 71–2.

65 Dina Edelson interview.

66 Lillian Katznelson interview.

67 "Favours Educating Jewish Children in Jewish Ideals," *The Ottawa Evening Citizen*, 25 November 1931," 22.

68 As Thelma Steinman recalled of her trips to and from public school, "many were the times we had to reroute, or slink around corners, to avoid the taunts and threats of the neighbourhood French children … The boys were especially at risk because the French boys would gang up, pick fights and beat them up." Steinman, *A Jewish Odyssey*, 25.

69 Draper and Karlinsky, "Abraham's Daughters," 77.

70 OJA, Lo, "The Path from Peddling," 40.

71 OJA, Hart, editor, *The Jew in Canada*, 399.

72 "Moses Doctor Young Lawyer Is Found Dead," *The Ottawa Evening Journal*, 21 March 1934," 13.

73 OJA, Lo, "The Path from Peddling," 40.

74 Alan Abelson interview. Alan is the son of Jess Abelson.

75 COA, Box 1 (69D04) – BPC, File – 29 April 1935, letter from Lillian Freiman to Chief Joliat, 25 April 1935. In an official report to Joliat, Boehmer recounted the events that motivated the charge against him, but fervently denied his guilt. A month prior, Boehmer had viewed a movie about the Great War. Sometime later, he spoke about the film with Mr A.E. Brown, a First World War veteran who had also seen it. Boehmer said, "Say Brownie tell me the truth as you should know, is this an honest to goodness picture? Or is it Jewish propaganda to stir up another war?" Boehmer insisted that he "did not make any statement that was detrimental to her [Freiman] or any other Canadian whether born in Canada or naturalized or any subject of His Majesty King George V." See COA, Box 1 (69D04) – BPC, File – 29 April 1935, Ottawa Police Department General Report to Chief Constable Emile Joliat from Constable H. Boehmer, 26 April 1935.

76 COA, Box 1 (69D04) – BPC, File – 29 April 1935, letter from Secretary, Board of Commissioners of Police to Lillian Freiman, 30 April 1935.

77 OJA, Rabinovich, "Isolated Actions," 7; COA, Box 1 (69D04) – BPC, File – 31 May 1935, letter from Chief Constable Emile Joliat to The Board of Commissioners of Police, 31 May 1935. Perhaps it was only a matter of luck that Detective Tissot, a member of the Ottawa police force in 1931, had not been assigned to the Edelson case.

78 OJA, Rabinovich, "Isolated Actions," 8–10.

79 Figler, *Lillian and Archie Freiman*, 262–3.

80 The trial scrutinized the *Talmud* and Jewish philanthropy and business practices as much as Tissot's misdeeds. Even with the legal defeat, and the general censure of Tissot by the Ottawa public and press, he remained steadfast in his anti-Semitic beliefs, encouraged by the fifty supporters who greeted him outside the courtroom. See Medres, *Between the Wars*, 92; Freiman, *Don't Fall off the Rocking Horse*, 54–5; OJA, Lo, "The Path from Peddling," 44; OJA, Rabinovich, "Isolated Actions," 8–10.

81 Giusti, "Building Foundations," 11. Most notably, Irving Abella has

advanced this argument. Like me, Giusti argues that the Ottawa Jewish
community was committed, organized, and unified.

82 Giusti, "Building Foundations," 21–2. In November of 1931, The *Citizen* reported on a talk delivered in New York by Dr Bernhard Kahn, the
European Director of the American Jewish Joint Distribution Committee. In an eerie prediction, Kahn declared that "Jews of eastern and central Europe face a crisis which may readily develop into an irremediable
catastrophe." The following month, the *Journal* reported that a two-day
campaign in Ottawa was launched to raise funds for Eastern European
Jews. Almost two hundred people attended an evening of addresses by
New York rabbi Jacob Wise, son of the famed rabbi Stephen Wise, and
chairman of the National Joint Distribution Committee, and by Ottawa
rabbis Nathan Kollin and A.H. Freidman. Rabbi Wise emphasized that
"the Jews in Eastern Europe today are facing economic slavery, slavery
as hard as that in ancient Egypt, the most ruthless, senseless, bitter thing
in the world today. Millions of our brethren in Eastern Europe tremble
today, not only for their daily bread, but for the simplest, most elementary rights." Rabbis Kollin and Freidman implored members of the community, many of whom were still affiliated with *landsmanshaftn* (mutual
aid societies whose membership was organized according to the village
from where one hailed) to help in offering relief. Their words were
echoed by activist and philanthropist Lillian Freiman, who also spoke
"of the wretched condition of the Jewish people abroad." Before the
evening was through, the community raised $2,030, almost half of the
projected two-day goal. Seventeen teams of fundraisers planned to blanket the city the next day to collect the remaining amount. See "Stirring
Appeals to Help Stricken Jewish People Made by Noted Leaders," *The
Ottawa Evening Journal*, 28 December 1931, 2.

83 OJA, Max Bookman Collection, Box 2, File – A History of Ottawa
Young Judaea – 1933, Max Bookman, "A History of Ottawa Young Judaea," Ninth National Convention of Canadian Young Judaea, September 2, 3, 4, 1933, 7. The Zionist Organization of Ottawa was formed in
January 1932. Its first president, Sam Berger, was installed at "a largely
attended meeting." See "Samuel Berger President Local Zionist Branch,"
The Ottawa Evening Citizen, 15 January 1932, 26.

84 Hadassah-Wizo Organization of Canada, *Seventy-Fifth Anniversary*, 91,

41, 53, 55. Young Judaea was the chief Zionist social and cultural youth group in Ottawa. Established in Ottawa in 1899, the group gained ground in 1924 when it united with the national federation, and secured effective local leadership. It attracted one hundred and thirty-five members. Although the group virtually disbanded by the late 1920s, in 1930 it returned revitalized, boasting a record membership of two hundred and fifty young men and women. By the autumn of 1931, Ottawa Young Judaea was the third largest such organization in Canada, just behind the much larger communities of Montreal and Toronto. See OJA, Max Bookman Collection, Box 2, File – A History of Ottawa Young Judaea – 1933, Max Bookman, "A History of Ottawa Young Judaea," Ninth National Convention of Canadian Young Judaea, September 2, 3, 4, 1933, 7–9, 11.

85 Draper and Karlinsky, "Abraham's Daughters," 77.

86 Draper, "The Role of Canadian Jewish Women," 5.

87 Draper and Karlinsky, "Abraham's Daughters," 79. The Labour Zionist Pioneer Women's Organization, in contrast, attracted immigrant, working-class women.

88 Alice's chapter oversaw the Palestine booth, while the three other Ottawa chapters ran booths devoted to traditional pursuits such as "fancy work," "aprons," flowers," "candy," and "dolls," and to more unconventional hobbies such as "smokes," and "fortune telling." Along with several other women, including her sister Rose, Alice supervised the stationery booth. After witnessing the efforts of these volunteers, Freiman's husband Archibald remarked that "Canadian Zionists and Hadassah members are an army." OJA, OHW, Box 6 – Anniversary and Milestone Series, Folder – Early Days, Part of an Exhibit, "Spirit of Generosity among Jewish Shown in Fine Bazaar," 17 November 1927 [newspaper article].

89 Adelene Hyman interview.

90 "Stirring Appeals to Help," 2.

91 Lionel Metrick interview.

92 Steinman, A Jewish Odyssey, 23-4.

93 They could borrow up to one hundred dollars, two dollars of which was used to pay interest to the bank. See OJA, Kershman, "Family, Friends, Lower Town" [side 2].

94 OJA, RSA, Box – Untitled Manuscript on Ten Decades of Jewish Life in
Ottawa [hereafter Untitled Manuscript], File – Decade of Immigration …
Saga of the Synagogues, 3.

95 In the late 1920s and early 1930s, Rabbi Nathan Kollin directed the
King Edward (1929–32), and Rabbis Berger (1902–27) and Doctor
(1902–34) led the Rideau Street. At the start of the century, both the
King Edward and Rideau Street *shuls* expanded: in 1904, the former re-
located from Murray Street to King Edward (375) just below Rideau
Street, and in 1921 built an extension; in 1912, the latter moved to another location on Rideau Street (417), between Friel and Chapel Streets.
The new building could accommodate four hundred congregants, and
added an extension in 1928. OJA, RSA, Box – Untitled Manuscript, File –
The Decade of Unification … 1922-1931, 5,6; OJA, RSA, Box – Untitled
Manuscript, File – Decade of Immigration … Saga of the Synagogues, 1,
2. RSA, Box – Untitled Manuscript, File – A Decade of Philanthropy …
1912-1929," 1; OJA, Finding Aid, Agudath Achim Congregation; Congregation Beth Shalom – Our History, http://www.bethshalom.ca/our_
history.htm.
    In 1911, Ottawa's fourth synagogue, B'nai Jacob (the James Street
shul) was established in Uppertown (otherwise known as Centretown)
for the growing, albeit still small, number of downtown Jews. See OJA,
RSA, Box – Untitled Manuscript, File – Decade of Immigration … Saga
of the Synagogues, 3; Lieff, *Gathering Rosebuds*, 27. In the 1920s, there
also existed the more fringe Folke Shul, established by Labour Zionist in-
tellectuals who promoted Yiddish culture. See Lieff, *Gathering
Rosebuds*, 45–6. In 1956, Adath Jeshuran and Agudath Achim merged
to form Beth Shalom, a congregation that occupied a newly built synagogue on Chapel Street. The former Adath Jeshuran building became the
Jewish Memorial Chapel where all of Ottawa's Jewish funerals were
held. The Agudath Achim building was torn down that same year.

96 Alan Abelson interview.

97 Ibid.; Goldberg, "Economic and Social Aspects." But none of these distinctions prevented teenagers on the holidays from "*shul*-hopping," happily traveling between synagogues to visit their friends.

98 Indeed, eleven-year-old Vivian Edelson was one of "nine dainty little
girls" who at the Sunday school Chanukah party "dressed in bright and
pretty costumes to represent the *Shamus* [the *menorah* candle used to

light the others] and the eight candles," and performed "the March of the Candles." OJA, Max Bookman Collection, Box 2, File – Young People's League News – 1930, "Young People's League News," 15 January 1930, 4, 3.

99 SE, *The Holy Scriptures*. Inside the book, the Rabbi inserted his business card. He wrote on the back of the card "December 1931," and wrote on the front of the card "For Mr. Edelson."

100 SE, "Benjamin Edelson Eulogy."

101 Lillian Katznelson interview.

102 SE, "Benjamin Edelson Eulogy"; OJA, IC, File – Young Men's Hebrew Association, Finding Aid; Lillian Katznelson interview; OJA, IC, File – Young Men's Hebrew Association, *The Bulletin* (November 1921– December 1921), 2 December 1921, 3. The Jewish women of Ottawa claimed their own bowling club – the Judean Ladies' Bowling League; "Bowling Summary," 23.

103 OJA, RSA, Box – Untitled Manuscript, File – Decade of Immigration … Saga of the Synagogues, 6; RSA, Box – Untitled Manuscript, File – A Decade of Philanthropy … 1912–1929," 6.

104 COA, "Tune in to Shalom Ottawa," advertisement, *Ottawa Jewish Bulletin*, 24 January 1986, 28; Tulchinsky, *Canada's Jews*, 215.

105 Lillian Katznelson interview; SE, "Benjamin Edelson Eulogy"; Benjamin Edelson, *Thirteenth Census of the United States Federal Census: 1910-Population*. On the 1907 postcard in which he outlined his sailing itinerary from Riga to America, Ben signed his name in Russian, English, and Yiddish. SE, picture postcard of *Noordland*, 1907, from Ben Edelson. Ben's knowledge of German was typical of Jews from the Courland region of Latvia where Friedrichstadt, his birthplace, was located. Their integration with the larger culture distinguished Courland Jews from many of their Eastern European brethren. See Liekis, "Courland," 358.

106 SE, "Benjamin Edelson Eulogy."

107 Ibid.

108 Adelene Hyman interview.

109 Mary Goldberg interview; Lillian Katznelson interview; Dina Edelson interview.

110 Lillian Katznelson interview; Joel and Sharon Edelson interview.

111 Lillian Katznelson interview.

112 Mary Goldberg interview; Ibid.; Dina Edelson interview.

113 "Parts of Bullet Found," *The Ottawa Evening Journal*, 15 January
    1932, 7.

114 Lillian Katznelson interview.

115 OJA, Lo, "The Path from Peddling," 51.

CHAPTER THREE

1 "Moses Doctor Young Lawyer Is Found Dead," *The Ottawa Evening
   Journal*, 21 March 1934, 13. Doctor was well connected. He was married to Rose Florence whose father, Avram (Abraham) Lazarus Florence,
   once a junk dealer who specialized in paper, was the owner of the Florence Paper Company, contracted by the Government of Canada. See
   OJA, 1C, File – A.L. Florence, Finding Aid.

2 Miriam Russ correspondence; Doreen Caplin Teichman telephone interview; Max Adler telephone interview; Lionel Metrick interview. Max
   Adler remembered his cousin's keen sense of justice and powers of per-
   suasion. In the mid-1920s, a teenage Adler worked on Ottawa trains selling newspapers and snacks. When his boss refused to pay him his full
   wages, his cousin Moe immediately dropped everything, closed his office,
   journeyed to Union Station, and got Max his money. Max Adler, telephone interview with author, 28 October 2007.

3 "Ben Edelson Found Not Guilty and Is a Free Man," *The Ottawa
   Evening Journal*, 18 January 1932, 13.

4 Auger endured five trials, which successively tackled charges of rape (trials one, two, and three), seduction (trial four), and perjury (trial five).
   Auger was acquitted in trial three largely due to Doctor's efforts to secure more francophone jurors to mitigate prejudice, and to redress
   flawed translation of witness testimony. In the end, Auger was found
   guilty only of seduction, and served two years in Kingston Penitentiary.
   See Constance Backhouse, "Calculated to Reflect on the Dignity of Parliament," 1, 17–18, 11.

5 "Ben Edelson Arraigned on Charge of Murder and Remanded a Week,"
   The Ottawa Evening Journal, 25 November 1931, 1.

6 "Hundreds in Last Tribute to Late Aubrey Macdonald [*sic*]," *The Ottawa Evening Citizen*, 20 May 1942, 12; OCA, Ottawa Police Force, Box
   1/7, *Annual Report of the Police Department of the City of Ottawa for
   the year 1931* (Ottawa: Commercial Printing), 141; "Edelsons Still Hold-

ing Key to Fatal Shooting," *The Ottawa Evening Citizen*, 26 November 1931, 3. Eulogized as a popular officer who held a "position of trust and comradeship," MacDonald served thirty-five years with the Ottawa police force before he died in May of 1942. Present at his funeral were detachments of the Ottawa police and fire departments, the Quebec Provincial Police, and the RCMP, in addition to the mayor of Ottawa and many lawyers, politicians, and judges. See "Hundreds in Last Tribute to Late Aubrey Macdonald [*sic*]," 12.

7   "Ben Edelson Arraigned," 3; "Employe[e] of Ben Edelson Tells of Calling Doctor to Attend Jack Horwitz," *The Ottawa Evening Journal*, 26 November 1931, 17.

8   "History of the Carleton County Gaol"; "Crime and Punishment Jail Tour," The Haunted Walk of Ottawa

9   Brown, *Behind Bars*, 52; Drolet, "Jails."

10 "Crime and Punishment Jail Tour"; Brown, *Behind Bars*, 52. Some cite 1932, not 1933, as the year of Seabrooke's execution. As well, some say that he was the last of the three men hanged. See "History of the Carleton County Gaol." The other two men hanged at the jail were Patrick James Whelan in 1869, for the assassination of politician Thomas D'Arcy McGee, and Eugene Larment in 1946, for the murder of police officer Thomas Stoneman.

11 White, *Negotiating Responsibility*, 72.

12 "History of the Carleton County Gaol"; "Crime and Punishment Jail Tour." The jail closed its doors in 1972. In 1973, with a visit from the Duke of Edinburgh, the building reopened as the Nicholas Street Jail Hostel (today the HI-Ottawa Jail Hostel), and has since undergone extensive renovations to improve conditions for guests, while preserving its historic character.

13 "Horwitz Estate Divided among Three Persons," *The Ottawa Evening Citizen*, 27 November 1931, 2.

14 *Coroner's Act, Revised Statutes of Ontario*, 15; "When to Call a Coroner," Ontario Coroners Association; "Mission Statement," Ontario Coroners Association.

15 *Coroner's Act, Revised Statutes of Ontario*, 15. Today, the inquest also performs a public service function, as the jury may make recommendations intended to prevent similar deaths.

16 Today, the coroner may close an inquest to the public if a person is

charged with an indictable offense connected to the death. *Coroner's Act, Revised Statutes of Ontario*, 15–16.

17 *Coroner's Act, Revised Statutes of Ontario*, 13.

18 "Horwitz Estate Divided," 2.

19 "Ritchie Says May not Take Story of Wife," *The Ottawa Evening Journal*, 30 November 1931, 1.

20 "Are Satisfied Three People Only in Store," *The Ottawa Evening Journal*, 30 November 1931, 7.

21 "Interest Roused in Tonight's Inquest," *The Ottawa Evening Citizen*, 1 December 1931, 1.

22 Lillian Katznelson interview.

23 "Hadassah Tea," *The Ottawa Evening Citizen*, 2 December 1931, 19; "Horwitz Estate Divided," 2.

24 "City Police Striving to Solve Mystery of Jewelry Store Drama," *The Ottawa Evening Citizen*, 25 November 1931, 7.

25 "17 Are Called to the Inquest as Witnesses, *The Ottawa Evening Journal*, 1 December 1931, 4; "Ritchie Says," 1; "Ben Edelson Goes to Trial at Assizes Next January; New Evidence Is Presented," *The Ottawa Evening Journal*, 16 December 1931, 15.

26 "Ritchie Says," 1.

27 "Edelsons Still Holding Key," 3; "Employe[e] of Ben Edelson," 17.

28 "Edelsons Still Holding Key," 3.

29 "Sensational Evidence Given at Horwitz Inquest," *The Ottawa Evening Journal*, 2 December 1931, 13.

30 "Horwitz Inquest Brings out Startling Evidence," *The Renfrew Mercury*, 3 December 1931, 1.

31 "Sensational Evidence Given," 13.

32 AO, RG 4-32 – J.A. Ritchie, Crown Attorney, Ottawa; "Sensational Evidence Given," 13. Emphasis mine.

33 "Sensational Evidence Given," 13.

34 Ibid., 14.

35 "Not to Proceed with Case until Inquest Ended," *The Ottawa Evening Journal*, 2 December 1931, 2.

36 "States Mrs. Edelson Kissed Dying Man," *The Toronto Daily Star*, 2 December 1931 (internet); "Sensational Evidence Given," 13.

37 "Lorenzo Lemieux," *The Ottawa Evening Journal*, 2 December 1931, 14.

38 "Not to Proceed with Case until Inquest Ended."

39 "Sensational Evidence Given," 13; "Lorenzo Lemieux," 14; "States Mrs. Edelson Kissed Dying Man."

40 "States Mrs. Edelson Kissed Dying Man."

41 "Unable to Hear Evidence until Inquest Closed," *The Ottawa Evening Citizen*, 2 December 1931, 2.

42 "Resume Inquest Tomorrow Night," *The Ottawa Evening Journal*, 8 December 1931, 1; Ibid., 1.

43 "Lorenzo Lemieux," 14.

44 "Resume Inquest Tomorrow Night," 1; "Murder Hearing Set for Tuesday," *The Ottawa Evening Journal*, 9 December 1931, 1.

45 "Resume Inquest Tomorrow Night," 1; "Unable to Hear Evidence," 1.

46 "Unable to Hear Evidence," 2.

47 "Ben S. Edelson Named Slayer of J. Horwitz," *The Ottawa Evening Citizen*, 10 December 1931, 4.

48 "Murder Hearing Set for Tuesday, 1; "Resume Inquest Tomorrow Night," 1.

49 "Ben S. Edelson Named Slayer," 4, 19.

50 Ibid., 4.

51 Ibid.

52 The jury included E.A. Beach (foreman), Norman Ross (coroner's clerk and later foreman), Thomas Stinson, Marshall Brooks, Robert Elliott, John Laurin, Ovila Archambault, and Edward Monette. See "City Police Striving," 7, and "Ben S. Edelson Named Slayer," 4.

53 "Sensational Evidence Given," 13; "Ben S. Edelson Named Slayer," 4. The 9 December proceedings lasted ninety minutes.

54 "Ben S. Edelson Named Slayer," 4.

55 Ibid.; "Verdict of Coroner's Jury Finds that Jack Horwitz Was Shot by Ben Edelson," *The Ottawa Evening Journal*, 10 December 1931, 2; "Coroner's Jury Says Edelson Shot Horwitz," *The Renfrew Mercury*, 10 December 1931, 1; "Ottawa Man Shot Rival Finding of Coroner's Jury," *The Toronto Daily Star*, 10 December 1931 (internet).

56 "Ben S. Edelson Named Slayer," 19.

57 "Lorenzo Lemieux," 14.

58 "Verdict of Coroner's Jury," 2.

59 "Sensational Evidence Given," 13.

60 "Ben S. Edelson Is Acquitted on Murder Charge," *The Ottawa Evening*

Citizen, 18 January 1932, 14. Curiously, as noted in Chapter 6, Danby would be called several years later to tend to Edelson lawyer Moses Doctor, a case which also puts into question the doctor's code of conduct.

61 "Police Court Hearing in Edelson Case Starts," *The Ottawa Evening Journal*, 15 December 1931, 1.

62 Ibid., 1.

63 Ibid.

64 "Graphic Story," *The Ottawa Evening Journal*, 15 December 1931, 30.

65 "Ben Edelson Goes to Trial," 15.

66 White, *Negotiating Responsibility*, 10; "Interest Roused," 1.

67 "Interest Roused," 1.

68 "Sensational Evidence Given," 13.

69 Ibid.

70 "Horwitz Estate Divided," 2.

71 "Ben S. Edelson Named Slayer," 4.

72 Ibid.

73 "Not To Proceed With Case," 1.

74 These themes are reflected in a bizarre story that appeared on page one of the *Journal* next to coverage of the Edelson/Horwitz case. The *Journal* reported that at a Manhattan party, "after hours of bridge and parlor games," the eight guests "decided on dramatic improvisation." One man "took the part of the philanderer-homewrecker," another "portrayed the role of the husband" who finds his wife "in the arms of another man," and a woman "was chosen to play the wife" who was shocked by her husband's arrival. As the actors played out the scene, they "proceeded with mock seriousness to the denouement" when the husband "summoned up an expression of outraged pride," reached for a revolver in his right coat pocket, and "shot" his wife's lover. Shockingly, the guest, a member of the National Rifle Association, mistakenly grabbed his .32 caliber pistol instead of the paper-cap gun, and shot his friend in the neck. The horrified party guests, who had simply been "playing 'theatre'" "just for jolly entertainment," were "in a panic" at what they had just witnessed. This story of friends seeking to enliven their stale gathering by dramatizing a sexually-charged and violent vignette suggests the high entertainment value for spectators in the Edelson/Horwitz murder case courtroom. See "Shooting Scene Was 'All in Fun,' but his Best Friend Is near Death," *The Ottawa Evening Journal*, 30 November 1931, 1.

75 "Ben S. Edelson Is Acquitted," 14. For the courtroom as theatre, see
    Dubinsky, *Improper Advances*, 90.

76 "Ben S. Edelson Named Slayer," 4.

77 Ibid.

78 "Verdict of Coroner's Jury," 2.

79 "Ben S. Edelson Named Slayer," 4.

80 Ibid.

81 "Ben Edelson Arraigned," 3.

82 Ibid.; "City Police Striving," 1, 7; "Edelsons Still Holding Key," 3.

83 "Murder Hearing Set for Tuesday," 1; "Further Remand For B. Edelson,"
    The Ottawa Evening Citizen, 9 December 1931, 2.

84 "Verdict of Coroner's Jury," 2.

85 Ibid.

86 SE, correspondence from Joseph Pinchus Edelson, Bronx, New York to
    Alice and Benny, 6 December 1931. The letter, written in Yiddish, reveals
    his deep faith in a compassionate God, his belief that the shooting was
    an accident, and his own capacity for optimism and kindness. He hoped
    that "with God's help the truth will emerge that Benny is innocent and
    will soon be released. As long as a person is alive, anything can happen.
    We have to remain courageous and strong and rely on God because no
    one is guilty here. It's an act of God. As we say, God's punishment, and
    the dear Lord will surely have mercy and we will overcome this and
    speak happily about it in the future." It is impossible to tell whether he
    knew of Alice's infidelity and its role in the shooting, but his letter never
    overtly blames her for Ben's fate.

87 SE, correspondence from Joseph Pinchus and Zelda Edelson, New York,
    to Alice and Benny, 24 December 1931.

88 SE, correspondence from Joseph Pinchus Edelson, Bronx, New York to
    Alice and Benny, 6 December 1931.

89 Lionel Metrick interview; Lillian Katznelson interview.

90 "Edelsons Still Holding Key," 3; Ben S. Edelson Is Acquitted," 14.

91 Adelene Hyman interview.

92 Lillian Katznelson interview.

93 The Haunted Walk of Ottawa, Crime and Punishment Jail Tour.

94 Lillian Katznelson interview.

95 Ward, AO, correspondence.

96 "Horwitz Estate Divided," 2.

CHAPTER FOUR

1 Francine Shaffer telephone interview; Suzie Gellman interview; Goldberg, "The Depression and War," 55.
2 Bookman, "Excerpts from A History of the Jew," 399.
3 OJA, Kershman, "Family, Friends, Lower Town" [side 1].
4 Ibid.
5 OJA, Kershman, "Family, Friends, Lower Town" [side 2].
6 They sang out the evening prayers, and made vulgar sexual comments
  in Yiddish about female customers. And instead of yelling out the usual
  "rags for sale," they broadcasted in Yiddish "thieves, thieves. Nothing
  but a bunch of thieves live here." With no one understanding their
  Hebrew chanting or their Yiddish ranting, with no family and friends
  to keep their behaviour in check, and generally uncaring about their
  impression on non-Jews, the men felt free to let loose. See OJA, Levine,
  In Lower Town.
7 OJA, RSA, Box – Untitled Manuscript on Ten Decades of Jewish Life in
  Ottawa [hereafter Untitled Manuscript], File – The Decade of Unification
  ... 1922–1931, 1; Goldberg, "The Depression and War," 72.
8 Goldberg, "The Depression and War," 77; OJA, Kershman, "Family,
  Friends, Lower Town" [side 1].
9 OJA, RSA, Box – Untitled Manuscript, File – The Decade of Unification
  ... 1922–1931, 1.
10 Max Bookman, "Excerpts from A History of the Jew," 395.
11 The last day of the Edelson trial was a Saturday, which meant that neither Doctor nor Ben could have observed the Sabbath if he had wanted
  to, and that the Jewish courtroom spectators opted not to.
12 OJA, Max Bookman Collection, Finding Aid; Max Bookman Collection,
  Box 1 – Ottawa Hebrew News March 1956–September 1965, File –
  Ottawa Hebrew News Mailing List 1937–1938, "Ottawa Hebrew
  News Mailing List – 1937–38."
13 Suzie Gellman interview; Joel and Sharon Edelson interview; Lieff,
  Gathering Rosebuds, 69.
14 Lillian Katznelson interview. One estimate had the school at 99% Jewish.
  See Steinman, *A Jewish Odyssey,* 22.
15 OJA, Kershman, "Family, Friends, Lower Town" [side 1].

16 Goldberg, "The Depression and War," 55.

17 OJA, IC, File – Young Men's Hebrew Association, *The Bulletin* (November 1921–December 1921), 2 December 1921, 3.

18 "Favours Educating Jewish Children in Jewish Ideals," *The Ottawa Evening Citizen*, 25 November 1931, 22.

19 Goldberg, "The Depression and War," 74.

20 This group also boasted close to one hundred members, and attracted at least half that number to its weekly Sunday afternoon meetings. See OJA, Young Jewish People's Association of Ottawa, Finding Aid. The demise of these Yiddish associations in the mid-1930s signaled not only the ravages of the Depression, but waning European Jewish immigration, the gradual acculturation of Ottawa's Jewish children, and the growing Zionist movement's emphasis on Hebrew, all of which facilitated the decline of Yiddish usage among Jews in North America. See Goldberg, "The Depression and War," 73–5. With regard to acculturation, for example, Yiddish-speaking, nine-year-old Thelma Rivers, who had just immigrated to Ottawa from Kiev, "mastered English quickly." See Steinman, *A Jewish Odyssey*, 22.

21 "Accused Man on Stand in Own Defence Tells Story [of] Fatal Struggle," *The Ottawa Evening Citizen*, 18 January 1932, 14; "Ben Edelson Found Not Guilty and Is a Free Man," *The Ottawa Evening Journal*, 18 January 1932, 16.

22 "City Police Striving to Solve Mystery of Jewelry Store Drama," *The Ottawa Evening Citizen*, 25 November 1931, 7.

23 The group met at the King Edward *shul*, where Alice and her committee set a table with pink tapered candles and a basket centerpiece of Columbia roses. In addition to conducting a brief business meeting, members discussed an agricultural school in Palestine and donated trees for planting in Palestine to new mothers in the group. See "Hadassah Tea," *The Ottawa Evening Citizen*, 25 November 1931, 18; "Are Joint Hostesses at Successful Tea for Hadassah Chapter," *The Ottawa Evening Journal*, 25 November 1931, 8.

24 He discussed the anti-Semitism experienced by Jews in Europe, and contrasted it to the relatively privileged life of Jews in the British Empire. See "Sam Berger Delivers Talk on Citizenship," *The Ottawa Evening Citizen*, 25 November 1931, 7.

25 "City Police Striving," 7.

26 "Wife of Ben Edelson Likely to be Called as Witness at Probe," *The Ottawa Evening Journal*, 26 November 1931, 1.

27 "Hundreds Pay Last Tribute to Victim of Store Tragedy," *The Ottawa Evening Citizen*, 26 November, 1931, 1. Jack Horwitz, Sam Berger, and Moses Doctor were childhood pals who grew up in the first decade of the century in Lowertown, and all came from large, immigrant families of eight children. Berger and Doctor were both the sons of rabbis, and were raised in devout and learned homes. In fact, it had been Rabbis Berger and Doctor who officiated at the 1925 wedding of Jack's sister, Sarah. See OJA, IC, File – Berger, Samuel, "J.N.F. Negev Dinner In Honour of Samuel Berger, Q.C.," 9 December 1968; OJA, J.C. Horwitz Collection, File 1 – Clippings, "Synagogue Is Scene of Pretty Wedding" [1925], reprinted in "Couple of the Year Celebrate 50th," *The Gazette* [Montreal], 11 January 1975.

28 "Moses Doctor Young Lawyer Is Found Dead," *The Ottawa Evening Journal*, 21 March 1934, 13.

29 Ibid.

30 "Late Moses Doctor Left behind Many Sorrowing Friends," *The Ottawa Evening Citizen*, 21 March 1934, 2; "Many at Funeral of Moses Doctor," *The Ottawa Evening Citizen*, 22 March 1934, 3.

31 "Moses Doctor Young Lawyer," 13; "Thousands Pay Fitting Tribute to Moses Doctor," *The Ottawa Evening Journal*, 22 March 1934, 3.

32 "Ben Edelson Arraigned on Charge of Murder and Remanded a Week," *The Ottawa Evening Journal*, 25 November 1931, 3.

33 "Hundreds Pay Last Tribute," 1.

34 OJA, IC, File – Young Men's Hebrew Association, *The Booster*, January 1921, *passim*, 5; OJA, IC, File – Young Men's Hebrew Association, *The Bulletin* (November 1921–December 1921), 2 December 1921, 1; OJA, IC, File – Young Men's Hebrew Association, *The Bulletin* (November 1921–December 1921),11 November 1921, 2–3; OJA, IC, File – Young Men's Hebrew Association, *The Bulletin* (November 1921–December 1921), 2 December 1921, 3.

35 Lillian Katznelson interview; Goldberg, "The Depression and War," 56.

36 Lillian Katznelson interview.

37 OJA, IC, File – Young Men's Hebrew Association, *The Booster*, January 1921, *passim*, 5; OJA, IC, File – Young Men's Hebrew Association, *The*

Bulletin (November 1921–December 1921), 2 December 1921, 1; OJA, 1C, File – Young Men's Hebrew Association, *The Bulletin* (November 1921-December 1921),11 November 1921, 2–3; OJA, 1C, File – Young Men's Hebrew Association, *The Bulletin* (November 1921–December 1921), 2 December 1921, 3. The paper also integrated photographs, lighthearted poems, puzzles, and inside jokes, as well as advertisements by local Jewish businesses, including that of Jack's father, M. Horwitz and Co. In November and December of 1921, there were six issues of the paper.

38 Alice wore a "nile green georgette, made in bouffant style," donned a hair "bandeau of silver and green," and carried a bouquet of Columbia roses. See OJA, J.C. Horwitz Collection, File 1 – Clippings, "Synagogue Is Scene of Pretty Wedding" [1925], reprinted in "Couple of the Year Celebrate 50th."

39 "Ben S. Edelson Is Acquitted on Murder Charge," *The Ottawa Evening Citizen*, 18 January 1932, 14; "Ben Edelson Goes on the Stand and Tells how Horwitz Was Shot," *The Ottawa Evening Journal*, 18 January 1932, 16.

40 "Ottawa Man Shot Rival Finding of Coroner's Jury," *The Toronto Daily Star*, 10 December 1931 (internet).

41 Lillian Katznelson interview; Dina Edelson interview.

42 Regrettably, the OJA did not possess relevant issues of Max Bookman's *Ottawa Hebrew News*, which published at this time. It is questionable, however, whether the paper would have reported such a devastating event.

43 "Ottawa Community Stunned by Mysterious Shooting," *The Canadian Jewish Chronicle*, 27 November 1931, 8, 13; "Principals in Ottawa's Mysterious Shooting Affray," *The Canadian Jewish Chronicle*, 4 December 1931, 17.

44 Eugene V. Orenstein, in Weinfeld et al., *The Canadian Jewish Mosaic* (1981), Jewish Virtual Library, "Canadian Literature," 5–6; Margolis, "The Yiddish Press in Montreal," 9.

45 JPL, *Keneder Adler*, 26–7, 29 November 1931, all page 1; 3, 11, 17 December 1931, all page 1; 15, 17 January 1932, both on page one.

46 SE, untitled, undated newspaper article in Yiddish.

47 Suzie Gellman interview; Lionel Metrick interview.

48 SE, untitled, undated newspaper article in Yiddish.

49 Prager and Telushkin, *The Nine Questions*, 46.

50 Ibid., 52, 69. In addition to the Laws of Ethics and Laws of Holiness categories, there are Reflexive Laws ("to elevate the performer of the law") and National Laws ("to identify with the Jewish nation and with its past"). See p. 46.

51 Rosenfeld, "Living in the World's View." Rabbi Rosenfeld underscores the point that the notion of *chillul Hashem* is not restricted to public misdeeds. Neither does it expect human perfection – sinning is inevitable, but it can be abated and forgiven. See page 2. In contrast to *chillul Hashem, kiddush Hashem* is the act of bringing glory, respect, and honour to God.

52 In an August 2009 issue, *The Canadian Jewish News* featured no less than four articles about the concept of *chillul Hashem*. In the face of recent scandals featuring crooked financiers, corrupt politicians, violent demonstrators, and kidney-selling rabbis, for example, the Jewish people, cites one article, are "united in shame." See Rosensweig, "The Jewish People: United in Shame," 35.

53 Rosenfeld, "Living in the World's View." Some Jewish academics and activists advocate for a more realistic and empowered understanding of contemporary Jewish life. Adrienne Asch, Director of the Center for Ethics at Yeshiva University, believes that "it is time for Jews to face the fact that there are criminals among them, just as there are criminals everywhere else." Moreover, notes Asch, "'Jews are powerful people … We have to stop acting as if every terrible thing someone does is a public relations nightmare for Jews, as if we are all about to be persecuted if one person does a bad thing." After all, adds one Jewish activist, "the anti-Semites don't need our help to be anti-Semitic." See Wiener, "How Communal Norms," 9.

54 Stanislawski, *A Murder in Lemberg*, 117.

55 As does the community's subsequent participation in *lashon hara* (literally meaning "evil tongue"), a grave transgression of perpetrating, listening to, or believing slanderous talk, whether true or not.

56 Rosenberg, *Canada's Jews*, 234.

57 OCA, Ottawa Police Force, Box 1/7, *Annual Report of the Police Department of the City of Ottawa for the Year 1931* (Ottawa: Commercial Printing), 125–6. To what extent these criminals made up the total number of their respective groups living in Ottawa was not stated.

58 Rosenberg, *Canada's Jews*, 234. The notable exception is the higher crime rate among Jews in mid-1930s Canada as compared with the general population regarding "breaches of revenue laws." These included drug offences, perjury, and conspiracy. Gambling offences were also proportionately more common in the Jewish community. Like many philosophers and commentators before them, Dennis Prager and Rabbi Joseph Telushkin attribute the Jewish aversion to violent crime to the religious laws of *kashrut* (keeping kosher) which encourage self-discipline and self-control. Jews are mandated to limit the type of animals they kill and consume, to slaughter animals humanely, and to prevent the consumption of blood. The authors note, for example, that "the unique practice of draining blood from meat consumed by Jews has had over thousands of years a profoundly moral impact. It has helped produce an extraordinary antipathy to bloodthirst" which, "in addition to the uniquely low incidence of violence among Jews," has meant the virtual nonexistence of hunting for sport among Jews." See Prager and Telushkin, *The Nine Questions*, 58–9.

59 COA, Larochelle, *The History of the Ottawa Police*, 83, 104, 99; "Chief Joliat Wants More Men on Force," *The Ottawa Evening Journal*, 15 December 1931, 1. Of course, the greater number of arrests may also be attributable to a more efficient, vigilant, and/or aggressive police force.

60 "Large Increase in Petty Crimes Reported in Year," *The Ottawa Evening Journal*, 26 January 1932, 5.

61 "Slow-Moving Justice" [letter to editor], *The Ottawa Evening Citizen*, 19 January 1932.

62 See for example, "Youth, Crime, Judges and Sentences" [editorial], *The Ottawa Evening Journal*, 16 December 1931, 6; "Service Station Hold-Ups" [letter to editor], *The Ottawa Evening Journal*, 16 December 1931, 6; "Slow-Moving Justice"; "Firearms" [letter to editor], *The Ottawa Evening Journal*, 25 January 1932, 6; "Drunkenness and Convictions" [letter to editor], *The Ottawa Evening Journal*, 25 January 1932, 6.

63 COA, Larochelle, *The History of the Ottawa Police*, 83, 104, 99; "Large Increase in Petty Crimes," 5; "Chief Joliat Wants," 1.

64 Ibid.

65 COA, Larochelle, *The History of the Ottawa Police*, 102, 104–5; "Crooks Appointed," 1; "Large Increase in Petty Crimes."

66 Lucia Goulet claimed that her mother had killed herself, a finding

supported by an alleged suicide note, and by an instant confirmation by the county coroner. On 27 November, Goulet was found guilty of manslaughter and sentenced to fourteen years at the Kingston Penitentiary. See "Judge Favours Goulet Trial Be Speedy One," *The Ottawa Evening Journal*, 25 November 1931, 7; "Court Sits Ten Hours in Trial of Lucia Goulet," *The Ottawa Evening Citizen*, 26 November 1931, 4; "Lucia Goulet Gets 14 Years for Manslaughter," *The Ottawa Evening Citizen*, 27 November 1931, 1.

67 This was Cassidy's second trial after winning an appeal following an execution order in November 1930. On 21 January 1932, after a gripping three-day trial, Cassidy was found guilty, and sentenced to hang behind the Hull jail on 8 April. See "Crown's Case Cassidy Trial Closing Today," *The Ottawa Evening Journal*, 19 January 1932, 13; "Cassidy Takes Overdose of Sleeping Medicine; Stabs Self with Knife," *The Ottawa Evening Journal*, 22 January 1932, 13.

68 "Cassidy Takes Overdose," 13; "Special Guards Assigned Cassidy during the Night," *The Ottawa Evening Journal*, 23 January 1932, 28; "Open Inquiry into Cassidy's Attempt on Own Life," *The Ottawa Evening Journal*, 23 January 1932, 1; "Hundreds See Cassidy Leave for Montreal," *The Ottawa Evening Journal*, 25 January 1932, 5.

69 JPL, "Prominent Ottawa Jew Shot; Another Jew Arrested," *Keneder Adler*, 26 November 1931, 1.

70 Steinman, *A Jewish Odyssey*, 25; Alan Abelson interview. Some Jewish boys could be equally scrappy. In the 1940s, for example, Larry Greenberg's nickname in 1940s Lowertown was "Killer," a name which indicated his fighting prowess, and his "leadership of a band of local French-Canadian and Jewish roughnecks." See OJA, IC, File – Minto, Wayne Skene, *Minto: A Tradition of Family Values: The First Fifty Years* (Canada: Tribute books, 2005), 14. See also Lieff, *Gathering Rosebuds*, 72.

71 Freiman, *Don't Fall off the Rocking Horse*, 15–16.

72 Campbell, *Respectable Citizens*, 17.

73 Dubinsky, *Improper Advances*, 95.

74 Ibid., 95, 98.

75 Weinfeld, *Like Everyone Else*, 135.

76 Ibid., 129. But the community was also aware of his more dubious reputation, especially regarding his perceived involvement, in early twentieth-

century American cities, in the business of white slavery and prostitution. See Hyman, *Gender and Assimilation*, 107.

77 Dubinsky, *Improper Advances*, 95.

78 Campbell, *Respectable Citizens*, 17.

79 Tulchinsky, *Canada's Jews*, 215.

80 Isaacson, "Matrimony," 111.

81 Weinfeld, *Like Everyone Else*, 127–8.

82 Draper and Karlinsky, "Abraham's Daughters," 75.

83 Weinfeld, *Like Everyone Else*, 127-8; Ibid., 75–6.

84 Isaacson, "Matrimony," 111.

85 Roth, editor-in-chief, "Adultery," 37. This distinction in the definition of adultery was related historically to the notion that a wife's adultery was a violation of the property rights of her husband, who had exclusive claim to her body. As well, a wife's adultery could put into question the paternity of children, creating questions regarding lineage and inheritance. A philandering husband, in contrast, was not viewed as legally transgressing against his wife (his property), but was deemed an adulterer only if he trespassed on another man's wife, transgressing against that husband's property. A husband could escape the adultery accusation by engaging unmarried women instead (although this scenario could be morally and physically ruinous for the women).

86 Lillian Katznelson interview; Dina Edelson interview with author.

87 Dina Edelson interview.

88 Mary Goldberg interview; Suzie Gellman interview.

89 se, "Benjamin Edelson Eulogy."

90 Lillian Katznelson interview.

91 Dina Edelson interview.

92 Lillian Katznelson interview.

93 Dina Edelson interview.

94 Adelene Hyman interview.

95 Dina Edelson interview.

96 Readily employed birth control methods included "natural" approaches such as continence, *coitus interruptus*, and the rhythm method, and more disreputable "mechanical" devices such as the condom, douche, and pessary. These strategies would have been used for long-term birth control, as well as for spacing out children within marriage. McLaren and McLaren, *The Bedroom and the State*, 18–22.

97 McLaren and McLaren, *The Bedroom and the State*, 18.

98 Lillian Katznelson interview.

99 Ibid.; Francis Shaffer telephone interview.

100 Sangster, *Regulating Girls and Women*, 92, 114.

101 Ibid., 119–20.

102 Mary Goldberg interview.

103 Antler, *You Never Call!*, 7, 15.

104 Ibid., 16.

105 Ibid., 16, 17; Hyman, *Gender and Assimilation*, 126–7.

106 Antler, *You Never Call!*, 17–25. The quotation appears on page 25.

107 Antler, *You Never Call!*, 35–6.

108 "Nathaniel Zalowitz, "Ungrateful Children of Sacrificing Parents: Many Parents Sacrifice Everything for Children who Reward Them by Contempt – Are Jewish Children Less Grateful to Their Parents than Any Others?" *Forward*, 14 June 1925, in Antler, *You Never Call!*, 37.

109 Mary Goldberg interview.

110 Hyman, *Gender and Assimilation*, 137–8; Antler, *You Never Call!*, 25–6.

111 Hyman, *Gender and Assimilation*, 137–41, 155.

112 Ibid., 142–3.

113 Jewish women, of course, assumed a significant role as pioneers in Palestine in their capacity as farm and field labourers, *ad hoc* soldiers, and household managers.

114 Hyman, *Gender and Assimilation*, 145, 150.

115 Ibid., 157.

116 Antler, *You Never Call!*, 25–34; Ibid., 159. See, for example, Philip Roth's 1969 book, *Portnoy's Complaint*.

117 Antler, *You Never Call!*, 39; Weinfeld, *Like Everyone Else*, 128, 138; Vincent, *Bodies and Souls*, 191. Poverty and juvenile delinquency were also problems that plagued Jewish families.

118 Antler, *You Never Call!*, 7. See note 22 in this introductory chapter for more sources on mother-blaming.

119 Mary Goldberg interview.

120 Sangster, *Regulating Girls and Women*, 107–8.

121 Adelene Hyman interview.

122 Suzie Gellman interview.

123 Ibid.

124 Ibid.

125 "Horwitz Estate Divided among Three Persons," *The Ottawa Evening Citizen*, 27 November 1931, 2.

126 "Ben S. Edelson Is Acquitted," 14.

127 Adelene Hyman interview.

128 Lillian Katznelson interview; Dina Edelson interview.

129 Adelene Hyman interview.

130 Suzie Gellman interview.

131 Lionel Metrick interview.

132 Dina Edelson interview.

133 Figler, *Lillian and Archie Freiman*, 199; Lillian Katznelson interview. In contrast to this allusion to Archibald Freiman's imperfect marriage, Figler wrote that Lillian Freiman "was not only his beloved wife but the very crown of his life, his pride and inspiration. Their married life was an example of harmony, love and devotion." 201.

134 OJA, Box – Agudath Achim Congregation, Membership/Seat Holders, File – Agudath Achim, Seat Sale, 1913; Seat Holders 1952, "Seat holders – Congregation United Brethren [1948]." The switch in synagogues, however, might be attributable to the Edelson's move in 1939 from Friel Street to Clarence Street near Wurtemburg, which was marginally closer to the Rideau Street *shul*.

135 Adelene Hyman interview.

136 Lillian Katznelson interview; Dina Edelson interview.

137 Lillian Katznelson interview.

138 Lionel Metrick interview; ibid.

139 Estelle Abelson interview.

140 Lillian Katznelson interview.

141 Ibid.

142 Suzie Gellman interview.

143 Ibid.

144 Francine Shaffer telephone interview.

145 Lillian Katznelson interview.

146 Although at an all-time high in 1932, and the cause of great concern to social observers, the number of divorces in Canada numbered only 1,007 (a rate of 9.6 per 100,000 population). See Table 4 in Strong-Boag, *The New Day Recalled*, 99.

147 Weinfeld, *Like Everyone Else*, 142. The divorce rate in Canada for Jews, however, was only marginally higher than for Canadians generally. See Rosenberg, *Canada's Jews*, 68.

148 Mary Goldberg interview.

149 Ibid.

150 Adelene Hyman interview.

CHAPTER FIVE

1 "Edelson Trial Opens with Court Room Crowded," *The Ottawa Evening Journal*, 14 January 1932, 1.

2 "Edelson Trial Opens," 1.

3 *Revised Statutes 1927*, Section 252, 746; "Had Edelson Any Unlawful Purpose in Producing Weapon, Judge Asks," *The Ottawa Evening Journal*, 18 January 1932, 15.

4 *Revised Statutes 1927*, Section 259, 747.

5 *Revised Statutes 1927*, Section 263, 748. Hanging was the only form of execution ever utilized in Canada, where a total of 710 people (697 men and thirteen women) were killed. The death penalty was abolished in Canada in 1976. See Department of Justice Canada, "Capital Punishment in Canada."

6 *Revised Statutes 1927*, Section 261, 748. It may be described as what happens when "a usually sane and normal person" is impulsively "driven by panic, love, or jealousy of an exaggerated or obsessive sort to kill a spouse, a rival or a lover." See Engel, 19, 27.

7 The perception surrounding crimes of passion is that they "are offenses not normally committed by criminals, but by *ordinary people*, who are criminalized only by these acts." They commit their crimes out of very specific set of circumstances, and are not likely to re-offend. Indeed, "someone who has suddenly or unexpectedly been betrayed by a loved and trusted partner ... is rarely treated as a common murderer." See Engel, 14, 21–2. Although a verdict of manslaughter for provocation could garner life imprisonment, an unwelcome result for both sides, the finding had its benefit. For the prosecution, it would at least ensure a conviction, and prevent Edelson from going free. For the defence, it would at least keep him off the gallows. See *Revised Statutes 1927*, Section 268, 749.

8 McEvoy had first made a name for himself by serving as defence counsel in the infamous 1901 and 1902 Joseph Sifton murder trials. Joseph's thirty-year-old son Gerald, angered by Joseph's plan to marry a pregnant servant girl, and fearing the loss of his wealthy father's inheritance, was accused, along with an impressionable farm hand, of hacking Joseph to death with an axe. Despite the farm hand's guilty plea and dubious witness testimony that Joseph, seen holding an axe, inadvertently caused his own death in the barn, Gerald was acquitted. The lead police investigator reflected that the verdict was "a miscarriage of justice and a disgrace to the country." See Hughes and Purdom, *History of the Bar*, 48; "Handwriting Complications," *The New York Times*; Le Caron, *Memoirs of a Great Detective*, 360–4.

   In profiling the forty-eight-year-old McEvoy in his 1912 history of the legal profession in Middlesex County, author Judge David John Hughes noted that "there is probably no member of the bar who appears oftener in court and in important, hard-fought trials ... As Mr. McEvoy is still a young man much may yet be looked for." With such accolades, it is not surprising that McEvoy was appointed a superior court judge in 1927. See Hughes and Purdom, *History of the Bar*, 48; "Ontario Courts," and "Former Judges of the Superior Courts."

9 "Brilliant, Effective Address by Moses Doctor," *The Ottawa Evening Citizen*, 18 January 1932, 15.

10 The insanity defence was never introduced by Doctor. Edelson, after all, did not exhibit, nor have a history of, bizarre or delusional behaviour – he came off as a rational man. Moreover, the insanity defence would have precluded legal consideration of "justified" actions by the accused, which necessarily required his sanity, and would have likely negated the empathy and affection that a jury had toward him. Most importantly, a "not guilty" verdict by reason of insanity would not have rendered him his freedom. Almost certainly, Ben – who later testified that he was in control of his emotions at the time of the shooting – would not have wanted to be perceived as having a mental disorder. William A.G. Simpson telephone interview. Because Doctor elected not to advance an insanity defence, psychiatrists made no appearance in the trial as expert witnesses, despite the fact that they increasingly did so in Canadian murder trials, albeit in a minor capacity, after 1910. Today, even without the

insanity defence, it is almost unimaginable to have a murder trial absent of psychiatric testimony. See White, *Negotiating Responsibility*, 35, 38.

11 "Defence Objections Sustained," *The Ottawa Evening Journal*, 14 January 1932, 19. Another possible reduced verdict was criminal negligence causing death. This decision allows for an accident, but would have affirmed that Edelson's actions fell below the reasonable standard of care, showing a "wanton and reckless disregard" for the safety of others.

12 Doctor's promotion of the "accident" theory might have also been a mark of his own insecurity as the junior lawyer trying his first case of murder. William A.G. Simpson telephone interview.

13 "Edelson Trial Opens with Court Room Crowded," "Ottawa Jeweler Faces Trial on Capital Charge," *The Ottawa Evening Citizen*, 14 January 1932, 2. That White and Doctor were positioned on opposing sides of the Edelson case seemed highly appropriate. Although both were Conservatives, the two lawyers could not have been more different. At sixty years old, White was a seasoned lawyer who graduated from law school before Doctor was born; the thirty-year-old Doctor was still a novice who had never defended a murder case. White's family hailed from Scotland, had been in Canada for three generations, and was staunchly Protestant. Doctor was born in Europe, immigrated to Canada, and was proudly Jewish. White was the son of a lumber mogul; Doctor the son of a rabbi. White was a rugged outdoorsman who hunted and fished; Doctor was bookish and scholarly. See "Ben Edelson Found Not Guilty and Is a Free Man," *The Ottawa Evening Journal*, 18 January 1932, 13; AO, C 81-5-0-7 – PW, "How Pembroke was founded by Peter White," *The Pembroke Bulletin*, 8 February 1943; AO, C 81-5-0-7 – PW, *Who's Who*, Peter White Sr.

14 Law Society of Upper Canada, "Jury Selection." Today, the challenge-for-cause process authorizes the lawyer exercising the objection to query a prospective juror for prejudice, and for him/her to be dismissed if it is deemed in evidence. For more information on the jury selection procedure in Canada, see Tanovich, et al., *Jury Selection in Criminal Trials*, and Granger, et al., *Canadian Criminal Jury Trials*.

15 AO, C 81-1-0-28 – OSOH, Interviews with Roydon Hughes, 46.

16 Ibid.

17 Phillips and Gartner, *Murdering Holiness*, 145, 148.

18 "Ottawa Jeweler Faces Trial," 2.

19 "Ben Edelson Found Not Guilty," 16.

20 "Statements of Horwitz Made on His Death Bed Are Not Given to Jury," *The Ottawa Evening Journal*, 16 January 1932, 14.

21 "Widow of Horwitz on Stand in Murder Trial," *The Ottawa Evening Citizen*, 16 January 1932, 1.

22 Ibid; "Mrs. Jack Horwitz Tells Story at Edelson Trial," *The Ottawa Evening Journal*, 16 January 1932, 1.

23 "Ben S. Edelson Is Acquitted on Murder Charge," *The Ottawa Evening Citizen*, 18 January 1932, 14.

24 "Ben Edelson Found Not Guilty and Is a Free Man," 13. Difficulties pertaining to crowd control at the Carleton County Courthouse were also attributable to the small, inadequate facility that was described by "many prominent jurists in Ontario" at this time as "absolutely intolerable." Judges complained, for example, that they "had to elbow their way through a crowd in the corridor to get to the bench," while others referenced the ways in which justice and confidentiality were compromised by the chronic lack of office and meeting space. There was much debate regarding the improvements required to make the courthouse more functional, and it would persist until the building was finally renovated in 1953. See "Demand Action in Improving Court House," *The Ottawa Evening Citizen*, 12 December 1931, 9; "Open House," *The Ottawa Evening Citizen*, 10 March 1953, 28.

25 White graduated from Osgoode Hall Law School in 1896, and was appointed King's Counsel in 1908. He practiced law in Pembroke for ten years before moving to Toronto in 1916, where he became a partner in the firm Bain, Bicknell, White and Bristol. See AO, C 81-5-0-7 – PW, *Who's Who*, Peter White Sr; AO, C 81-5-0-7 – PW, "How Pembroke was founded by Peter White," *The Pembroke Bulletin*, 8 February 1943; AO, C 81-5-0-7 – PW, "The First Family of Pembroke Left a Fine Tradition," *Pembroke Observer*, 28 February 1963. White was the grandson of Pembroke's founder and pioneering lumber entrepreneur.

26 "How Pembroke Was Founded by Peter White."

27 In 1931, for example, he was a member of the Special Committee of the House of Commons investigating the Beauharnois Power Project scandal, a case in which the Liberal party was accused of accepting sizeable donations from the power company in exchange for government consent to reroute water from the St Lawrence River for hydro-electricity. See

AO, C 81-5-0-7 – PW, "Memorial to the Late Peter White K.C.," The
Law Society of Upper Canada, 1949; Thompson, "Beauharnois Scandal." See Canada. Parliament. House of Commons. Special Committee
on Beauharnois Power Project, 1931. White also sat on the Royal
Commission investigating the 1915 sinking near Ireland of the *Gypsum
Queen*, a freighter whose Nova Scotian captain had received a generous
settlement from the Canadian government in 1931, after his bogus claim
that the ship was torpedoed by a German submarine. "Memorial to
the Late Peter White K.C.," "Gypsum Queen," *Time*.

28 "Brilliant, Effective Address by Moses Doctor," *The Ottawa Evening
Citizen*, 18 January 1932, 15. Why White was called in from Toronto to
be the chief prosecutor in this case, relegating Ottawa Crown prosecutor
Ritchie to the sidelines, is difficult to know. It's likely that for such a
high-profile case (a murder in the capital involving both a middle-class
perpetrator and victim), the Crown wanted a more experienced lawyer.
It's also possible that White's connections earned him political and professional sway in Ottawa. Whatever the reason, his son noted in 1980
that White often tried cases in other cities. See AO, C 81-1-0-14 – OSOH,
Interviews with Peter White [Jr.], 15 April 1980, 71, 74, 76.

29 "Brilliant, Effective Address," 15. Many of these disputes were over
technical issues regarding firearms, ballistics, and the physical layout of
the store. Doctor argued, for example, that the prosecution's photographs of the store's interior were not sufficient for the jury to judge size
and distance, especially if the furnishings in the store were positioned differently than on the night of the shooting. The judge agreed, and allowed
just one photograph to be used for "identification purposes only." See
"Edelson Trial Opens with Court Room Crowded," "Defence Objections Sustained," 19.

30 Only one witness, police-commissioned photographer William J. Whiteside, who took pictures of Edelson Jewellers two days after the incident,
completed his testimony. See "Edelson Trial Opens," 1; "Defence Objections Sustained," 19.

31 "Edelson Trial Opens," 1; "Ottawa Jeweler Faces Trial," 2.

32 See Paciocco and Stuesser, *The Law of Evidence*, 103–8.

33 "Edelson Trial Opens," 1; "Ottawa Jeweler Faces Trial," 2. Despite
White's insistence to the judge that he was not leading his witness, the
deft prosecutor quickly scoped out another spot in the testimony where

Danby could be permitted to utter "someone said he's been shot." The exasperated judge responded with "Now, now, Mr. White," and refused to accept further discussion of the subject. "Ottawa Jeweler Faces Trial," 2.

34 White became so infuriated with Lemieux's befuddled answers that at one point the prosecutor "threw up his hands in dramatic fashion and said to the bench: 'My Lord, you drive a horse to water but you can't make him drink.'" It was expected that Lemieux's testimony would last longer, but his appearance was curtailed "owing to the extreme difficulty the Crown prosecutor had in dragging out of him many points." There were times that Lemieux's confusing testimony actually provoked laughter in the courtroom. See "New Testimony by Lemieux at Edelson's Trial," *The Ottawa Evening Citizen*, 15 January 1932, 13.

35 "New Testimony by Lemieux," 13.

36 "Hope to Finish Edelson Trial Tomorrow Night," *The Ottawa Evening Citizen*, 15 January 1932, 1.

37 "Second Bullet Evidence Given at Trial Today," *The Ottawa Evening Citizen*, 15 January 1932, 1.

38 "Jury Today to Decide Fate of Ben S. Edelson," *The Ottawa Evening Citizen*, 16 January 1932, 7.

39 Ibid.

40 "Hope to Finish," 1; Ibid.

41 "Jury Today to Decide Fate," 7. The credibility of this testimony is dubious given that Jack, in talking to his brother, would not have referred to his childhood pal as "Mr. Berger."

42 "Hope to Finish," 1.

43 "Jury Today to Decide Fate," 7. In the absence of the jury, and being questioned by White, Berger agreed that Horwitz knew he was dying: "He told me he was sure he would not survive. I believe any communications made to me were made with the expectations he was going to die." But during cross-examination by Doctor, Berger affirmed that Horwitz held out "the faint hope" of recovery. Berger quoted Jack as having said "'if I get better, it [the shooting] was an accident.'" (The statement also hinted at Jack's desire to suppress, if he survived, the related adultery/paternity scandal, as well as scrutiny of Ben and Alice.) See "Statements of Horwitz Made," 14.

44 "Second Bullet Evidence," 1.

45 "Jury Today to Decide Fate," 7.

46 In addition to the Edelson trial, the itinerary comprised another criminal
    case and thirty-eight civil actions, including seventeen non-jury cases
    (four of these divorce suits) and twenty-one jury cases. The *Journal* noted
    that only a month had been allocated to the winter assizes, and that
    "Mr. Justice McEvoy will endeavor to clear the long list up." See "Have
    17 Non-Jury Cases Listed for Assizes in Ottawa," *The Ottawa Evening
    Citizen*, 9 January 1932, 4; "Trial of Edelson on Murder Count on
    Assizes Docket," *The Ottawa Evening Journal*, 8 January 1932, 11.

47 "Lawyers Agree to Unique Step in Exam Case," *The Ottawa Evening
    Journal*, 25 January 1932, 1. McEvoy would suffer a stroke at the end of
    January, and would die in 1935. See "Meets with Accident," *The Mon-
    treal Gazette*, 6 February 1932, 11; "Ontario Courts," "Former Judges
    of the Superior Courts."

48 "Widow of Horwitz on Stand in Murder Trial," 1; "Mrs. Horwitz Tells
    Story of Family Trouble," *The Ottawa Evening Citizen*, 16 January
    1932, 10. Doctor asked "Do you keep a record of marks and bruises on
    prisoners' faces?" to which Levigne was compelled to state "No." The
    day before, Doctor had also drilled Detective-Sergeant MacDonald and
    Sergeant-Major Hardon about the existence of the mark. When Mac-
    Donald testified that he noticed no mark, Doctor referenced the dark-
    ened streets at the time of the arrest, and the poor lighting at Edelson's
    Friel Street home, in the police car, and at the police station. Hardon
    agreed that there was no mark, at which point an unremitting Doctor
    asked, "Even a policeman is human and can err at times, can he not?"
    Hardon firmly replied "Not in this instance, though." See "Jury Today
    To Decide Fate," 7.

49 "Crowded Court Tense as Accused Tells Dramatic Story," *The Ottawa
    Evening Journal*, 18 January 1932, 14.

50 "Mrs. Horwitz Tells Story," 10. As the investigation was performed in
    the absence of defence counsel, the irritated judge condemned police
    for neglecting "to invite Mr. Doctor down to these tests," but the judge
    nevertheless entertained the testimony.

51 "Mrs. Horwitz Tells Story," 10.

52 "Ben S. Edelson Is Acquitted," 18.

53 "Crowded Court Tense," 14. Boasting fourteen-years experience with
    firearms, Sherman Hardisty was head of the gun department and a gun

salesman at a sporting goods store. See "Cassidy Close to Collapse in Trial's Closing Stages New Evidence about Coat," *The Ottawa Evening Journal*, 20 January 1932, 3.

54 Sergeant Stephen Dykeman interview.

55 "Widow Relates Details of," *The Ottawa Evening Journal*, 16 January 1932, 22.

56 "Ben Edelson Found Not Guilty," 16.

57 "Had Edelson Any Unlawful Purpose in Producing Weapon, Judge Asks," *The Ottawa Evening Journal*, 18 January 1932, 18.

58 "Widow of Horwitz on Stand," 1; "Mrs. Jack Horwitz Tells Story," 1;

59 "Mrs. Jack Horwitz Tells Story," 1; "Widow of Horwitz on Stand," 1.

60 "Widow of Horwitz on Stand," 1; "Mrs. Horwitz Tells Story," 10; "Ben S. Edelson Is Acquitted," 15.

61 "Widow Relates Details of," 22. As the paper recorded no stunned reaction from the courtroom crowd, Yetta might have previously articulated this suspicion on the stand.

62 "Ben S. Edelson Is Acquitted," 14, 15; "Crowded Court Tense," 14.

63 "Crowded Court Tense," 14; "Ben S. Edelson Is Acquitted," 14.

64 Dubinsky, *Improper Advances*, 79.

65 "Crowded Court Tense," 14; "Ben S. Edelson Is Acquitted," 14.

66 "Mrs. Horwitz Tells Story," 1; "Ben S. Edelson Will Take Stand in Own Defence," *The Ottawa Evening Journal*, 13 January 1932, 1.

67 Defence Objections Sustained," 19; "Crown Exhibit Ruled out in Ben Edelson Case," *The Ottawa Evening Citizen*, 14 January 1932, 1; "Ben S. Edelson Is Acquitted," 14.

68 Backhouse, "'Calculated to Reflect on the Dignity of Parliament,'" 1, 17–18, 11.

69 "Brilliant, Effective Address," 15.

70 Frondorf, *Death of a "Jewish American Princess*," 204.

71 "Ben S. Edelson Is Acquitted," 14.

72 Ibid.

73 "Ben Edelson Found Not Guilty," 13.

74 "Ben Edelson Goes on the Stand and Tells how Horwitz Was Shot," *The Ottawa Evening Journal*, 18 January 1932, 13.

75 "Ben S. Edelson Is Acquitted," 14.

76 Ibid.

77 Sergeant Stephen Dykeman interview.

78 "Ben S. Edelson Is Acquitted," 14.

79 Ibid.

80 Ibid.

81 "Crowded Court Tense," 14.

82 Lillian Katznelson interview.

83 Ibid.

84 "Sensational Evidence Given," 13.

85 "Ben S. Edelson Is Acquitted," 14.

86 Ibid.

87 "Ben S. Edelson Is Acquitted," 14; "Crowded Court Tense," 14.

88 "Ben S. Edelson Is Acquitted," 14.

89 Ibid., 15.

90 Ibid., 14.

91 Ibid.

92 In order to draw attention away from the possibility that an incensed
    Ben had tracked Jack's actions previously, Doctor made nothing of the
    fact that Edelson had already known Jack's license plate number. When
    asked about the matter by White, Ben simply stated that "I had seen him
    driving before." See "Ben Edelson Goes on the Stand," 16, and
    "Crowded Court Tense," 14.

93 "Ben S. Edelson Is Acquitted," 14.

94 Ibid.

95 Ibid.

96 Ibid.

97 Frondorf, *Death of a "Jewish American Princess,"* 258–9. Frondorf, an
    attorney, explains that in the 1981 Steven Steinberg case, in which Stein-
    berg was tried for stabbing his wife to death, the Judge insisted that the
    time required for premeditation was more than sufficient – it occurred in
    the mere minutes that it took Steinberg to walk the sixty-six feet from
    the bedroom to the kitchen (where he retrieved the murder weapon), and
    back to the bedroom where he killed her.

98 "Ben S. Edelson Is Acquitted," 14; "Ben Edelson Found Not Guilty," 13.

99 "Crowded Court Tense," 14.

100 "Ben S. Edelson Is Acquitted," 15.

101 Ibid.

102 Ibid.

103 "Ben Edelson Found Not Guilty," 13.

104 "Ben S. Edelson Is Acquitted," 15. White asked Ben "You are sure that this was the exact position? ... I am giving you every chance to tell me just what happened. I may take you at your word?" Ben repeatedly replied, "Yes."

105 "Ben Edelson Found Not Guilty," 13.

106 "Ben S. Edelson Is Acquitted," 14.

107 "Brilliant, Effective Address," 15.

108 "Verdict More than Expected Says Edelson," *The Ottawa Evening Journal*, 18 January 1932, 13.

109 "Brilliant, Effective Address," 15.

110 "Ben Edelson Found Not Guilty," 13.

111 "Brilliant, Effective Address," 15.

112 Ibid.

113 Ibid.

114 *Horwitz v. Loyal Protective Ins. Co.*

115 "Brilliant, Effective Address," 15.

116 These missteps suggest that White neglected to focus on a few key and compelling arguments. Instead, he "nitpicked," seeing "too many trees and not the forest." William A.G. Simpson telephone interview.

117 "Brilliant, Effective Address," 15. For example, at the start of the trial, White told the jury that "it may be necessary for you to consider provocation." See "Defence Objections Sustained," 19.

118 "Edelson Back at Store Today after Acquittal," *The Ottawa Evening Journal*, 18 January 1932, 1.

119 Women would not be legally allowed to sit on juries in Ontario until 1952, and would not appear as jurors in Ottawa until 1953. In contrast, Jewish men had been jurors in British North America since the late seventeenth century: Asser Levy of New York was the first in 1671. But given the close and interrelated Jewish community in Ottawa, there was little chance that a Jew would have been selected by either the prosecution or defence for Edelson jury duty. See "Judge Helen Kinnear"; "New Quarters Not Ready for Assizes," *Ottawa Evening Citizen*, 10 January 1953, 32; Jewish Virtual Library, "New Amsterdam's Jewish Crusader," 2. Jews in Nova Scotia and Quebec began serving on juries as early as the eighteenth century. See Godfrey and Godfrey, *Search Out the Land*, 76 (Nova Scotia), 97 (Quebec).

120 The jurors were builder Edward Kingsbury (Cambridge Street, Ottawa),

tailor F. Lauzon (Rideau Street, Ottawa), carpenter James Johnston (Isabella Street, Ottawa), culler J.B. Larocque (Louisa Street, Ottawa), Edmund Jeanveau (his occupation was not named) (St Patrick Street, Ottawa), and merchant James H. Laishley (Lionel Street, Ottawa), and farmers Daniel Wilson (March Township), A.N. Anderson (Gloucester Township), Robert Taylor (Marlborough Township), Alan Wilson (Gloucester Township), Norman Missell (Osgoode Township), and Hartley Miller (Fitzroy Township). "Edelson Trial Opens," 1; "Defence Objections Sustained," 19; "Ottawa Jeweler Faces Trial," 2. Discrepancies exist in the newspapers regarding the names of some jurors: James H. Laishley is also listed as James H. Lishley, James Johnston as James Johnson, Edmund Jeanveau as Edward Janveau, Alan Wilson as Allan Wilson, and Norman Missell as Norman Mussell.

121 McLaren, "Males, Migrants, and Murder," 168.
122 Campbell, *Respectable Citizens*, 118, 121.
123 White, *Negotiating Responsibility*, 99; "Ben S. Edelson Is Acquitted," 14.
124 "Late Moses Doctor Left behind Many Sorrowing Friends," *The Ottawa Evening Citizen*, 21 March 1934, 2.
125 "Thousands Pay Fitting Tribute to Moses Doctor," *The Ottawa Evening Journal*, 22 March 1934, 3; "Moses Doctor Young Lawyer Is Found Dead," *The Ottawa Evening Journal*, 21 March 1934, 13.
126 "Many at Funeral of Moses Doctor," *The Ottawa Evening Citizen*, 22 March 1934, 3.
127 "Late Moses Doctor Left behind," 2.
128 "Portion of Bullet Was Taken from Woodwork at Scene of Shooting," *The Ottawa Evening Citizen*, 15 January 1932, 2.
129 "Crowded Court Tense," 14; "Ben S. Edelson Is Acquitted," 15.
130 "Ben S. Edelson Is Acquitted," 14.
131 See, for example, Walker, "Killing the Black Female Body," 94–5.
132 See, for example, Ibid., 100.
133 White, *Negotiating Responsibility*, 12. The Edelson/Horwitz case was not a domestic murder case, *per se*, but revolved around a domestic relationship, and incorporated many of the same elements.
134 Working-class men, along with immigrant and native men, were regularly denied the status entrenched in the perceived sanctity of the family. See White, *Negotiating Responsibility*, 13. Trial testimony and arguments

never indicated, however, that the middle-class Edelson family, by virtue
of its Jewish immigrant background, was in any way inferior to nativist
Canadian families.

135 Evidence that James Johnston and Hartley Miller were married include
Johnston-Matthews (1895), http://granniesgenealogygarden.com; and
Miller-Smith (1943), http://www.rootsweb.ancestry.com/~onlanark/
NewspaperClippings

136 *1911 Census of Canada*, Province of Ontario, Carleton County, Nepean
Enumeration District, #25, 12.

137 Horn, "The Menace of Single Men," 306–8.

138 "Chief Blames Transients for Crimes Here," *Ottawa Evening Citizen*,
29 December 1934, 1. It seems M. Horwitz Limited was itself a victim
of these criminals. In December of 1936, two or more bandits broke
into the front door of the Bank Street store at 1:00 am and stole $1,800
worth of jewellery, cigarette lighters, and fountain pens. See "Thieves
Get Away with Big Haul in Jewelry Robbery," *The Ottawa Evening
Citizen*, 4 December 1936, 8.

139 "Mother Denies Son Had Ever Owned Any Gun," *The Ottawa Evening
Journal*, 31 December 1931," 1.

140 "Police Press Man-Hunt for Lavigne's Murderer." *The Ottawa Evening
Journal*, 14 December 1931, 1; "Service Station Employe[e] Killed during
Struggle with Unknown Gun-Man." *The Ottawa Evening Citizen*, 14
December 1931, 11.

141 COA, Larochelle, *The History of the Ottawa Police*, 105. In contrast to
the Edelson trial, the Attorney General Central Registry Criminal and
Civil Files for the period 1873 to 1976 [RG 4-32] includes a file on the
Seabrooke trial. Perhaps this was because the case concluded with a
hanging, which A.W. Nichol, who downsized the collection for the AO,
probably found compelling. See "A Note on Sources."

142 Campbell, *Respectable Citizens*, 137–8, 49, 131–2.

143 McLaren, "Males, Migrants, and Murder," 162.

144 Gartner and Phillips, "The Creffield-Mitchell Case," 69.

145 Ibid., 74; Engel, *Crimes of Passion*, 21, 27. In the 1949 romantic-comedy
Adam's Rib, lawyer Amanda Bonner (Katharine Hepburn) defends a
woman who shoots (but doesn't kill) her philandering husband. Unconventional and feminist, Bonner argues that the unwritten law has served
to exonerate unlawful men who seek to safeguard their families, and that

the same consideration should be extended to her female client. The film makes it easy, however, to dismiss the credibility of Bonner's gendered argument: the case is reduced to a series of courtroom antics in the name of sex equality, and is essentially used as a vehicle for a comedic battle of the sexes between Amanda and her husband Adam, who is prosecuting the case. This lighthearted mood is enhanced by the unlikely verdict: the female defendant is acquitted of attempted murder, based on the unwritten law. This legal victory, a hallmark of a new, greater equality between women and men, seems hollow in light of Amanda's volatile marriage, and is all the more absurd given the general post-war promotion of women's return to their traditional (that is, domestic and unremunerated) gender roles. See *Adam's Rib*, MGM, Director George Cukor, 1949.

146 Gartner and Phillips, "The Creffield-Mitchell Case," 74. Even after a murder conviction, husbands who killed adulterous wives or their lovers (as well as women who killed abusive husbands or their babies) "were usually candidates for mercy." Until the 1960s in Canada, the federal Cabinet regularly exercised its royal prerogative, reducing death penalty sentences or granting full pardons. See Strange, "Mercy for Murderers?" 562, 568.

147 "Brilliant, Effective Address," 15.

148 McLaren, "Males, Migrants, and Murder," 175.

149 Gartner and Phillips, "The Creffield-Mitchell Case," 69.

150 For examples of defendants professing their adherence to the unwritten law, see Phillips and Gartner, *Murdering Holiness*, 122–3, and Uruburu, *American Eve*, 331.

151 Phillips and Gartner, *Murdering Holiness*, 134–7.

152 The quotation comes from Ibid., 159. The authors assert that the unwritten law was usually argued "under the guise" of the insanity defence, as in the Mitchell Case. 159–62.

153 White, *Negotiating Responsibility*, 103.

154 Phillips and Gartner, *Murdering Holiness*, 159. The authors make this point with regard to the defence lawyers and the insanity defence in the Mitchell case.

155 "Brilliant, Effective Address," 15.

156 "Crown Prosecutor Declares Edelson's Account of Shooting an Impossibility," *The Ottawa Evening Journal*, 18 January 1932, 15.

157 "Brilliant, Effective Address," 15.

158 Gartner and Phillips, "The Creffield-Mitchell Case," 69–73, 75, 79, 80.

159 "Augustino Declares He Used Knife in Defence," *The Ottawa Evening Citizen*, 14 January 1937, 13.

160 Ibid; "M. Augustino Not Guilty of Murder Charge," *The Ottawa Evening Citizen*, 14 January 1937," 1.

161 "Augustino Declares He Used Knife," 13; "Augustino Named as Wife's Slayer," *Montreal Gazette*, 29 September 1936, 6; "Augustino Case to Be Adjourned," *The Ottawa Evening Citizen*, 12 September 1936, 4.

162 "Augustino Declares He Used Knife," 13. The diminutive Augustino, referred to by the press as "mild-mannered," was described by his boss as "industrious, sober, and punctual," and by police as "very fond of children." He was so dedicated to the welfare of his marriage that upon first hearing of the affair, he sought out a job in a different city, ready and willing to relocate his family. After finding his wife at the hotel with McKluskey, he even telephoned police and requested that they come to escort Mary from the bar so he could take her home, but the police refused to get involved. Augustino later testified that Mary "broke her promise to 'mend her ways,' and hosted McKluskey in their home when Augustino worked nights. As well, she was accused of neglecting her children: on the eve of her death, Augustino came home to find that Mary had gone out, and had left all seven children alone.

163 "M. Augustino Not Guilty," 7.

164 Ibid.; Ibid., 1.

165 "Ben S. Edelson Is Acquitted," 14; Phillips and Gartner, *Murdering Holiness*, 189.

166 As Engel points out, the unwritten law has been employed in some southern U.S. states to protect husbands who have murdered their unfaithful wives. See *Crimes of Passion*, 27.

167 Gartner and Phillips, "The Creffield-Mitchell Case," 74; Uruburu, *American Eve*, 358.

168 Horn, "Introduction," 15.

169 Gartner and Phillips, "The Creffield-Mitchell Case," 74, 76.

170 Ibid.

171 Comack and Balfour, *The Power to Criminalize*, 61.

172 McLaren, "Males, Migrants, and Murder," 175.

173 White, *Negotiating Responsibility*, 103.

174 "Ben S. Edelson Is Acquitted," 14.

175 "Ben Edelson Found Not Guilty," 13.
176 AO, C 81-1-0-28 – OSOH, Interviews with Roydon Hughes, 28 October
     1983, 45–6.
177 Ibid.
178 "Brilliant, Effective Address," 15.
179 Ibid.
180 Dubinsky, *Improper Advances*, 132.
181 "Brilliant, Effective Address," 15; "Three-Day Trial Ends when Crowd
     Applauds Verdict of Not Guilty," *The Ottawa Evening Journal*, 18 Janu-
     ary 1932, 15.
182 "Three-Day Trial Ends," 15.
183 Backhouse, "'Calculated to Reflect on the Dignity of Parliament,'" 17.
184 "Ben S. Edelson Is Acquitted," 14.
185 "Three-Day Trial Ends," 15; "Brilliant, Effective Address," 15.
186 "Brilliant, Effective Address," 15; "Three-Day Trial Ends," 15
187 "Brilliant, Effective Address," 15.
188 "Three-Day Trial Ends," 15. Doctor named Ben Edelson, Yetta Horwitz,
     and their children – another glaring omission was the dead Jack Horwitz.
     According to one family member, true to his claim that a husband should
     not forgive a woman like Alice, Doctor "was very disappointed when the
     defendant went back to his wife." See Miriam Russ correspondence.
189 "Brilliant, Effective Address," 15.
190 Ibid.
191 Ibid. White's remark, of course, is unintentionally heterosexist.
192 Dubinsky, *Improper Advances*, 26.
193 Ibid., 26–8.
194 Ibid., 30, 69.
195 Ibid., 98.
196 Lusty, "Is There a Common Law Privilege against Spouse-Incrimina-
     tion?" 6–7; Stewart, "Spousal Incompetency and the Charter," 412–13,
     416–17; Huhn, "Ohio's 'Sacred Seal of Secrecy,'" 443–5. The chief ex-
     ception to the incompetency rule was if the crime by the spouse had
     threatened the other's freedom, health, and safety.
197 Medine, "The Adverse Testimony Privilege," 521–2; Stewart, "Spousal
     Incompetency and the Charter," 414, f.n. 15; *Canada Evidence Act*,
     R.S.C. 1985.
198 Medine, "The Adverse Testimony Privilege," 543. Although some of the
     rationales related to spousal incompetency have since been contested,

and although some of the related laws have been dropped or revised, "the common law rule that a spouse is not a competent witness for the prosecution remains in force." See Stewart, "Spousal Incompetency and the Charter," 413–14.

199 Huhn, "Ohio's 'Sacred Seal of Secrecy,'" 434, 448–9.

200 Ibid., 443; Lusty, "Is There a Common Law Privilege against Spouse-Incrimination?" 3.

201 *Canada Evidence Act*, in *Batary v. Saskatchewan*, Supreme Court of Canada; Medine, "The Adverse Testimony Privilege," 523. In the United States, the Supreme Court ruled in 1933 that a defendant's spouse could testify on his behalf (*Funk v. United States*). In Canada, the relevant contemporary statute can be found in *Canada Evidence Act*, s. 4(1).

202 Hamish Stewart correspondence; Stewart, "Spousal Incompetency and the Charter," 416, f.n. 21. The likely presumption here was that a wife would naturally be desirous to take the stand if it meant saving her husband (and herself, due to wives' economic dependence on husbands).

203 Hamish Stewart correspondence; Stewart, "Spousal Incompetency and the Charter," 414, f.n. 15.

204 Kramer and Mitchell, *Walk towards the Gallows*, 168. Also see Dubinsky, *Improper Advances*, 132–3, and Little, *'No Car, No Radio, No Liquor Permit,'* 76.

205 Little, *'No Car, No Radio, No Liquor Permit,'* 77–8, 105. One reason a patriarchal society views this female dependence on men as desirable is the otherwise unremunerated productive and reproductive labour that women perform in exchange for this security.

206 Kimmel, *Manhood in America*, 132–3; Campbell, *Respectable Citizens*, 130.

207 "Verdict More than Expected," 13.

208 See, for example, "Ben Edelson Arraigned," 1.

209 "Edelson Back at Store," 1.

210 Ibid.

211 "Ben S. Edelson Is Acquitted," 14.

212 Ibid.

213 Ibid.

214 Ibid.

215 Ibid.

216 "Edelson Grateful for Treatment Given Him," *The Ottawa Evening Citizen*, 18 January 1932, 1.

217 "Verdict More than Expected," 13.

218 "Edelson Back at Store," 1.

219 Ibid.

220 Perhaps it was no coincidence that B'nai Brith president Ben Goldfield, the Horwitz family lawyer, was absent from the meeting that night. See "Ovation Is Given to Ben Edelson," *The Ottawa Evening Journal*, 19 January 1932, 3. The *Journal* reported that "All morning people were peering into the store through the glass window of the door in an effort to get a glimpse of Mr. Edelson." As he was attending the showcase closest to the door, "an ample opportunity was afforded them." And despite the presence of sales staff, there were even those who "waited to be served by him personally." See "Edelson Back at Store," 1.

221 "Ben Edelson Found Not Guilty," 13.

222 Francine Shaffer telephone interview.

223 Mary Goldberg interview, and Sid Kronick interview; Adelene Hyman interview.

224 Sid Kronick telephone interview.

225 Francine Shaffer telephone interview. Adelene Hyman shared this sentiment. Adelene Hyman interview.

226 Suzie Gellman interview.

227 Lionel Metrick interview.

228 Suzie Gellman interview.

229 Ben's family felt differently about the verdict. As daughter Lillian later declared, "I think we always expected him to be found 'not guilty.'" After all, with Ben so "upstanding" and "hardworking," "he wasn't the kind of man that you attach this kind of event to." Lillian Katznelson interview.

230 "Edelson Grateful for Treatment," 1.

231 "Verdict More than Expected," 13.

232 Ibid.

CHAPTER SIX

1 Irwin-Zarecka, *Frames of Remembrance*, 57.

2 The memory scholarship that flourished in the 1990s was produced by historians, anthropologists, sociologists, psychologists, and neuroscientists. For examinations on memory and the Holocaust, see, for example,

ibid; Kirmayer, "Landscapes of Memory," 173–98; Kugelmass, "Missions to the Past," 199–214; Spitzer, "'Back through the Future,'" 87–104.

3 Kirmayer, "Landscapes of Memory," 190.

4 Antze and Lambek, "Forecasting Memory," xii.

5 Ibid., xxix.

6 Kirmayer, "Landscapes of Memory," 175.

7 Ibid., 191.

8 Antze and Lambek, "Forecasting Memory," xxix.

9 Bjork, Bjork, and MacLeod, "Types and Consequences of Forgetting," 136, 134. David Gross asserts that several advantages come with forgetting the collective past, including overcoming old hostilities and antagonisms, viewing the world through "fresh eyes," and discerning new opportunities. See Gross, *Lost Time*, 140–1.

10 Kirmayer, "Landscapes of Memory," 188.

11 Irwin-Zarecka, *Frames of Remembrance*, 54–5.

12 Gross, *Lost Time*, 112.

13 Irwin-Zarecka, *Frames of Remembrance*, 118; Kirmayer, "Landscapes of Memory, 190.

14 "Edelsons Still Holding Key to Fatal Shooting," *The Ottawa Evening Citizen*, 26 November 1931, 3.

15 "Horwitz Estate Divided among Three Persons," *The Ottawa Evening Citizen*, 27 November 1931, 2.

16 "Edelsons Still Holding Key," 3.

17 "Are Satisfied Three People Only in Store," *The Ottawa Evening Journal*, 30 November 1931, 7.

18 "Legal Battle over Horwitz Estate Looms," *The Ottawa Evening Journal*, 28 November 1931, 4.

19 "Edelson Back at Store Today after Acquittal," *The Ottawa Evening Journal*, 18 January 1932, 1.

20 Adelene Hyman interview. During the course of the interview, Hyman used this expression repeatedly to describe life in the Edelson home after Ben's acquittal.

21 SE, photograph of Ben and Alice Edelson, Quebec 1932.

22 AO, RG 22-1304-03 – Carleton County Supreme Court Procedure Book, 1931–1933, 61; *Horwitz v. Loyal Protective Ins. Co.*

23 *Horwitz v. Loyal Protective Ins. Co.*

24 "Slain Man's Heirs to Get Insurance," *The Toronto Daily Star*, 28 May
   1932 (internet). The insurance case was covered by the Toronto paper
   likely because the judge's decision was rendered at Toronto's Osgoode
   Hall.

25 COA, *1932 ocd*, 263.

26 Steven Chernove telephone interview; Steven Chernove correspondence.

27 "Register of Marriages of Congregation Shaare Zion (Gates of Zion),"
   1935, *Quebec Vital and Church Records*; "Engagements – Chernove-
   Fenster," A6. Interestingly, the wedding was officiated by Rabbi Julius
   Berger, the brother of lawyer Sam Berger, who had abandoned Yetta as a
   client several years before. See also *Quebec Vital and Church Records*;
   OJA, "Ottawan Air Force Chaplain," *Ottawa Jewish Bulletin*, 22 December 1943, 4.

28 Steven Chernove telephone interview.

29 "Index to Register of Voters," 1944, *California Voter Registrations*.
   Thanks to Sharon Edelson for locating this document.

30 "Ben Edelson Brings Charge against Hertz." *The Ottawa Evening Citizen*, 17 June 1932, 3.

31 "Edelson-Horwitz Feud Must Stop Court Asserts," *The Ottawa Evening
   Journal*, 28 December 1932, 1.

32 Dina Edelson interview.

33 In December of 1934, for example, Hertz, who ran a second Horwitz
   family jewellery store at 46 Rideau Street, claimed that as he was working in his shop, a lone thug entered the store at 9:30 pm, whacked him
   unconscious with a piece of iron pipe, and robbed the register of forty
   dollars. Two days later, the *Citizen* reported that police were pursuing a
   "new angle" in the case, and were terminating their search for a suspect.
   The newspaper now referred to the incident as an "alleged holdup," and
   more than implied that police were now doubtful the pipe had served as
   a weapon. See "Rideau Street Jeweler Knocked Out by Bandit and
   Robbed," *The Ottawa Evening Citizen*, 29 December 1934, 4; "Police
   Working on New Angle in Holdup Case," *The Ottawa Evening Citizen*,
   31 December 1934, 2. In July of 1936, just hours after Hertz had been
   placing window-display diamonds into the vault, a fire engulfed the rear
   of the store. The origin of the blaze was never discovered. See "Trans-
   portation Building Store Scene of Blaze," *The Ottawa Evening Citizen*,
   14 July 1936, 13.

34 Frank Slover, a men's clothing store owner, died in August 1933, leaving
    a robust estate of more than $117, 000. Just two days before he died, the
    litigious Slover executed a will at 6:30 pm, and then, according to Hertz,
    dictated a final will to him at 10:17 pm. The numerous trial witnesses in-
    cluded brother-in-law Charles Horwitz, who corroborated Hertz's story,
    and several handwriting experts who examined the wills' signatures.
    "Judge's Ruling Is that Later Will Not Valid," *The Ottawa Evening Citi-
    zen*, 28 November 1933, 12.

35 "Moses Doctor Young Lawyer Is Found Dead," *The Ottawa Evening
    Journal*, 21 March 1934, 13.

36 Ibid., 13; "Moses Doctor's Sudden Passing Shocks Ottawa," *The Ottawa
    Evening Citizen*, 21 March 1934, 12.

37 Ibid.

38 "Moses Doctor Young Lawyer," 13.

39 Ibid.; "Moses Doctor's Sudden Passing," 12.

40 "Moses Doctor Young Lawyer," 13.

41 AO, RG 22-354 – Carleton County Surrogate Court Estate Files, Estate
    File for Moses Doctor, 16686/1934. They resided at 68 Sweetland
    Avenue.

42 "Moses Doctor Young Lawyer, 13; "Moses Doctor's Sudden Passing,"
    12.

43 Doreen Caplin Teichman telephone interview. Teichman's grandmother,
    Eva Adler, was the sister of Rabbi Doctor, which made Teichman's
    mother Alice and Moses Doctor first cousins; Diane Payne (Abe Lieff)
    correspondence. Payne interviewed her ninety-two-year-old father, Abra-
    ham Harold Lieff, whose mother Mindel (Minnie) was a sister of Moses
    Doctor; AO, C 81-1-0-28 – OSOH, Interviews with Roydon Hughes, 28
    October 1983, 13, 22.

44 Miriam Russ correspondence. Russ is a niece of Moses Doctor; Diane
    Payne (Abe Lieff) correspondence.

45 Diane Payne (Abe Lieff) correspondence; Alan Abelson interview; Lionel
    Metrick interview. Metrick's mother was a first cousin of Moses Doctor's
    wife Rose Florence; Interviews with Roydon Hughes, 28 October 1983,
    22. Doctor's estate was valued at $12,573.46, with liabilities valued
    at over $20,000. Assets had first been assessed at $21,591.56, but
    $9,018.10 was deducted from the original $18,252.06 in life insurance
    monies, possibly due to the cause of death. See Estate File for Moses

Doctor, 16686/1934. Doctor's law partner Roydon Hughes attributed Doctor's debt to his unstinting philanthropy: "he was a great spender ... And he was very generous towards all people ... towards all religious things ... he gave money away like a drunken sailor. No matter how much money was brought into the firm, he could spend it all and more." Hughes noted that Doctor "was always borrowing from the bank," and from "the Jewish money lenders around Ottawa in those days" who loaned Doctor money "at high rates of interest." Interviews with Roydon Hughes, 28 October 1983, 22.

46 Diane Payne (Abe Lieff) correspondence; Alan Abelson interview; Lionel Metrick interview. It certainly seems possible that Doctor had indeed used the place for afternoon trysts, since he had no children to disturb his legal studies at home. Miriam Russ correspondence. His alleged affair casts a hypocritical light on his indictment of Alice, although within a patriarchal culture, a discreet man with no children bore little similarity to an imprudent woman with seven.

47 Doreen Caplin Teichman telephone interview.

48 OJA, IC, File – Doctor, Rev. Louis, "Rev. Louis Doctor Called by Death," *The Ottawa Citizen*, 20 September 1934; Miriam Russ correspondence. Rabbi Doctor died on 19 September 1934, which was Yom Kippur, the holiest day of the Jewish calendar.

49 As well, an autopsy would have delayed burial, which in traditional Judaism is supposed to transpire within a day after death. Indeed, Moses Doctor stipulated in his will that this timeline be followed. See Estate File for Moses Doctor, 16686/1934.

50 Attempted suicide was, in fact, a crime, and could garner a two-year prison sentence. See *Revised Statutes of Canada 1927*, Section 270.

51 Suicide is regarded as a serious offence in Judaism because it undermines the notion of life as a divine gift whose duration is ordained by God. In traditional Judaism, one who possesses mental and physical health and commits suicide is denied Jewish mourning and burial rituals. One who suffers from extreme mental or physical distress and commits suicide is regarded as not responsible for his/her actions, and is accorded full mourning and burial rites. Today, the latter approach predominates. See Rabbi Louis Jacobs, "Suicide in Jewish Tradition and Literature."

52 Lillian Katznelson interview.

53 Francine Shaffer telephone interview.

54 Mary Goldberg interview.

55 SE, Ben Edelson's "Address Book." Another person also wrote entries in the book, as Ben's own death in 1988 is recorded.

56 SE, Ben Edelson's "Address Book."

57 Lillian Katznelson interview.

58 Ibid.; Francine Shaffer telephone interview; Suzie Gellman interview. Francine Shaffer and Lillian Edelson were friends in the 1930s and 40s, but never spoke of the shooting. Suzie Gellman and Vivian Edelson attended school together, but also never spoke of the incident.

59 Joel and Sharon Edelson interview.

60 Lillian Katznelson interview; Dina Edelson interview.

61 Ibid. Dina agreed

62 Lillian Katznelson interview.

63 Ibid.

64 COA, *1940 ocd*, 187; Joel and Sharon Edelson interview.

65 Jeff Keshen, "World War Two and the Making of Modern Ottawa," 387.

66 Lillian Katznelson interview; Dina Edelson interview.

67 Dudley, "Downtown Jeweller Winds Down," E1. One of the employees worked there for forty-seven years.

68 "National Building Is Swept by Fire," *The Ottawa Evening Citizen*, 25 November 1950, 1. This was not the first time the Edelson store had been robbed. See, for example, "Smash and Grab Robbery at Rideau Street Store," *The Ottawa Evening Citizen*, 2 September 1940, 15, and "Lawyers Seeking Money Taken from Convicted Robber," *The Ottawa Evening Citizen*, 2 October 1943, 12. Neither was this fire a first for Edelson. See "15-Year-Old Boy Started Blaze," *The Ottawa Evening Citizen*, 26 November 1947, 2.

69 Dudley, "Downtown Jeweller Winds Down," E1.

70 Mary Goldberg interview.

71 Lillian Katznelson interview.

72 Ibid.

73 Adelene Hyman interview.

74 Mary Goldberg interview.

75 Sam got married in 1938, and Lillian, Vivian, and Jack all got married in 1941. See Ben Edelson's "Address Book."

76 Sam, Jack, Vivian, and Lillian all had children. The single Dina and the divorced Shirley and Eli never had children.

77 Joel and Sharon Edelson interview.

78 Pioneer Women was a labour Zionist group started in Palestine in 1925 that launched a chapter in Ottawa in 1938. See OJA, "Na'amat Canada's 75th anniversary," *Ottawa Jewish Bulletin*, 11 September 2000, 9.

79 Lillian Katznelson interview.

80 See, for example, OJA, OHW, Box 12, File – Publicity Series – *Hadassah Highlights*, Ottawa, 1955–1964, "Lillian Freiman Chapter," October 1957, 3; November 1957, 3; October 1958, 5–6; January 1956, 3; and January 1962, 4.

81 Dina Edelson interview.

82 OJA, OHW, Box 12, File – Publicity Series – *Hadassah Highlights*, Ottawa, 1955-1964, "Lillian Freiman Chapter," *Hadassah Highlights*, June 1955, 2; OJA, OHW, Box 6 – Anniversary and Milestone Series, File – Anniversary Golden Jubilee – Canadian Hadassah-Wizo, 1917–1967, "Report on Hadassah's 50th Anniversary," program, 23 October 1967, 10; OJA, OHW, Box 12, File – Publicity Series – *Hadassah Highlights*, Ottawa, 1965–1977, "Lillian Freiman Chapter," *Hadassah Highlights*, October 1971, 3.

83 OJA, OHW, Box 12, File – Publicity Series – *Hadassah Highlights*, Ottawa, 1965–1977, January–February 1973, 4.

84 OJA, Box – Judge Jacie Charles Horwitz, File 2 – Clippings, marriage announcement, 26 November 1939, and "Married in Toronto," 26 November 1939.

85 OJA, Box – Judge Jacie Charles Horwitz, File 9 – Eulogy for Charles Horwitz, "Eulogy – Charles Horwitz." Oddly enough, the 1998 obituary for Jacie Horwitz referenced no siblings at all. See OJA, Box – Judge Jacie Charles Horwitz, File – Clippings, "Judge Jacie Charles Horwitz, QC: Judge Fought for Human Rights," *The Ottawa Citizen*, 5 April 1998, A9.

86 Jack Horwitz interview; Jonathan Horwitz interview. According to Jonathan, some of his cousins heard the story for the first time as adults when a family member who had no knowledge of the shooting hired Ben and Alice's son Jack, a professional caterer, for a Horwitz family gathering. Older family members who attended were dismayed by the presence of an Edelson. The next generation of Edelsons were also told next to nothing about the incident. For example, Joel Edelson, son of Ben and Alice's oldest child, Samuel, only learned about the homicide when he got into a fight with some local bullies as a teenager and the father of

one of the boys shouted, "You're going to be a killer, just like your grandfather!" Joel and Sharon Edelson interview. In the meantime, Joel, and Philip Horwitz's son, Bobby, became excellent friends, but never spoke of the topic. Joel only learned fully of the event in the mid-1960s after his new bride Sharon researched the newspaper coverage. Natalie Edelson, the adult daughter of Ben and Alice's son Jack, noted that the shooting was "a very well-kept secret in my family – one that I only circuitously found out about when I was eleven or twelve years old." Natalie Edelson correspondence.

87 In the 1940s, for example, Jacie and his family lived in a house right across the street from Lillian's family. Lillian Katznelson interview; Jack Horwitz interview. There were many other overlapping events in the two families' lives: for instance, in the 1950s, Jacie was a member of B'nai Brith along with Eli Edelson. OJA, Box 1 – B'nai Brith, File – B'nai Brith Ottawa Lodges – Ottawa Lodge No. 885. Membership Lists and Lodge Rosters – 1945, 1972–1976, 1980–1981, "Ottawa Lodge B'nai Brith #885 List of Membership, May 25 1954." Jacie Horwitz's wife Jeanne and Alice worked on several Hadassah luncheons together. OJA, OHW, Box 12 – Publicity Series – History – *Hadassah Highlights* – News Clippings, File – Publicity – Newspaper Clippings, 1927–1992, "Martin Speaks on Polio at Hadassah Luncheon," *The Ottawa Citizen*, no date, likely 1955, 19. Also in the 1950s, Ben and Alice's teenage grandson Joel worked for an engraver, and on his bicycle picked up from and delivered orders to Horwitz Jewellers on Bank Street. Joel and Sharon Edelson interview. In the 1970s, Jack Edelson did some catering for Philip's Beacon Arms Hotel, and Jacie's son Jack patronized Edelson Jewellers. Jack Horwitz interview.

88 Jack Horwitz interview; Jonathan Horwitz interview

89 Steven Chernove telephone interview.

90 Wertsch, *Voices of Collective Remembering*, 40.

91 Ibid., 31, 41–2; Irwin-Zarecka, *Frames of Remembrance*, 9, 25.

92 Irwin-Zarecka, *Frames of Remembrance*, 127.

93 Kirmayer, "Landscapes of Memory," 191–2.

94 Freiman, *Don't Fall Off the Rocking Horse*, 67–70.

95 Greenberg, *My Memoirs*, 30–1, 34.

96 Lieff, *Gathering Rosebuds*, 40–1, 43, 92, 107, 205–8, 191–5, 98, 112–14. Lieff and Doctor both attended Osgoode Hall, the only law

school in Ontario at the time, and one with no admission restrictions regarding Jews. See p.92.

97 Adelene Hyman interview.

98 Shirley Berman correspondence.

99 Ibid.

100 Goldberg, "The Depression and War," 46–115. Other than a 1930 *City Directory* listing of Ben's store on page 59, and a brief caption which identifies Alice in a reprinted 1948 photograph of her volunteer women's group (Gary May, "The Golden Age," 126), Ben and Alice assume virtually no role in the book's narrative.

101 Suzie Gellman interview. It is not surprising that Lindbergh, in particular, loomed large for Gellman. In 1927, on the heels of his continuous solo flight across the Atlantic, Lindbergh arrived in Ottawa to much fanfare, a visit which must have made his subsequent personal misfortune all that more heartbreaking for his Ottawa admirers. Moreover, although Gellman didn't mention it, this trip proved the occasion of another Lindbergh-related calamity. In celebration of Canada's diamond jubilee, Lindbergh, Prime Minister King, and tens of thousands of adoring Lindbergh fans watched in horror during an air show over Parliament Hill as one of the participating planes dropped from the sky and crash landed. The pilot was killed instantly, and the Ottawa revelers were left in shock. The event had been broadcast live on radio by the Château Laurier, and heard by five million people. See Rankin, *Meet me at the Château*, 41.

102 Suzie Gellman interview.

103 They also assumed that when they used the term "we" and "community," I, as a fellow Jew, knew exactly who they meant.

104 Engel, *Crimes of Passion*, 44.

105 Sharon Edelson correspondence. Sharon later heard the woman tell this story.

106 Lionel Metrick interview; Francine Shaffer telephone interview.

107 Lionel Metrick interview.

108 Anonymous source.

109 Mary Goldberg interview.

110 Lionel Metrick, interview with author, Ottawa, 27 August 2006. Metrick recalls that for his bar mitzvah in August of 1930, his Aunt Olive gave him a monogrammed ring from Jack Horwitz's store. When Jack congratulated the bar mitzvah boy, and shook his hand so earnestly that the

ring's metal initials fell to the floor, Jack immediately picked up the small piece, and had it rewelded. Jack's gift to Lionel was a tie pin in the shape of a horseshoe. Both the ring and the tie pin remain in Metrick's possession to this day.

111 Francine Shaffer telephone interview.

112 Jack Horwitz interview; Jonathan Horwitz interview.

113 For example, Lionel Metrick interview.

114 Jack Horwitz interview.

115 Estelle Abelson interview; Mary Goldberg interview; Jonathan Horwitz interview; Francine Shaffer telephone interview; Adelene Hyman interview with author. Estelle Abelson first made me aware of this rumour, which her mother, a confidante of Alice, had relayed to her at least four or five decades ago.

116 Jonathan Horwitz interview; Francine Shaffer telephone interview.

117 Jonathan Horwitz interview; Adelene Hyman interview.

118 Joel and Sharon Edelson interview. In deference to both the Edelson and Horwitz families, I do not explore the paternity issue further.

119 Lillian Katznelson interview.

120 Sid Kronick telephone interview; Lionel Metrick interview.

121 Francine Shaffer telephone interview.

122 Suzie Gellman interview.

123 In order to protect the privacy and confidentiality of these Edelson and Horwitz family members, I am unable to reveal their names.

124 Lillian Katznelson interview; SE, "Hulse and Playfair Funeral Directors," statement of interment for Alice Edelson, 2 January 1972.

125 Joel and Sharon Edelson interview.

126 Steven Chernove interview.

127 Max Fenster, *Social Security Death Index*; Yetta R. Fenster, *Social Security Death Index*.

128 "Engagements – Chernove-Fenster," A6; "Robert B. Chernove: A Los Angeles Man You'll Like to Know" [advertisement], 6; Steven Chernove interview.

129 Kenneth Chernove and Steven Chernove, *California Birth Index*; "Panhellenic Group," A4.

130 Steven Chernove interview.

131 Ibid.

132 Dudley, "Downtown Jeweller Winds Down Store after 85 Years," *The*

Ottawa Citizen, 22 April 2005, E1; "Rideau Street Loses a Gem," *The Ottawa Citizen*, 5 April 2004, D1; Scanlan, "72-year Stint on Rideau Strip Ends for Jeweller," *The Ottawa Citizen*, 30 June 1992, B3.

CONCLUSION

1 Strange, "Wounded Womanhood and Dead Men," 176, 151.
2 White, *Negotiating Responsibility*, 25.

A NOTE ON SOURCES

1 See, for example, "Murder and Justice," *The Ottawa Evening Journal*, 22 January 1932, 8; "The Cassidy Case," *The Ottawa Evening Journal*, 23 January 1932, 8; "More Queer Justice," *The Ottawa Evening Journal*, 26 January 1932, 6.
2 See, for example, Phillips and Gartner, *Murdering Holiness*, 121–40; Uruburu, *American Eve*, 306–8, 312–14.
3 White, *Negotiating Responsibility*, 10; "The Cassidy Case," *The Ottawa Evening Journal*, 26 January 1932, 6, and "The Cassidy Case," *The Ottawa Evening Journal*, 29 January 1932, 3; "Service Station Hold-Ups," [letter to editor]. *The Ottawa Evening Journal*, 16 December 1931, 6.
4 See, for example, "Jack Horwitz, Victim of Shooting, and His Wife," *The Ottawa Evening Journal*, 25 November 1931, 1.
5 See, for example, RG 22-517-0-195, Supreme Court Registrar's Criminal Indictment Files, Carleton, Winter Assize 1932 – Folder "Criminal Indictments" Winter 1932, "Report of Criminal Business ... Ottawa Winter Assizes, 1932."
6 Attorney General Central Registry Criminal and Civil Files, AO, "Search Groups of Archival Records, "About these records," http://ao.minisisinc. com; AO, RG 4-32 – Attorney General Central Registry Criminal and Civil Files, 1871–1976.
7 "Customer Service Guide 109," AO, Freedom of Information and Protection of Privacy, www.archives.gov.on.ca. This site offers a link to a copy of the *Freedom of Information and Protection of Privacy Act*.
8 Other papers which provide no coverage of the case (in the days after the shooting and Ben's acquittal) include *Le Soleil* (Quebec City), *Le Quotidien de Lévis* (Quebec City), *Le Progrès du Golfe* (Lower St Laurent and

Gaspésie regions), *Le Gazette du Nord* (north-western Quebec), and *Le Colon* (Roberval). With the exception of *Le Droit* (Ottawa), which also included no stories, the Ottawa-area French-language press proved difficult to research as publications were generally small, infrequent, or sporadic, and thus often no longer available.

9 See "Jack Horwitz est Tué Chez un Bijoutier" ["Jack Horwitz is Killed at a Jeweller's"]. *L'Action catholique*, 25 Novembre 1931, 1; "Edelson n'a pas Fait de Déclaration" [Edelson did not Make a Statement"], *L'Action catholique*, 26 November 1931, 1; "Le Petit Jury Accepte la Version de Ben S. Edelson" ["The Small Jury Accepts Ben S. Edelson's Version"], *L'Action catholique*, 18 January 1932, 1; "Du Mystère autour de la Mort du Bijoutier Horwitz" ["Mystery surrounds the death of jeweller Horwitz"] *La Patrie*, 26 November 1931, 9.

10 OJA, Rhinewine, "The Jewish Press in Canada," 457.

Bibliography

ARCHIVAL SOURCES

Archives of Ontario (AO)

RG 4-32 – Attorney General Central Registry Criminal and Civil Files, 1871–1976

RG 22-1304-03 – Carleton County Supreme Court Procedure Book, 1931–1933

RG 22-354 – Carleton County Surrogate Court Estate Files. Estate file for Moses Doctor, 16686/1934

C 81-5-0-7 – Documentation Pertaining to the Legal Career of Peter White Jr. [clippings].

C 81-1-0-28 – Osgoode Society Oral History Programme. Interviews with Roydon Hughes.

C 81-1-0-14 – Osgoode Society Oral History Programme. Interviews with Peter White.

RG 4-32 – J.A. Ritchie, Crown Attorney, Ottawa

RG 22-517-0-195, Supreme Court Registrar's Criminal Indictment Files, Carleton, Winter Assize 1932 – Folder "Criminal Indictments."

City of Ottawa Archives (COA)

Fletcher, Katherine. *Capital Walks: Walking Tours of Ottawa*. Second edition. Toronto: Fitzhenry and Whiteside, 2004.

Larochelle, Gilles M. *The History of the Ottawa Police 1826–1993*. Gloucester, Ontario: Tyrell Press, 1994.

Meeting, Board of Police Commissioners, Box 1

Ottawa Police Force, Box 1/7

Ottawa City Directory, 1931, 1932, 1934, 1935, 1936, 1937, 1938, 1940, 1945, 1946, 1947, 1948, 1949, 1950, 1951, 1956

Jewish Public Library (Montreal), Archives (JPL)
Keneder Adler (Jewish Daily Eagle), 26, 27, 29 November 1931; 3, 11, 17 December 1931; 15, 17 January 1932.

New York Public Library (NYPL)
1910/11 Jersey City, New Jersey City Directory

Ottawa Jewish Archives (OJA)
Adath Jeshurun Congregation Minutes (1892–1956)
Agudath Achim Congregation, Membership/Seat Holders
– Minutes, 1928–1954
Rabbi Saul Aranov Collection
B'nai Brith
Max Bookman Collection
Goldberg, Samuel Lawrence. "Economic and Social Aspects of the Location of Jews in Ottawa (1891–1931)." Undergraduate essay, Geography. Carleton University, 1976.
Greenberg, Bess. *My Memoirs* [as told to Cynthia Nyman Engel] [self-published], 1995.
Hart, Arthur Daniel, editor. *The Jew in Canada: A Complete Record of Canadian Jewry from the Days of the French Regime to the Present Time.* Toronto and Montreal: Jewish Publications Limited, 1926.
J.C. Horwitz Collection
Judge Jacie Charles Horwitz
Individual Collections: Samuel Berger; Rev. Louis Doctor; A.L. Florence; Minto; Young Men's Hebrew Association
Kershman, Sylvia. "Family, Friends, Lower Town" [audio cassette]. Ben Karp Memorial Lecture, Ottawa Jewish Historical Society, 8 May 2002.
– "Lower Town Tour" [audio cassette], 2001.
Levine, Norman. *In Lower Town*. Ottawa: Commoners Publishing, 1977.
Lo, Laurelle C. "The Path from Peddling: Jewish Economic Activity in Ottawa prior to 1939." M.A. thesis, History. University of Ottawa, 2000.
Ottawa Hadassah-Wizo Collection
Ottawa Jewish Bulletin

Rabinovich, Jonah. "Isolated Actions: A.J. Freiman, and Anti-Semitism in Ottawa during the mid 1930s." Undergraduate essay.

Rhinewine, A. "The Jewish Press in Canada." *The Jew in Canada: A Complete Record of Canadian Jewry from the Days of the French Régime to the Present Time.* Compiled and edited by Arthur Daniel Hart, 457. Toronto and Montreal: Jewish Publications Limited, 1926.

Steinman, Thelma. *A Jewish Odyssey* [self-published memoir], 2002.

Young Jewish People's Association of Ottawa

Private Collections

Sharon Edelson

Steven Chernove

CORRESPONDENCE WITH AUTHOR

Berman, Shirley. 9, 11, 16 June 2009

Chernove, Steven. 13 June 2008

Edelson, Natalie. 12 April 2010

Edelson, Sharon. 19 February 2006; 14 August 2006; 18, 19 June 2008; 16 September 2008; 9 February 2009

Payne, Diane. 24 October 2007

Russ, Miriam. 3, 17 October 2007

Shaver, Michael (through Miriam Russ). 24 October 2007

Slone, Eric. 22, 24 November 2007

Stewart, Hamish. 13 November 2007

Ward, Ron, AO. 20 June 2008, pertaining to AO, Ottawa Jail Punishment Register, RG 20-84-2

INTERVIEWS

Abelson, Alan. Ottawa, 1 May 2006

Abelson, Estelle. Ottawa, March 2004

Adler, Max. Telephone interview with author, 28 October 2007

Backhouse, Connie. Ottawa, 29 August 2007

Chernove, Steven. Telephone interview with author, 9 June 2008

Citron, Murray. Ottawa, 25 May 2009

Dykeman, Sergeant Stephen. London, 2 October 2009

Edelson, Dina. Ottawa, 30 April 2006

Edelson, Joel and Sharon. Ottawa, 29 April 2006

Gellman, Suzie. Ottawa, 26 August 2006

Goldberg, Mary. Ottawa, 5 July 2006

Horwitz, Jack. Ottawa, 6 July 2006

Horwitz, Jonathan. Ottawa, 6 July 2006

Hyman, Adelene. Cambridge, Ontario, 4 July 2009

Katznelson, Lillian. Ottawa, 29 August 2005

Kronick, Sid. Telephone interview with author, 27 August 2007

Metrick, Lionel. Ottawa, 27 August 2006

Shaffer, Francine. Telephone interview with author, 4 September 2006

Simpson, William A.G. Telephone interview with author, 8 April 2010

Teichman, Doreen Caplin. Telephone interview with author, 22 October 2007

NEWSPAPERS

L'Action catholique

The Boca Raton News

The Canadian Jewish Chronicle

The Canadian Jewish News

The Canadian Jewish Review

The Cornwall Standard

The Detroit Almanac

The Jewish Daily Forward

The Los Angeles Times

The Montreal Gazette

The New York Times

The Ottawa Citizen

The Ottawa Evening Citizen

The Ottawa Evening Journal

La Patrie

The Renfrew Mercury

The Toronto Daily Star

The Toronto Globe

OTHER SOURCES

Adam's Rib, MGM, Director George Cukor, 1949.

The Haunted Walk of Ottawa. Crime and Punishment Jail Tour [Nicholas Street Jail], 28 August 2008.

ARTICLES AND BOOKS

Abella, Irving. *A Coat of Many Colours: Two Centuries of Jewish Life in Canada*. Toronto: Key Porter Books, 1990; rpt. 1999.

– and Harold Troper. *None Is Too Many: Canada and the Jews of Europe, 1933–1948*. Toronto: Lester and Orpen, 1983; rpt. 1986.

Antler, Joyce. *You Never Call! You Never Write!: A History of the Jewish Mother*. New York: Oxford University Press, 2007.

Antze, Paul and Michel Lambek. "Forecasting Memory." *Tense Past: Cultural Essays in Trauma and Memory*. Ed. Paul Antze and Michel Lambek, xi–xxxviii. New York: Routledge, 1996.

Attorney General Central Registry Criminal and Civil Files, AO, "Search Groups of Archival Records, "About these records." http://ao.minisisinc.com.

Aunt Eva [Eva Bilsky], *What Happened After: Some Familiar Fairy Tales Continued*. Montreal: The Mercury Press Limited, 1942.

Auster, Paul. *The Invention of Solitude*. Sun Press, 1982; rpt. New York: Penguin Books, 1988.

Backhouse, Constance. "Rape in the House of Commons: The Prosecution of Louis Auger, Ottawa, 1929." *Essays in the History of Canadian Law*, Volume X, A Tribute to Peter N. Oliver. Ed. Jim Phillips et al., 33–66. Toronto: The Osgoode Society for Canadian Legal History, University of Toronto Press, 2008.

– "'Calculated to Reflect on the Dignity of Parliament': Rape in the House of Commons, Ottawa 1929." www.lawsite.ca

Betcherman, Lita-Rose. *The Swastika and the Maple Leaf: Fascist Movements in Canada in the Thirties*. Toronto: Fitzhenry and Whiteside, 1975.

Bjork, Elizabeth L., Robert A. Bjork, and Malcolm D. MacLeod. "Types and Consequences of Forgetting: Intended and Unintended." *Memory and Society: Psychological Perspectives*. Ed. Lars-Goren Nilsson and Nobuo Ohta, 134–58. East Essex, England: Psychology Press, 2006.

Bookman, Max. "Excerpts from A History of the Jew in Canada's Capital." *Canadian Jewish Reference Book and Directory 1963*. Ed. Dr Eli Gottesman, 387-405. Montreal: Jewish Institute of Higher Research, Central Rabbinical Seminary of Canada, 1963.

Boyle, Terry. *Fit to Be Tied: Ontario's Murderous Past*. Toronto: Polar Bear Press, 2001.

Brodkin, Karen. *How Jews Became White Folks & What That Says about Race in America*. New Brunswick, New Jersey: Rutgers University Press, 1998.

Brown, Ron. *Behind Bars: Inside Ontario's Heritage Gaols*. Toronto: Natural Heritage Books, 2006.

Brym, Robert J. "The Rise and Decline of Canadian Jewry?" *The Jews in Canada*. Ed. Robert J. Brym et al., 22-38. Toronto: Oxford University Press, 1993.

California Birth Index, 1905–1995. Ancestry.com.

California Voter Registrations, 1900–1968. Ancestry.com.

Campbell, Lara. *Respectable Citizens: Gender, Family, and Unemployment in Ontario's Great Depression*. Toronto: University of Toronto Press, 2009.

Canada Evidence Act, R.S.C. 1985, c. C-5, s. 4 (3).

Canada Evidence Act, 6, Ed. VII, c. 10, s. 1, 1906, in *Batary v. Saskatchewan (Attorney General)*, Supreme Court of Canada, 1965.

"Capital Punishment in Canada," Department of Justice Canada. http://www.justice.gc.ca.

Cobban, James. "Families of South-West Middlesex. "John M. McEvoy." http://jamescobban.net/FamilyTree/Web.

Comack, Elizabeth and Gillian Balfour. *The Power to Criminalize: Violence, Inequality and the Law*. Halifax: Fernwood Publishing, 2004.

Conley, Carolyn A. *The Unwritten Law: Criminal Justice in Victorian Kent*. New York: Oxford University Press, 1991.

Coroner's Act, Revised Statutes of Ontario, 1990, Chapter 37. www.e-laws.gov.on.ca

"Customer Service Guide 109." AO, Freedom of Information and Protection of Privacy. www.archives.gov.on.ca.

Davies, Blodwen. *The Charm of Ottawa*. Toronto: McClelland and Stewart, 1932.

Dick, Caroline. "A Tale of Two Cultures: Intimate Femicide, Cultural Defences, and the Law of Provocation." *Canadian Journal of Women and the Law*, 23 (2011): 519–47.

Dinnerstein, Leonard. *The Leo Frank Case*. New York: Columbia University Press, 1968; rpt. Athens: The University of Georgia Press, 1987.

Draper, Paula. "The Role of Canadian Jewish Women in Historical Perspective." *Canadian Jewish Women of Today: Who's Who of Canadian Jewish Women*. Ed Edmond Y. Lipsitz, 3–10. Downsview, Ontario: J.E.S.L. Educational Products, 1983.

– and Janice B. Karlinsky. "Abraham's Daughters: Women, Charity, and Power in the Canadian Jewish Community." *Looking into My Sister's Eyes: An Exploration in Women's History*, Ed. Jean Burnet, 75–90. Toronto: Multicultural History Society of Ontario, 1986.

Dubinsky, Karen. *Improper Advances: Rape and Heterosexual Conflict in Ontario, 1880–1929*. Chicago: The University of Chicago Press, 1993.

– and Franca Iacovetta. "Murder, Womanly Virtue, and Motherhood: The Case of Angelina Napolitano, 1911–1922." *Canadian Historical Review*, LXXII, 4 (1991): 505–31.

Engel, Howard. *Crimes of Passion: An Unblinking Look at Murderous Love*. Toronto: Prospero Books, 2007.

Fido, Martin. *Deadly Jealousy: Men and Women Driven by Passion to Kill*. London: Constable and Robinson, 1993.

Figler, Bernard. *Lillian and Archie Freiman: Biographies*. Montreal: 1962.

Frager, Ruth A. *Sweatshop Strife: Class, Ethnicity, and Gender in the Jewish Labour Movement of Toronto, 1900–1939*. Toronto: University of Toronto Press, 1992.

"Framing Canada: A Photographic Memory." ArchiviaNet: On-line Research Tool. Library and Archives Canada, Photographic Collections. http//data4.collectionscanada.gc.ca.

Freiman, Lawrence. *Don't Fall Off the Rocking Horse*. Toronto: McClelland and Stewart, 1978.

Frondorf, Shirley. *Death of a "Jewish American Princess."* New York: Berkley Books, 1988.

Gartner, Rosemary and Jim Phillips. "The Creffield-Mitchell Case, Seattle, 1906." *Pacific Northwest Quarterly* (Spring 2003): 69–82

Gilgoff, Dan and Eric Marrapodi, "Child's Grisly Murder Shocks Brooklyn Neighborhood." CNN Belief Blog. http://religion.blogs.cnn.com/2011/07/14/.

Giusti, Marissa. "Building Foundations: The Ottawa Jewish Community 1930–1950." Undergraduate paper, Laurentian University, 2004.

Godfrey, Sheldon J. and Judith C. Godfrey. *Search Out the Land: The Jews and the Growth of Equality in British Colonial America, 1740–1867*. Montreal and Kingston: McGill-Queen's University Press, 1995.

Goldberg, Ruth Kahane. "The Depression and War." *A Common Thread: A History of the Jews of Ottawa*. Compiled by Anna Bilsky, 47–115. Ottawa: Ottawa Jewish Historical Society, 2009.

Gottesman, Dr Eli. *Who's Who in Canadian Jewry, 1964*. Montreal: The Canadian Jewish Literary Foundation for the Jewish Institute of Higher Research of the Central Rabbinical Seminary of Canada, 1964. http://dsp-psd.pwgsc.gc.ca.

Granger, Christopher, et al. *Canadian Criminal Jury Trials*. Agincourt, Ontario: Carswell, 1989.

Gross, David. *Lost Time: On Remembering and Forgetting in Late Modern Culture*. Amherst: University of Massachusetts Press, 2000.

"The Guardsman." Classic Film Guide. www.classicfilmguide.com.

"The Guardsman." IMDb. www.imdb.com.

"Gypsum Queen." *Time* (31 May 1937). www.time.com.

Hadassah-Wizo Organization of Canada. *Seventy-Fifth Anniversary Commemorative Book*, 1993.

Halpern, Monda. *And on That Farm He Had a Wife: Ontario Farm Women and Feminism, 1900–1970*. Montreal and Kingston: McGill-Queen's University Press, 2001.

Harlow, Rabbi Jules, ed. *Siddur Sim Shalom* [prayerbook]. New York: Rabbinical Assembly, 1985.

"History of the Bar of Middlesex." Internet Archive. http://www.archive.org/stream/historyofbarofcooohughuoft.

"History of the Carleton County Gaol." The Carleton County Gaol. www.carletoncountygaol.com.

Horder, Jeremy. *Provocation and Responsibility*. Oxford: Clarendon Press, 1992

Horn, Michiel, ed. *The Dirty Thirties: Canadians in the Great Depression*. Toronto: Copp Clark Publishing, 1972.

Horwitz v. Loyal Protective Ins. Co. [1932] 3 D.L.R. 378. Ontario Supreme Court, Logie, J., 27 May 1932.

Hughes, Judge David John and T.H. Purdom. *History of the Bar of the County of Middlesex*. London? n.p., 1912.

Huhn, Wilson R. "Ohio's 'Sacred Seal of Secrecy': The Rules of Spousal Incompetency and Marital Privilege in Criminal Cases." *Akron Law Review*, 20 (1987): 433–53.

Hyman, Paula. *Gender and Assimilation in Modern Jewish History: The Roles and Representation of Women*. Seattle: University of Washington Press, 1995.

Ignatiev, Noel. *How the Irish Became White*. New York: Routledge, 1995.

"Index to Register of Voters," 1944. *California Voter Registrations, 1900–1968*. Ancestry.com.

Irwin-Zarecka, Iwona. *Frames of Remembrance: The Dynamics of Collective Memory*. New Brunswick, New Jersey: Transaction Publishers, 1994.

Isaacson, Dr Ben. *Dictionary of the Jewish Religion*. New York: Bantam Books, 1979.

Jacobs, Rabbi Louis. "Suicide in Jewish Tradition and Literature." http://www.myjewishlearning.com/life/Life_Events/Death_and_Mourning/Contemporary_Issues/Suicide.shtml?p=1.

Johnston-Matthews (1895). http://granniesgenealogygarden.com.

Joseph, Norma Baumel. "Jewish Women in Canada: An Evolving Role." *From Immigration to Integration: The Canadian Jewish Experience: A Millenium Edition*. Ed. Ruth Klein and Frank Dimant, 182–95. Toronto: Institute for International Affairs, B'nai Brith Canada, 2001.

"Judge Helen Kinnear." www.heronwoodent.ca/content/Helen%20Kinnear.htm.

"Jules Alexandre Castonguay Fonds." ArchiviaNet: On-line Research Tool. Library and Archives Canada, http://data4.archives.ca.

"Jury Selection." Bar Admission Course Materials. Criminal Procedure. Toronto: Law Society of Upper Canada, 2009.

Keshen, Jeff. "World War Two and the Making of Modern Ottawa." *Ottawa: Making a Capital*. Ed. Jeff Keshen and Nicole St-Onge, 383–410. Ottawa: University of Ottawa Press, 2001.

Kimmel, Michael S. *Manhood in America: A Cultural History*. Second edition. New York: Oxford University Press, 2006.

Kirmayer, Lawrence J. "Landscapes of Memory: Trauma, Narrative, Dissociation." *Tense Past: Cultural Essays in Trauma and Memory*. Ed. Paul Antze and Michel Lambek, 173-98. New York: Routledge, 1996.

Kirsch, Adam. "Edward Kitzler's History of Jewish Pirates Is Uneven."
    JewishJournal.com (10 December 2008). www.jewishjournal.com.

Knowles, Valerie. "Pioneers and Peddlars." *A Common Thread: A History
    of the Jews of Ottawa.* Compiled by Anna Bilsky, 1-44. Ottawa: Ottawa
    Jewish Historical Society, 2009.

Kramer, Reinhold and Tom Mitchell. *Walk towards the Gallows: The Tragedy
    of Hilda Blake, Hanged 1899.* Don Mills, Ontario: Oxford University Press,
    2002.

Le Caron, Major Henri. *Memoirs of a Great Detective: Incidents in the Life
    of John Wilson Murray.* London: William Heine Mann, 1904.

Lenarcic, Dorothy A. "Jewellery and Silverware Industry." The Canadian
    Encyclopedia HISTOR!CA. www.canadianencyclopedia.ca.

Lessard, Suzannah. *The Architect of Desire: Beauty and Danger in the Stan-
    ford White Family.* New York: Dell Publishing, 1996.

Lester, David and Gene Lester. *Crime of Passion: Murder and the Murderer.*
    Chicago: Nelson Hall, 1975.

Levitt, Cyril and William Shaffir. *The Riot at Christie Pits.* Toronto: Key
    Porter Books, 1987.

– "The Swastika as Dramatic Symbol: A Case-Study of Ethnic Violence in
    Canada." *The Jews in Canada.* Ed., Robert J. Brym, et al., 77–96. Toronto:
    Oxford University Press, 1993.

Lieff, Abraham (Abe). *Gathering Rosebuds.* Toronto: Gall-Papenburg Com-
    puter Systems, 1991.

Liekis, Šarunas. "Courland." *The YIVO Encyclopedia of Jews in Eastern
    Europe,* vol. 2. Ed. David Hundert, 357-8. New Haven: Yale University
    Press, 2008.

Little, Margaret Jane Hillyard. *'No Car, No Radio, No Liquor Permit': The
    Moral Regulation of Single Mothers in Ontario, 1920–1997.* Toronto:
    Oxford University Press, 1998.

Lusty, David. "Is There a Common Law Privilege against Spouse-Incrimina-
    tion?" *UNSW Law Journal,* 1 (2004): 1–41.

Margolis, Rebecca. "The Yiddish Press in Montreal, 1900–1945." *Canadian
    Jewish Studies,* XVI/XVII (2008/9): 3–26.

May, Gary. "The Golden Age." *A Common Thread: A History of the Jews
    of Ottawa.* Compiled by Anna Bilsky, 117–87. Ottawa: Ottawa Jewish
    Historical Society, 2009.

McLaren, Angus. "Males, Migrants, and Murder in British Columbia, 1900–

1923." *On the Case: Explorations in Social History*. Ed. Franca Iacovetta and Wendy Mitchinson, 159–80. Toronto: University of Toronto Press, 1998.

– and Arlene Tigar McLaren. *The Bedroom and the State: The Changing Practices and Politics of Contraception and Abortion in Canada, 1880–1980*. Toronto: McClelland and Stewart, 1986.

Medine, David. "The Adverse Testimony Privilege: Time to Dispose of a 'Sentimental Relic.'" *Oregon Law Review*, 67 (1988): 519–60.

Medres, Israel. *Between the Wars: Canadian Jews in Tradition*. Translated from the Yiddish by Vivian Felsen. Montreal: Eagle Publishing, 1964; rpt. Montreal: Véhicule Press, 2003.

Menkis, Richard. "Antisemitism in the Evolving Nation: From New France to 1950." *From Immigration to Integration: The Canadian Jewish Experience: A Millennium Edition*. Ed. Ruth Klein and Frank Dimant, 31–51. Toronto: Institute for International Affairs, B'nai Brith Canada, 2001.

Miller-Smith (1943). http://www.rootsweb.ancestry.com/~onlanark/NewspaperClippings.

"Mission Statement." Ontario Coroners Association. www.ontca.ca

Morton, James C., "Jury Nullification?" http://www.smhilaw.com/Publications/ART-0507-JuryNullification.pdf.

Morwood, Jean. "Automated Genealogy." "1911 Census of Canada." Province of Ontario, Carleton County. http://automatedgenealogy.com/census11.

Moss, Wendy and Elaine Gardner-O'Toole, "Aboriginal People: History of Discriminatory Laws" (1987), rev. ed., Government of Canada: 1991. http://www.multiculturalcanada.ca

Ontario, Canada Births, 1869–1909. Ancestry.com.

Ontario, Canada Deaths, 1869–1932. Ancestry.com.

Ontario, Canada Marriages, 1857–1924. Ancestry.com.

"Ontario Courts." "Former Judges of the Superior Courts." http://www.ontariocourts.on.ca/coa/en/former judges/.

Orenstein, Eugene V. "Canadian Literature." *The Canadian Jewish Mosaic* (1981). Ed. M. Weinfeld et al., 5–6. www.jewishvirtuallibrary.org/jsource/judaica.

"Our History." Congregation Beth Shalom. www.bethshalom.ca/our_history.htm.

Paciocco, David M. and Lee Stuesser. *The Law of Evidence*. Fifth edition. Toronto: Irwin Law, 2008.

Phillips, Jim and Rosemary Gartner. *Murdering Holiness: The Trials of Franz Creffield and George Mitchell*. Vancouver: UBC Press, 2003.

Prager, Dennis and Joseph Telushkin. *The Nine Questions People Ask about Judaism*. New York: Touchstone, 1986.

Rankin, Joan E. *Meet Me at the Château: A Legacy of Memory*. Toronto: Natural Heritage, 1990.

"Register of Marriages of Congregation Shaare Zion (Gates of Zion)." 1935. *Quebec Vital and Church Records (Drouin Collection), 1621–1967*. Ancestry.com.

Revised Statutes of Canada 1927, Criminal Code, Chapter 36, Part VI

Roediger, David R. *The Wages of Whiteness: Race and the Making of the American Working Class*. London: Verso, 1991.

Rome, David. *Clouds in the Thirties: On Anti-Semitism in Canada, 1929–1939: A Chapter on Canadian Jewish History*. Montreal: Canadian Jewish Congress, 1977.

Roodman, Herman S. *The Ottawa Jewish Community: An Historical Chronicle of Our Community for the Years 1857–1987 5617–5747: One Hundred and Thirty Years of Progress and Achievement in the Annals of Ottawa Jewry*, April 1989.

Rosenberg, Louis. *Canada's Jews: A Social and Economic Study of Jews in Canada in the 1930s*. Bureau of Social and Economic Research, Canadian Jewish Congress, 1939; rpt. edited by Morton Weinfeld. Montreal and Kingston: McGill-Queen's University Press, 1993.

Rosenfeld, Rabbi David. "Living in the World's View," Pirkeis Avos – Torah.org. www.torah.org.

Rosenthal, Herman. "Friedrichstadt." www.jewishencyclopedia.com

Rosin, Joseph. "Panevezys (Ponevezh) Lithuania." www.shtetlinks.jewishgen. org.

Rosser, Frederick. *London Township Pioneers, Including a Few Families from Adjoining Area*. Belleville: Mika Publishing, 1975.

Roth, Cecil, editor-in-chief. *The Standard Jewish Encyclopedia*. Garden City, New York, 1962.

Rubin, Harold. *Those Pesky Weeds*. Edited by Shirley Berman. Ottawa: Ottawa Jewish Historical Society, 1992.

Sangster, Joan. *Regulating Girls and Women: Sexuality, Family, and the Law in Ontario, 1920–1960*. Don Mills, Ontario: Oxford University Press, 2001.

Sharp, Rosalie, et al. *Growing Up Jewish: Canadians Tell Their Own Stories*. Toronto: McClelland and Stewart, 1997.

"The ShipsList – L Archives." www.rootsweb.com.

"Shooting outside West Boca Synagogue." www.dancharnas.com.

Smith, Helmut Walser. *The Butcher's Tale: Murder and Anti-Semitism in a German Town*. New York: W.W. Norton and Company, 2002.

Social Security Death Index. Ancestry.com.

South River Historical and Preservation Society, "Aftermath of the 1908 South River Fire," and "South River Population, 1880–2000." www.rootsweb.ancestry.com/~njsrhps

Srebnick, Amy Gilman. *The Mysterious Death of Mary Rogers: Sex and Culture in Nineteenth-Century New York*. New York: Oxford University Press, 1995.

"S/S Noordland, Red Star." www.norwayheritage.com.

Stanislawski, Michael. *A Murder in Lemberg: Politics, Religion, and Violence in Modern Jewish History*. Princeton: Princeton University Press, 2007.

– "Spousal Incompetency and the Charter." *Osgoode Hall Law Journal*, 34 (1996): 411–60.

Strange, Carolyn. "Mercy for Murderers? A Historical Perspective on the Royal Prerogative of Mercy." *Saskatchewan Law Review*, 64 (2001): 559–72.

– "Wounded Womanhood and Dead Men: Chivalry and the Trials of Clara Ford and Carrie Davies." *Gender Conflicts: New Essays in Women's History*. Ed. Franca Iacovetta and Mariana Valverde, 149–88. Toronto: University of Toronto Press, 1992.

Strong-Boag, Veronica. *The New Day Recalled: Lives of Girls and Women in English Canada, 1919-1939*. Mississauga, Ontario: Copp Clark Pitman, 1988.

Sudarsky, Mendel and Uriah Katzenelenbogen, eds. *Lite*. Volume 1. New York: Jewish-Cultural Society, 1951. www.jewishgen.org.

"Synagogue Shooting Shocks Rosh Hashana Worshippers." Local10.com, 5 October 2005. www.local10.com.

Tanovich, David M., et al. *Jury Selection in Criminal Trials: Skills, Science, and the Law*. Concord, Ontario: Irwin Law, 1997.

Thirteenth Census of the United States Federal Census: 1910-Population. AncestryLibrary.com.

Thompson, John Herd. "Beauharnois Scandal." *The Canadian Encyclopedia Historica*. www.thecanadianencyclopedia.com.

Troper, Harold. *The Defining Decade: Identity, Politics, and the Canadian Jewish Community in the 1960s*. Toronto: University of Toronto Press, 2010.

Tulchinsky, Gerald. *Branching Out: The Transformation of the Canadian Jewish Community*. New York: Stoddart Publishing, 1998.

– *Canada's Jews: A People's Journey*. Toronto: University of Toronto Press, 2008

– "The Contours of Canadian Jewish History." *The Jews in Canada*. Ed. Robert J. Brym et al., 5–21. Toronto: Oxford University Press, 1993.

Uruburu, Paula. *American Eve: Evelyn Nesbit, Stanford White, the Birth of the "It" Girl, and the Crime of the Century*. New York: Riverhead Books, 2009.

Vincent, Isabel. *Bodies and Souls: The Tragic Plight of Three Jewish Women Forced into Prostitution in the Americas*. Toronto: Random House Canada, 2005.

Walker, Barrington. "Killing the Black Female Body: Black Womanhood, Black Patriarchy, and Spousal Murder in Two Ontario Criminal Trials, 1892–1894." *Sisters or Strangers? Immigrant, Ethnic, and Racialized Women in Canadian History*. Ed. Marlene Epp, Franca Iacovetta, and Frances Swyripa, 89–107. Toronto: University of Toronto Press, 2004; rpt. 2007.

– *Race on Trial: Black Defendants in Ontario's Criminal Courts, 1858–1958*. Toronto: Osgoode Society for Canadian Legal History, 2010.

Weinfeld, Morton. "The Ethnic Sub-Economy: Explication and Analysis of a Case Study of the Jews of Montreal." *The Jews in Canada*. Ed. Robert J. Brym., et al., 218–37. Toronto: Oxford University Press, 1993.

– *Like Everyone Else … But Different: The Paradoxical Success of Canadian Jews*. Toronto: McClelland and Stewart, 2001.

Wertsch, James V. *Voices of Collective Remembering*. Cambridge: Cambridge University Press, 2002.

"When to Call a Coroner." Ontario Coroners Association. www.ontca.ca.

White, Kimberley. *Negotiating Responsibility: Law, Murder, and States of Mind*. Vancouver: UBC Press, 2008.

"Yousuf Karsh collection." ArchiviaNet: On-line Research Tool.Library and Archives Canada, Photographic Collections, http//data4.collections canada.gc.ca.

Index

Abelson, Estelle, 113
Abelson, Jess, 47. *See also* Tel Aviv Tennis Club
accident theory, 8, 10, 117, 122, 228n12; and Alice, 24, 35; and Ben, 58, 115; self-inflicted, 26–7
acquittal, 8, 159–60, 174–5; Ben's status, 132–50; as a defence strategy, 8, 117, 124, 132, 141; and the prosecution, 123. *See also* justifiable homicide
Adam's Rib, 237n145
adultery, 13, 25, 115, 139, 173; and Alice's immorality, 3, 108–9, 142, 160; defined, 103, 223n85; Jewish custom regarding, 96–9, 103; and sexuality, 10, 102, 167; Yetta's report about, 16
affair, the, 3–4, 13–17; 53, 96; and Alice, 19, 28, 104–10, 113; knowledge of, 58, 93–4, 127–9; remembered, 153–4, 158, 165, 168; and the trial, 104–13, 123, 126–9, 149–50; and Yetta, 28, 31–2. *See also* adultery; paternity; womanhood
Alexander, Nate, 19
anti-Semitism, 5–7, 109, 165, 186n8, 205n75; absence of, 9, 36, 46–8, 135, 173–4, 178, 187n24; blamed on Jews, 101; and class, 37; in Europe, 107, 205n80, 217n24; Jewish community responses to, 46, 98–9;

and masculinity, 107–8; resistance to, 48, 220n53; in the trial, 109, 118, 135, 173–4, 178; and violence, 101–2, 165, 185n8. *See also* scholarship; Tissot case
Arcand, Adrien, 6
assimilation, 109, 174, 209n105, 217n20; and Ben, 133–4. *See also* class; respectability
Auger case, 54, 124, 142, 188n28, 210n4
Augustino case, 138–40, 239n62. *See also* the unwritten law

Bank Street store, 13, 19, 157, 202n45, 249n81; Berger's involvement, 30–2; cellar incident, 15; closing of, 27; crime at, 237n138; "becoming white," 8, 10. *See also* Brodkin, Karen; Ignatiev, Nigel
Berger, Sam, 31, 60, 153, 193n80, 206n83; and anti-Semitism, 217n24; character of, 32; as Jack's lawyer, 26–8; and Jack's will, 26–8, 120–1; leaves case, 196n123; personal history, 193n79, 217n27; as a witness, 56; as Yetta's lawyer, 31–2, 94
Bilsky, Moses, 43, 102, 170
Bookman, Max, 48, 91–2. *See also* scholarship
The Booster, 95

Brodkin, Karen, 8. *See also* scholarship

The Canadian Jewish Chronicle, 32, 48, 96–7
capital punishment, 3, 61, 136; hanging, 55, 136, 211n10, 226n5; and jury selection, 117–18; and racial prejudice, 55
Carleton County, 54, 100, 115
Castonguay, Jules Alexandre, 147
charity, 48–9, 162; Alice's work on behalf of, 52, 56, 94, 162. *See also* Hadassah; Pioneer Women; womanhood
Château Laurier, 19, 43, 46, 93–4
Chateau Pharmacy, 19, 21–3, 44, 56, 58; Lemieux's testimony about, 62, 94
Chernove, Robert, 170
Chernove, Steven, 163
Christie Pits riot, 6
class. *See* middle class
chillul hashem, 98, 220n51; 220n52
Coblentz, Chaya, 39, 114, 201n29
Coblentz, Samuel, 43, 156. *See also* feud
coroner. *See* Craig, J.E.
coroner's inquest, 27, 35, 53–62, 119, 122; current approaches, 211n15, 211n16. *See also* Craig, J.E.
Craig, J.E., 55, 57, 59, 63, 157
crime, 3, 6, 9; during the Depression, 100; at the Horwitz store, 244n33; and the Jewish community (immigrants), 97, 99–102, 169, 175, 221n8; and the law, 9, 116–17; and Lowertown, 41; "of passion," 64, 116–17, 149, 167, 226n7, 237n145; scene, 22–3, 25–6, 34, 59, 61–2, 126, 129; statistics, 183n2

The Criminal Code, 57, 116–17
crown attorney. *See* Ritchie, J.A.
culpable homicide, 116, 124, 137

Danby, S.L. Everett, 157; called to treat Jack, 21–2, 25, 27; multiple roles of, 56, 61–2; testimony of, 34, 119, 213n60
defence. *See* Doctor, Moses; Hughes, Roydon
Depression, the, 64, 133, 156, 160; and anti-Semitism, 6, 99; and character, 51, 133, 135, 173; end of, 160–1; and class, 11, 42–4, 46, 49; and gender, 109, 114–16, 135, 146, 172–4; rise in crime during, 100, 135–6; Victorian culture, 139; and women, 146–7
Doctor, Louis, 158
Doctor, Moses, 7–8, 23–4, 33, 56–8, 132, Ben's defence by, 123–7, 141, 153, 156; career 53–4, 94; case against Hertz, 156; death of, 134–5, 154, 157–9; hurts Alice's reputation, 141–3, 167, 174; and the jury, 117–18, 143; and manly honour, 141; personal history of, 46,192n61; reasonable doubt, 131–2; verdict, 148. *See also* Auger case
dominant culture, 8, 11, 37, 103, 175; and anti-Semitism, 101; and the Jewish community, 51, 93, 134, 174. *See also* gender; middle class
Dubinsky, Karen, 8, 11

Edelson, Alice, 3, 7; after trial, 161–2; blamed, 141–3, 146; beauty, 51–2, 200n20; character, 91–8, 105, 142, 144, 146; early life, 38–9; death, 169; image, 106–7, 174; immorality, 141–2, 172; ill, 56; not blamed, 215n86; ostracized, 112; pregnancies, 105; relationship with

Ben, 39, 103–6; relationship with Jack, 14–17; remembered, 151, 167; respectability, 105; 61–2; seclusion, 35; unable to testify, 56–7, 144–6. *See also* adultery; paternity; womanhood

Edelson, Ben, 3, 7, 9, 13; character, 123–4, 130–1, 133, 135–6, 167; charged with murder, 33; death, 170; early life, 37–8; and the Jewish community, 166–7; knowledge of affair, 15–16, 58, 123, 127–9; takes Alice back, 113, 160, 240n188; testifies, 124–30; loss of manly honour, 136–8, 140; not guilty, 147; sues Hertz, 156. *See* Edelson, Alice; middle class; shooting

Edelson children, 3, 25, 35, 104–8, 110; and the affair, 14–15, 18–20; Jewish children, 93, 96; and the Jewish community, 50–2, 112–14, 148; in Lowertown, 44–5; in Montreal, 41–2; ostracized, 112, 156–7, 161; visit jail, 67. *See also* Edelson, Dina; Edelson, Lillian (Lillian Katznelson); Edelson, Samuel

Edelson, Dina, 44–6, 156, 160–1, 165, 169–70; on the affair, 14; blames Alice, 23; and the press, 35; works at family store, 66, 104, 112. *See also* Edelson Jewellers

Edelson Jewellers, 19, 26–8, 34, 57, 66, 96; and Alice, 52, 162; in case against Hertz, 156; closes, 170; as crime scene, 12–14, 21, 34; established, 43–4; fire, 161; insurance claims, 156; thriving, 44, 112, 161. *See also* crime; feud; jewellers

Edelson, Lillian (Lillian Katznelson), 44–6, 66–7, 93, 111, 162; on Alice's role, 23, 35, 51–2, 56, 106; on Ben's gun, 126; ostracized, 112–

13; silence about event, 154, 159–60, 165; suspected affair, 14, 17. *See also* Edelson children

Edelson, Samuel (son), 34, 44, 66–7

ethnicity, 5, 7, 172, 175. *See also* anti-Semitism; Jewish community

evidence, 57–65, 117, 124–5, 146, 155; ballistics, 121–2; bruises as, 232n48; contaminated, 34, 120–2, 126–7; gun casings, 34; gunpowder, 22; unsecured, 26, 34; versus social status, 8, 10, 115. *See also* crime; guns

Fenster, Max, 155, 170

feud, 32, 65, 154–7; legacy of, 163–4. *See also* insurance

Frank case, 5, 186n24

Freiman, A.J., 47–8, 112

Freiman, Lawrence, 164–5

Freiman, Lillian, 47–50, 162. *See also* Hadassah

Freiman's Department Store, 6–7

French Canadians, 6–7, 32, 101, 132, 135; in Lowertown, 41–3; picking on Jewish children, 204n68

French language press, 33, 177, 179–80

Friel Street, 51, 104, 161, 165; Lowertown, 42, 45–6; night Jack was shot, 18

funeral, 7, 28–9; of Doctor, 134, 157–8; and the Jewish community, 94–5; of Jack, 29–30

gallows. *See* capital punishment

Gauthier's Undertaking Parlors, 27

Gellman, Susie, 111–13, 149, 166, 169

gender, 5, 11–12, 139, 172–3; changing roles, 146–7; marriage, 102–3; men, 136–7, 140; women, 109–10, 136–7, 146. *See also* the Depression; dominant culture; unwritten law

German Jews, 5, 91–2

Goldberg, Mary, 107, 113–14, 159, 161

gossip, 13–14, 114, 151, 159, 220n55; Alice as the focus of, 111, 175; diminished, 164; impact, 168; and the jury, 63. *See also* paternity

Goulet case, 222n66

The Guardsman, 25, 193n74

guns, 34; autopsy findings, 59; ballistics, 58, 121–2; Ben's experience with, 116, 125–6; in Edelson shooting, 20, 27; tampered with, 24. *See also* accident theory; evidence

Hadassah, 48–9, 52, 56, 218n37; Alice as member, 94, 162, 207n88; Lillian Frieman Chapter, 48–9, 162, 205n82. *See also* charity; womanhood; Zionists

halachah (Jewish law), 96

Hertz, Harry, 25; against Edelson family, 32, 153, 155, 157, 159; at hospital with Jack, 34; as witness, 56, 59, 120–1. *See also* feud

Holocaust, the, 5–6, 108, 151–2

homicide, 3, 5–6, 9–10, 16; cause of death, 27; Ben charged with, 33, 59, 62; defined in legal proceedings, 116; inquest, 53–90; trial, 115–50; as unusual, 172. *See also* coroner's inquest; crime; *The Criminal Code*; evidence

Horwitz, Anita (Anita Fenster Chernove), 111, 151, 155, 163–4, 168; Jack's death, 27–8; Jack's will, 30, 32; later life, 170

Horwitz, Charles, 21, 25–8, 34–5, 155, 163; against Edelson family, 32; crime scene, 31–2; insurance, 54–5; intercedes, 16, 27; Jack's will, 26–7, 30–2; night of the

shooting, 13, 25; testimony of, 56, 120, 126, 153. *See also* feud

Horwitz, Jacie, 156, 163

Horwitz, Jack, 3, 7, 23, 33, 57; community response to, 149; death, 25–7, 151, 194n88; financial arrangement with Ben, 123; funeral of, 29; killed, 17–18, 60, 62, 116; legacy, 151, 154–5, 163–4, 167–8; participation in community, 95; protects Alice, 26; as business man, 29–30; status, 45, 95; and Yetta, 17, 27. *See also* adultery; affair; Sandy Hill

Horwitz, Jack (nephew), 163

Horwitz, Jonathan, 163

Horwitz, Max, 14, 96, 123; death, 197n132; store, 202n45

Horwitz, Philip, 123, 155

Horwitz, Yetta, 29, 34, 64, 97, 149; assimilation, 45; blames Alice, 15, 28; and Jack's death, 27–8; and Jack's will, 30–2; learns about affair, 14–17; leaves Ottawa, 17, 32–3, 197n129; legacy, 151, 154–6, 163–4, 170; ostracized, 33, 111, 168; talks with Ben, 16, 19, 27, 128, 191n33; testimony of, 56, 58–9, 63, 122, 128, 168; as victim, 28, 58–9, 110, 142–3. *See also* Sandy Hill

Hughes, Roydon, 118, 123, 140. *See also* defence

Hyman, Adelene, 105, 154, 161; gossip, 111–12; remembers the Edelsons, 46, 51, 165

Ignatiev, Nigel, 8

immigrants, 4–8, 52, 107, 139, 172–4; acculturation, 10–11, 45, 133; Ben as, 7, 37, 133, 135; and Jewish community, 91–3, 101; neighbour-

hoods, 40–1, 43; in Ottawa, 4–6, 49, 99, 165. *See also* crime; Jewish community; middle class
insurance, 26, 30–2, 131, 154–6, 159. *See also* feud

The Jazz Singer, 107
Jewish community, 4, 23, 36, 52, 63, 217n20; Alice, 10–11, 95, 97, 105–6, 113, 161; and Anglo-Protestant culture, 7; and Ben, 11, 44, 67, 95, 101, 147–9; in Canada, 41, 46, 49, 109, 163; "coming of age," 7, 10; and crime, 99–100; discusses case, 12, 63, 111, 171; as imagined killers, 5; legacy of the Edelson/Horwitz case, 151, 164–6, 169, 173, 175; ostracizes Edelson family, 112–13, 149–50, 161; representation of, 6; silence about Edelson/Horwitz case, 153–60; as united, 44, 91, 93–4, 98, 107, 114, 205n81, 220n52. *See also* Jews, Ottawa
Jewish law, 29, 46, 50, 96, 98–9, 103. See also *chillul hashem*; *halachah*; *kashruth*; *Talmud*; *Torah*
"Jew on Jew violence," 101, 149–50, 184n6, 220n53; Finkel case, 184n8. *See also* Jewish community
jewellers, 43–4, 56, 96, 133, 169; from Europe, 37–8, 202n45. *See also* Edelson, Ben; Edelson Jewellers; Horwitz, Jack
Jews, European, 4, 40, 103, 107, 199n15, 200n16. *See also* Jewish community
Jews, Ottawa, 12, 92–3, 95, 201n30; Ben and Alice, 113, 150, 164, 169; Lowertown, 41, 52; Palestine, 48; population, 200n27
Judaism, 4, 37, 135, 158–9; community, 92–3; in Ottawa, 37; and mar-

riage, 102–3, 113. *See also* Jewish community; Jewish law; religion
judges, 131, 134, 137, 165; J. Logie, 155; Glenn E. Strike, 156–7. *See also* McEvoy, John Millar
jury members, 8–10, 116–50; selection, 117, 228n14, 235n43. *See also* coroner's inquest; gender; middle class
jury nullification, 9–10, 189n34
justifiable homicide, 117, 132, 136

kaddish (mourner's prayer), 92
kashruth (kosher), 42, 55, 95
Katznelson, Lillian. *See* Edelson, Lillian
Keneder Adler (*Jewish Daily Eagle*), 97, 101

Laishley, James H., 118. *See also* jury members
Laframboise, J.B., 21–2, 56, 58
lawyers: T.A. Beament, 153; Benjamin Goldfield, 31–2, 46, 153–4. *See also* Berger, Sam; Doctor, Moses; Ritchie, J.A; White, Peter
Lemieux, Lorenzo, 29, 50, 112; and shooting, 17–23, 25, 125–7, 129; testimony, 119– 20, 125–7, 191n32–191n40, 231n34; as a witness, 56–8, 61–3
Lieff, Abe, 45, 165
Lisgar Collegiate, 66, 93
love triangles, 3–4, 64, 97, 143
Lowertown, 12–14, 18, 48–50, 52, 96, 119; described, 41; Edelsons leave, 161; as Jewish neighbourhood, 37, 41–2, 45, 91–3, 133; religion, 49–50; as tough neighbourhood, 13–14, 18, 135, 204n63
Loyal Protective Insurance Company, 154

manly honour, 8–10, 13; and Ben, 45, 53, 115–17, 132, 149; and defence, 137. *See also* gender; respectability; masculinity

manslaughter, 9, 100, 116–17, 130–2, 149

marriage, 118, 138, 140, 142–3, 145; of Alice and Ben, 39–41, 104–6, 113–14; and divorce, 225n146, 226n147; Jack and Yetta, 17, 32; in the Jewish community, 11, 103–5; legacy, 159, 163, 168, 170, 173. *See also* affair; paternity

masculinity, 91, 103, 108, 133–5, 137, 173; male character, 10, 146; violence, 140; and the Depression, 146–7. *See also* gender; justifiable homicide

McEvoy, John Millar, 117, 119–24, 135, 148; and the jury, 131, 137; Sifton case, 227n8; withdraws from trial, 121

McLaren, Angus, 10, 140

memoirs, 152, 164–5. *See also* Jewish community; memory

memory, 12, 243n9; collective, 12, 153, 164, 166, 169; and Jews, 151–3; scholarship, 152, 242n2; of shooting, 159, 161. *See also* Jewish community

Metrick, Lionel, 149, 167–9

middle class, 5, 49, 139, 147, 236n134; Alice's status as, 10, 162, 167, 173; as a problem, 188n28; Ben's status as, 7–8, 10–11, 33, 42–4, 132–6, 173–4; Jewish status and, 8, 114, 132–6; values, 102, 106. *See also* masculinity; respectability

Mitchell case, 138, 238n146, 238n152, 238n154

Montreal, 6, 17, 41

motherhood, 11, 105–9, 112; and

Alice, 223n96. *See also* gender; womanhood

murder. *See* homicide

My Yiddishe Mama, 107

Myrand Street, 18, 127

Nesbit, Evelyn, 4

newspapers, 3, 6–7, 13, 57, 100, 122; on acquittal, 147–8; on Ben's testimony, 124–5; coverage, 96–7, 118; death of Doctor, 158–9; on jury selection, 117–18; praise of Moses Doctor, 143; re-enactment of shooting, 129–30; sensationalizing case, 28, 36. *See also* Keneder Adler; The Ottawa Evening Citizen; The Ottawa Evening Journal; The Toronto Daily Star

Nicholas Street Jail, 67, 136, 179; about, 54–5, 102; Alice's absence from, 56; Ben in, 50, 59, 111, 150

Ontario Supreme Court, 115

The Ottawa Evening Citizen: on Alice, 36, 57, 59–60; on Ben, 33, 55, 111, 124, 148; on Jack, 30; sensationalizes case, 3; and the trial, 64, 134, 143; on Yetta, 28. *See also* newspapers

The Ottawa Evening Journal: on Alice, 36, 60, 150; and aftermath of case, 154; on Ben, 124, 130, 147; on Jack, 30, 32; on Doctor, 94–5, 158; about Ottawa, 100; publicity about the case, 63–5, 118–19; sensationalizes case, 3; on Yetta, 28, 58. *See also* newspapers

Ottawa General Hospital, 94, 120, 153; Alice visits, 34, 62, 111, 197n142; Hertz visits, 59; and Jack, 12, 22–3, 25–7

Ottawa Hebrew News, 93

paternity, 41, 105, 122–3, 141, 168; Jack's denial of, 15; Jack as father, 190n13; tied to adultery, 223n85. *See also* adultery; Edelson, Alice; motherhood

patriarchy, 66, 104, 162, 174. *See also* gender; masculinity; respectability

Le Patriote, 6–7. *See also* newspapers

Pioneer Women, 162, 248n78

police, 61, 63–5, 102, 138, 147–8; Sherman Hardisty, 122, 124; Joseph Hardon, 33–4; Charles H. Howe, 59, 121–2; in Edelson/Horwitz case, 22, 24, 26–8, 31, 56; Emile Joliat, 47, 100, 135; Hector Levigne, 121; Aubrey MacDonald, 24, 33, 54, 59; profiling criminals, 135–6; Reginald Raby, 34. *See also* Edelson, Ben; Tissot case

prosecution, 62, 118–23. *See also* White, Peter; Ritchie, J.A.

provocation. *See* manslaughter

rabbis, 37, 44, 134, 163; and Ben, 49–50; on family life, 103–4; on suicide, 158–9; and Yiddish, 93

Regent Theater, 14, 21–2, 24–5, 126. *See also* crime

religion, 98, 107, 113, 134–5. *See also* Judaism

respectability, 7–8, 10–12, 52, 115, 132, 187n25; female, 10, 144, 162; leniency because of, 33, 178; lost, 67, 160; male, 8–9, 11, 133–4, 173, 175; and violence, 135. *See also* adultery; assimilation; middle class

Rideau Street, 3, 34, 42, 45, 156, 165; altercation on, 18, 26, 127; Edelson Jewellers, 43–4, 156, 161, 170; and Lowertown, 41; mer-

chants, 6. *See also* Nicholas Street Jail; shooting; synagogues/*shuls*

Ritchie, J.A., 24, 56–8, 60, 62–3, 116. *See also* culpable homicide; prosecution

rumour. *See* gossip

Sandy Hill, 18, 31, 45–6, 52, 93, 158. *See also* Jewish Community; Horwitz, Jack

scandal, 6, 12–13, 16, 91, 165–6; public, 35–6, 175. *See also* gossip; silence

scholarship: on anti-Semitism 5–7, 9; on collective memory, 152, 164–5; on crime, 4–5; on deviance, 4; on Jew-on-Jew violence, 5; on Jewish history in Ottawa, 92; on Jewish subversion, 172; on Jewish success, 8, 48; on unwritten law, 10

Seabrooke case, 55, 100, 135–6

sexuality, 102–3, 106, 146; misconduct, 173. *See also* adultery; marriage

sexual misconduct. *See* adultery

Shaffer, Francis, 149, 169

shandeh (disgrace), 175

Shapiro, Charles, 25, 134

shochet (ritual slaughterer), 42, 192n61

shooting, 30, 33–5, 45–6; as an accident, 3, 117; Alice's role in, 23–5, 98, 142, 146; described, 17–26; inquest into; 53–4, 56–61, 66; Jewish community response to, 93–4, 97–8, 103–5, 138, 149; as justifiable, 115–17; debated, 9–10, 129–33; trial, 119–33; remembered, 152–5, 157, 159–60, 163–9, 173. *See also* crime; Edelson, Ben; Edelson family; evidence; Horwitz, Jack

shtetl (eastern European village), 42, 107

shvitz (steam bath), 42

silence, 19, 67, 105, 149, 151–71. *See also* Freiman, Lawrence; memory

spousal incompetency, 144–5, 240n196, 240n198, 241n202

Steinberg case, 185n8, 234n97

Strathcona Park, 14

synagogues/*shuls*, 37, 49–50, 92, 94–6, 103; Adath Jeshurun (King Edward Street shul), 29, 50, 112; Agudath Achim (Rideau Street shul), 50, 208n95; Machziki Hadath (Murray Street shul), 50, 208n95. *See also* charity; Jewish community

Talmud, 98

Talmud Torah, 92, 94

Tel Aviv Tennis Club, 47

testimony, 53–89, 91–114

Thaw case, 3–4

Tissot case, 6–7, 47–8, 173; and anti-Semitism, 205n80. *See also* anti-Semitism

Torah, 98

Toronto, 6, 41, 99, 116, 179–80

The Toronto Daily Star, 36, 96, 154–5

unwritten law, 8–10, 115, 132–50, 173–5; in the United States, 239n166

Vaad Ha'lr (Jewish Community Council), 48

White, Peter, 116, 119, 124, 143; and Alice, 143; and cross-examination, 128–30; death of, 184n4; doubts Ben's testimony, 130–1; and premeditation, 129; and re-enactment of shooting, 129–30. *See also* prosecution

White, Stanford, 4

Wiesel, Elie, 12

womanhood, 114, 170, 224n113; Alice as poor example of, 91, 175; and character, 10, 103–4, 142, 144, 175; and charity, 48–9, 91, 103; images of, 109, 174; seductresses, 141–2; and the law, 144–5; and respectability, 10. *See also* charity; gossip; Jewish community

Yehoash Folke Schule, 93–4

Yiddish, 66, 126, 135, 165, 187n24; Alice and Ben, 51; freedom to speak, 216n6; theatre, 184n8; unites community, 93. *See also* Jewish community; newspapers; religion

York Street School, 93

Young Judea, 50, 206n84

Young Men's Hebrew Association, 50, 95

Young People's League, 92, 94

Zionists, 6, 47–9, 93, 108; and Berger, 194n79, 206n83; and Doctor, 192n61. *See also* Hadassah; Pioneer Women; Young Judea